D1360516

CURRENT ISSUES IN
INDUSTRIAL ECONOMICS

CURRENT ISSUES IN ECONOMICS

General Editor: David Greenaway, University of Nottingham

Current Issues in Microeconomics
Edited by John D. Hey

Current Issues in Macroeconomics
Edited by David Greenaway

Current Issues in Labour Economics
Edited by David Sapsford and Zafiris Tzannatos

Current Issues in International Monetary Economics
Edited by David T. Llewellyn and Chris Milner

Current Issues in Development Economics
Edited by V. N. Balasubramanyam and Sanjaya Lall

Current Issues in Financial and Monetary Economics
Edited by Kevin Dowd and Mervyn K. Lewis

Current Issues in Public Sector Economics
Edited by Peter M. Jackson

Current Issues in the Economics of Welfare
Edited by Nicholas Barr and David Whynes

Current Issues in Agricultural Economics
Edited by A. J. Rayner and David Colman

Current Issues in Industrial Economics
Edited by John Cable

Current Issues in Industrial Economics

Edited by

John Cable
Professor of Economics
University of Wales, Aberystwyth

St. Martin's Press   New York

First published in the United States of America in 1994

Printed in Hong Kong

ISBN 0–312–09664–X

Library of Congress Cataloging-in-Publication Data
Current issues in industrial economics / edited by John Cable.
p.   cm. — (Current issues in economics)
Includes bibliographical references and index.
ISBN 0–312–09664–X
1. Industrial organization (Economic theory)   I. Cable, John.
II. Series.
HD2326.C88   1994
228.5—dc20   93–18909
                                                      CIP

Contents

v

Contents

List of Figures

List of Tables

Series Editor's Preface

As I said in the Preface to *Current Issues in International Trade*, which was the pilot to the *Current Issues* series, the reason for its creation was the difficulty of finding suitable references on 'frontier' subjects for undergraduate students. Many of the issues which excite professional economists and which dominate the journal literature take quite a time to percolate down into texts, hence the need for a volume of *Current Issues*. The reception which *Current Issues in International Trade* received persuaded me that it may be worth doing something similar for the other subject areas we teach. Macmillan agreed with my judgement, hence the series. Thus each volume in this series is intended to take readers to the 'frontier' of the particular subject area. Each volume contains nine or ten essays, one of which provides a general overview whilst the remainder are devoted to current issues.

As series editor the main challenge I faced was finding suitable editors for each of the volumes – the best people are generally the busiest! I believe, however, that I have been fortunate in having such an impressive and experienced team of editors with the necessary skills and reputation to persuade first-class authors to participate. I would like to thank all of them for their cooperation and assistance in the development of the series. Like me all of them will, I am sure, hope that this series provides a useful service to undergraduate and postgraduate students as well as faculty.

Current Issues in Industrial Economics is the tenth in the series. Industrial economics is a core subject area and a prominent component of undergraduate programmes. It has also been a very fertile field for research over the last ten years, with major developments in the analysis of product differentiation, innovation, entry and game theory. Much of this work is only just beginning to percolate into the textbooks. John Cable therefore faced a real challenge in putting together an appropriate range of topics and a suitable group of authors – a challenge which he has met admirably. The blend of topics chosen covers the range of current issues very effectively and complements *Current Issues in Microeconomics* nicely. I hope that readers find it as informative and interesting as I did.

University of Nottingham   DAVID GREENAWAY

Notes on the Contributors

John Beath is Professor of Economics at the University of St Andrews.

J. D. Byers is Lecturer in Economics at the University of Wales, Aberystwyth.

John Cable is Professor of Economics at the University of Wales, Aberystwyth.

Alan Carruth is Reader in Economics at the University of Kent.

Avinash Dixit is John J. F. Sherrerd '52 University Professor of Economics, Princeton University.

Saul Estrin is Associate Professor of Economics at the London Business School, and Director of the Programme on Post-Communist Reform at the Centre for Economic Performance, London School of Economics.

C. D. Fraser is Lecturer in Economics at the University of Warwick.

P. A. Geroski is Professor of Economics at the London Business School.

Yannis Katsoulacos is Associate Professor at the Athens University of Economics and Business.

D. A. Peel is Professor of Economics at the University of Wales, Aberystwyth.

Geoff Stewart is Lecturer in Economics at the University of Southampton.

xiii

David Ulph is Professor of Economics at University College, London.

Michael Waterson is Professor of Economics at the University of Warwick.

Thomas G. Weyman-Jones is Senior Lecturer in Economics at Loughborough University.

1 Introduction and Overview: Recent Developments in Industrial Economics

JOHN CABLE

1.1 THE SCOPE AND CURRENT STATE OF INDUSTRIAL ECONOMICS

Industrial economics – 'industrial organisation' in the USA and sometimes elsewhere – may be thought of not as a separate subject area (Stigler, 1968, p. 1) but as a supply-side perspective on the workings of the economy, 'particularly those markets in which business firms are sellers' (Schmalensee, 1988, p. 643). As an approach, it has always embraced theory, measurement, the empirical testing of hypotheses and policy application, albeit with varying degrees of emphasis.

It is popular to regard the present state of industrial economics in terms of the supersession of an old-style, structure–conduct–performance (SCP) paradigm by, in particular, a 'new industrial organisation' (new I-O), focussing on game-theoretic analysis of the strategic behaviour of rational agents within markets and firms. However this is only part of the picture. The SCP paradigm never completely filled the domain of industrial economics. Even in its country of origin, the USA, the work of Stigler and the 'Chicago School', for example, maintained a separate tradition from that of the SCP approach (Stigler's own *A Theory of Oligopoly*, 1964, remaining a model for the theory-to-empirics approach); and in Britain and continental Europe other distinctive

1

strands also flourished (see e.g. Hay and Morris, 1991; de Jong, 1986). Moreover, there are important lines of post-SCP development other than 'the new I-O', notably the Coasian transactions cost-based 'new institutional economics' developed in particular by Williamson, and brought together and summarised in Williamson (1985, 1989). Nevertheless, it is true that SCP was for many years widely embraced, influencing a whole generation of scholars and policy-makers. It is also the case that the application of game theory has made industrial economics one of the most exciting and vigorous areas of economics since the mid-1970s.

The SCP approach had its origins in the work of Mason (1957) and others in the 1930s, and drew in particular on the Chamberlinian strand of theoretical development. Its formulation and elevation to paradigm status, however, owed most to Bain's (1956) seminal work on entry, and his subsequent text (Bain, 1959) which structured many an undergraduate and not a few graduate courses over the next two decades. The great attraction of the SCP framework was that, once its causal assumptions were accepted, if stable, general relationships could be established between observable (and on the whole slowly-moving) structural variables such as seller concentration, entry conditions, and the degree of product differentiation, and performance variables such as excess profit, selling costs, and the rate of technological progress, then understanding could be gained, and policy-making informed, without the necessity of direct enquiry into the inherently more intractable, and largely unobservable, process of market conduct. Thus while conduct remained the crucial link in a causal flow running from structure to performance, and assumptions about the nature of conduct generated the *a priori* expectations concerning the empirical results (and indeed informed the specification of the relationships estimated), regularities in observed structure–performance relationships would justify the suppression of conduct in what in effect became a reduced-form analysis.

The SCP approach lent itself both to case studies of individual industries (the preferred method of the early Harvard school – though also of the Chicago school) – generating innumerable PhD theses and published studies, and also to inter-industry studies. After Bain's shaping of the subject, the latter then began to predominate; and with the advent in the mid-to late 1960s of a new generation of scholars trained (or hastily retooling) in econometric methods, coupled with rapidly expanding access to computers and to econometric software packages, cross-sectional regression analysis of structure–performance models became for a time almost the hallmark of I-O. Schmalensee (1989) and Cubbin (1988) provide extensive surveys of the literature and the results obtained.

The decline of SCP that subsequently began in the second half of the 1970s has yet to be definitively chronicled. No doubt there were several factors at work. Of less importance than some might expect, analysis may suggest, was the lack of stronger and more. explicit theoretical foundations. It is true that pre-1980s' industrial economics has often been lambasted for its atheoretic nature. But the criticism was never quite fair and, more importantly, more formal and greatly improved theoretical underpinnings for structure–performance relationships were emerging at the very time that SCP passed its zenith, for example following the influential paper by Cowling and Waterson (1976). (See also Schmalensee's, 1982a, account of the development of theory in industrial economics at this time.) More damaging, perhaps, were problems of causality within the SCP framework concerning 'feedbacks' from conduct and performance and, for these and other reasons, the endogeneity of structure, leading to much controversy over the interpretation of statistical results. Certainly it is the case that, at least partly in reaction to what had gone before, the new directions which industrial organisation subsequently took were ones in which, as Chapter 5 in this book puts it, 'conduct moves to centre stage, and structure (in particular seller concentration) is found jointly with prices, profits, output and welfare, as part of an equilibrium determined by preferences, behaviour and technology' (p. 100 below). Other difficulties with the SCP approach included problems in handling the multidimensional concept of market performance, particularly as a dependent variable in regression analyses; limitations imposed by the heavy reliance on statistical artifacts (SIC industries) as the unit of analysis in empirical work; and other data and measurement problems (later exponents of the approach often resorting to crude proxies, in contrast to Bain's scrupulous and painstaking early work). Above all, however, in accounting for the supplanting of SCP, was perhaps the fact that in practice the hoped-for panoply of stable, general and incontrovertible relationships proved reluctant to materialise.

Given that the 'old I-O' had grown out of dissatisfaction with received microeconomic theory in the 1930s, and its limitations in explaining the growth and behaviour of large-scale firms and increasingly concentrated industries, it is perhaps ironic that it was to be to the theorists that SCP would eventually itself yield place in industrial economics in the late 1970s. The intellectual impetus for this succession derived from the regeneration of game theory which was concurrently occurring, and the realisation that strategic behaviour by firms in markets and, later, individual agents within firms, provided rich opportunities for its application. The work of Spence (1977), Salop (1979b), Dixit (1979, 1980, 1982) and others on entry, for example, was indicative of what was to follow, and much did. At first, analysis tended to be in terms of games of full information, and later, games of incomplete information. Roberts (1987, p. 157) captures something of both the scope of the new developments, and the excitement surrounding them:

> we are beginning to get a theoretical handle on some aspects of the rich variety of behaviour that marks real strategic interactions but that has previously resisted analysis. For example, the only theoretically consistent analyses of predatory pricing available five years ago indicated that such behaviour was pointless and should be presumed to be rare; now we have several distinct models pointing in the opposite direction. These not only formalize and justify arguments for predation that had previously been put forward by business people, lawyers, and students of industrial practice; they also provide subtle new insights that call into question both prevailing public policy and legal standards and various suggestions for their reform. In a similar fashion, we now have models offering strategic, information-based explanations for such phenomena as price wars, the use of apparently uninformative advertising, limit pricing, patterns of implicit cooperation and collusion, the breakdown of bargaining and delays of agreement, the use of warranties and service contracts, the form of pricing chosen by oligopolists, the nature of contracts between suppliers and customers, and the adoption of various institutions for exchange: almost all of this was unavailable five years ago.

Surveys of, and references to, the literature of this and the immediately following periods may be found in Fudenberg and Tirole (1986), Schmalensee and Willig (1989) and Tirole (1988).

Before long, however, it became apparent that the wealth of new models and results were by no means hanging together in a coherent overall story. For some this is cause for celebration:

> The fact that in The New Industrial Economics there is no general theory encompassing the whole gamut of industrial behaviour should not be seen as a limitation, but rather as an achievement (Norman and La Manna, 1992, p. 2).

Others however take a different view and urge a return to empirics. Scherer (1988, p. 517) for example observed:

> the 'new industrial organisation' is profusely overdetermined . . . It is now widely recognised that a sorting out, based on solid empirical work, qualitative and quantitative, is needed.

Schmalensee (1988, pp. 675–6) concurred, summarising the state of the art as follows:

> our understanding of a number of classic problems, including entry deterrence and cartel stability, has been considerably advanced. But we have also learned two unpleasant features of the game-theoretic approach to the analysis of imperfect competition.
>
> First, even apparently simple multi-period games of incomplete information have multiple (perfect Bayesian–Nash) equilibria that can be uncovered only by very sophisticated analysis. The assumption that boundedly rational humans can solve the much more complex games they face in real life seems to push the rationality principle very far indeed . . . But it is not clear how to replace that assumption. Nor is it clear . . . how to deal in general with models possessing multiple perfect Bayesian–Nash equilibria.
>
> Second, the predictions of game-theoretic models seem delicate and are often difficult to test. Important qualitative features of equilibria often depend critically on whether prices

or quantities are choice variables, on whether discrete or continuous time is assumed, on whether moves are sequential or simultaneous, and, perhaps most disturbing of all, on how players with incomplete information are assumed to alter their beliefs in response to events that cannot occur in equilibrium.

Schmalensee went on to express the view that:

Until game-theoretic analysis either begins to yield robust general predictions or is replaced by a mode of theorising that does so, it seems a fair bet that most major substantive advances in industrial economics will come from empirical research. Only empirical studies can reveal which theoretical models are 'empty boxes' and which have wide domains of applicability. And without the discipline provided by a solid base of facts, theorists cannot be expected to concentrate on deducing the implications of empirically interesting assumptions.

By the time these views appeared in print a resurgence of empirical work had in fact already begun. For example, a special issue of the *Journal of Industrial Economics* in 1987 had been given over to a selection of studies which, the editors explained, though diverse in their scope, 'share elements of style and approach that clearly mark them as work of the 1980s' (Bresnahan and Schmalensee, 1987, p. 377). More recently, the exquisite blend of theory and empirics in Sutton (1991) may prove a model for future work.

Thus, in a way, the wheel has turned full circle; as in the 1930s industrial economists are turning to empirics to resolve ambiguities, fill lacunae and focus ideas. But 'wheel' is perhaps the wrong metaphor; 'spiral' would be better. For over the intervening sixty years progress has been made, and the differences between then and now are enormous. The burst of theorising over the past decade or more has left us with an incomparably richer understanding of at least 'what may happen' in markets and firms (and empirical researchers have never been loathe to take up the challenge of finding out what actually does happen). Empirical techniques and facilities are likewise of an entirely higher order, empirical data of both higher quality and greater accessibility, and empiricists wiser for the experience of what happened last time round. Most important of all, perhaps, the Chinese wall that has appeared to divide theorists and empiricists at times in the past appears to be crumbling; empiricists are increasingly willing to exploit recent advances in economic theory and econometric method, and theorists to get involved with the empirics.

1.2 THE CONTENTS OF THIS BOOK

The studies in this volume are a necessarily limited selection from the large number which could have been drawn from the area of industrial economics. The selection principle has been to lay down platforms and identify themes on or around which further exploration of the subject can take place or be structured.

Chapters 2 and 3 focus on the firm, reflecting its rediscovery within the last two decades as an institution worthy and indeed demanding of analysis, and the growing willingness there has been over this period to enquire into the 'black box' of traditional theory. In Chapter 2 Geoff Stewart deals with a mostly very modern literature on the contractual relationships between entrepreneurs, agents and input suppliers, emphasising the focal issues of incentives and insurance in situations which involve uncertainty and/or, as is typically the case, investments which are specific to the relationship, and 'lock in' one or more contracting parties.

One important issue in Chapter 2 concerns who receives the residual and, by extension, profit-sharing. This and related issues are taken further in Chapter 3, where Saul Estrin surveys a large literature that deals with the theory and practice of 'alternative' productive enterprises. Starting from the much-analysed labour-managed firm (LMF), Estrin moves on to more realistic configurations of ownership, management and investment, and ultimately to the more traditionally owned but participatory firm. Assessing the prospects for the small but rapidly growing alternative production enterprise sector, he contrasts the generally gloomy predictions of the theoretical literature with the considerably greater optimism of (largely orthogonal) empirical work.

Chapters 4 and 5 turn our attention from intra-firm issues to the behaviour of firms in markets. In different ways, both chapters overview classical oligopoly theory which, despite the theoretical revolution of industrial economics that has been described, remains a cornerstone in modern analyses of market behaviour. Thus, for example, second-stage equilibrium is routinely characterised as Cournot or Bertrand in multi-period games. In Chapter 4 Clive Fraser presents an exposition and critique of the conjectural variations approach to oligopoly theory, using this focus to trace a path through the multiplicity of alternative models of both homogenous-goods and differentiated-goods markets. The idea of consistent or rational expectations is found to offer only an incomplete solution to the problem of selecting amongst alternative models. Interestingly, in the context of recent theoretical developments, some apparently simple static oligopoly solutions are shown to derive from much more complicated game-theoretic scenarios.

Using a similar, CV-based unifying framework, John Cable, Alan Carruth and Avinash Dixit offer in Chapter 5 a further perspective on oligopoly models showing how, for a series of given underlying cost and demand conditions, these may be ranked in terms of price and output levels and above all welfare on the spectrum between perfect competition and pure monopoly. The numerical simulations reveal that, in particular, the form of oligopolistic rivalry and the degree of product differentiation in the market exert a major influence on the level of welfare generated, but cost and demand asymmetries as between rivals generally have little effect. Importantly for policy, measures of market structure are confirmed as providing a very unreliable guide to welfare levels.

The social welfare implications of product differentiation receive further attention from Mike Waterson in Chapter 6 – the first of three chapters addressing themes that, as subject matter, remain as much to the fore in the new industrial economics as they did in the old (the other two being market entry (Chapter 7) and technical innovation (Chapter 8)). Waterson finds that the advances in the theoretical product differentiation literature of the 1970s and 1980s have done much to clear up some earlier puzzles and inaccuracies. However, as in the industrial economics literature more generally, the new product differentiation models tend to generate a range of alternative predictions and be sensitive to 'subtle modelling nuances', leading to an endorsement by the author of the call for a search for empirical regularities.

Paul Geroski's treatment of market entry in Chapter 7 reflects the long history of the literature, from Bain's early work to the present. Three main sources of entry barriers are identified, and the relationship between entry and market performance examined, in particular profits, productivity and innovation. The empirical literature is reviewed as well as the theoretical framework, and the discussion is extended to the related, in a sense more general, issue of market share mobility and intra-industry dynamics, involving all firms in the market rather than entrants and exitors alone.

In Chapter 8 John Beath, Yannis Katsoulacos and David Ulph distinguish the firm's strategic incentive for R&D and innovation – as a 'competitive threat' – from the pure profit motive the firm would have for investing in R&D on a 'stand alone' basis. Their analysis focuses on three paradigms in the literature: auction models of R&D, non-tournament models, and finally tournament models in which, with technological uncertainty and a stochastic relationship between R&D effort and innovative success, the profit motive and competitive threat can be separated out. Once again, the models considered generate what the authors describe as 'a surprisingly varied tapestry of potential outcomes'.

In the foregoing chapters, policy isues are sometimes treated explicitly as they arise, and otherwise frequently implicitly in the discussion as it proceeds. Chapter 9, however, takes us squarely into the policy arena. With the widespread privatisation of public utilities in Britain and elsewhere, the subset of antitrust policy dealing with the theory and practice of regulating dominant firms has gained the importance there it has long had in the USA. Moreover, as Tom Weyman-Jones points out in his introduction, the introduction of game theory and incentive issues into this literature, as elsewhere, has revolutionised traditional ideas about regulation. His survey of the theory of regulation begins with the traditional ideas of cost of service and Ramsey pricing, proceeding to governance structures for natural monopolies and incentives regulation. The key issue of informational asymmetry between regulator and regulated then leads to principal–agent analysis of different types of regulatory contract, one of which takes us to the leading practical regulatory innovation, namely price caps.

The final chapter of the book concerns empirical methodology. As we have seen, case studies and inter-industry analyses have tended to be the stock-in-trade of empirical industrial economics in the past. With the current widespread emphasis on game theory at the theoretical level, the case study approach seems set to continue and indeed grow in relative prominence, while cross-section regression analysis recedes. There are also two other promising avenues for future empirical work. One is the experimental method, explained and surveyed by Plott (1989). The other is the application of time-series analysis, which has seen dramatic development in the 1980s and been widely applied in macroeconomics. In Chapter 10 David Byers and David Peel provide an introduction to some of the latest available methods in this field with illustrations from industrial economics. Their survey covers linear and non-linear methods, embracing both cointegration and error correction models (ECMs), and bilinear, threshold autoregressive and chaotic models. Time series analyses of markets are just beginning to appear in the journals; as improved longitudinal data sets become more widely available, they seem likely to be encountered with increasing frequency in the future.

2 Economics of the Firm

GEOFF STEWART

2.1 INTRODUCTION

It is often pointed out that whilst Industrial Organisation is concerned with the behaviour of firms in industries, the analysis generally stops short of the internal organisation of the firms themselves. Instead, very simple models of the firm tend to be used so that attention can be focused on the interactions between them. Thus a typical representation of a firm is an entity, i, which chooses its product price or output level to

$$\max \pi_i = p_i(q_1 \ldots q_n)q_i - c_i(q_i), \qquad i = 1 \ldots n \qquad (2.1)$$

where p_i denotes the price of firm i's product, q_i its output level, c_i its costs and n the number of firms in the industry. This type of model has been used to explore, for example, the differences between prices and quantities as decision variables, and how prices, quantities and profits vary with the number of firms in the industry. For our purposes the important point to note is that the firm is a collective entity, and that there is no explicit consideration of the behaviour of the *individual* agents who are involved. Such models are therefore sometimes termed 'black box' representations of the firm. However there has always been an important strand of the industrial organisation literature – the *economics of the firm* – that has sought to look inside the black box by taking the individual as the basic unit of analysis. This chapter, then, is about the ways in which individual agents coordinate their actions to produce a good or service.

One of the simplest ways to organise production is for a single entrepreneur to purchase or hire all of the necessary inputs from the various factor markets. This is explored in section 2.2, where it is shown that, if there is also a market in entrepreneurial services, then inputs will be combined with the objective of maximising profit; but if there is not then the outcome depends upon the preferences of the particular entrepreneur. One of the reasons that this latter market – and labour markets more generally – might not function smoothly is that it can be difficult for others to observe the quantity or quality of input. A main concern of the literature has been to explore methods of coordination under such conditions. Attention has focused, in particular, on the inefficiencies that can arise when the individual undertaking a given action does not receive all of the benefits, or incur all of the costs, that are generated. This may be because the action is an investment that is specific to another party (and so gives them some bargaining power), or because some assets that are necessary for production are owned by others (which again confers bargaining power), or, finally, because the individual requires some insurance in the face of an uncertain benefit. These cases are examined in sections 2.3, 2.4 and 2.5 respectively. Section 2.6 then draws upon standard oligopoly theory to demonstrate that, where there is rivalry in the product market, the contracts that individuals use to coordinate their actions may have strategic effects, and that recognition of this fact can then be expected to feed back to the contract design stage.

2.2   ENTREPRENEURIAL PRODUCTION

Production typically requires a variety of inputs. These might include, for example, factory space, raw materials, machinery and workers able to operate the machines. But the mere existence of such inputs will not generate a finished product in the hands of the consumers. *Coordination* is required. First of all there has to be a realisation that these various elements can usefully be combined, and then arrangements need to be made, for example, to secure the inputs in the correct proportions. At its simplest this may be carried out by a single individual – who may be termed the entrepreneur – as follows.

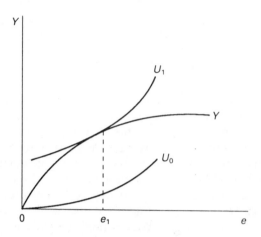

FIGURE 2.1 Residual income and effort

The entrepreneur E, first signs contracts with the input suppliers determining specifications, prices and delivery dates. A potential difficulty with the labour input is that it may be difficult to specify precisely what must be provided. For example, John Cable could not know exactly what would be in this chapter at the time we made our agreement for me to contribute to the book. We shall return to this point shortly, but for the moment suppose that the task that the worker is expected to perform in exchange for the wage can be tightly defined. In addition to contracting with the input suppliers, E must also sign one or more contracts to sell the finished product. The next stage is that the transactions specified in the contracts take place. For each of the input suppliers and consumers these are single exchanges of money for a commodity or task. By contrast, the return to E is the residual after all contracts have been put into effect. E is thus common to all of the bilateral contracts and is the *residual claimant*.

On what basis will E determine the contracts to be written? One might suppose that the objective will be to maximise the residual. However, as Scitovsky (1943) pointed out, the act of generating a residual will involve time and effort on the part of the entrepreneur. In Figure 2.1 the curve Y traces the relationship between the residual or 'gross income' (revenue *less* all costs except the input from E) and the effort expended by E. It seems reasonable to suppose that Y will be increasing in effort (at least initially) but that the rate of increase will diminish as the effort level increases. At some point, as fatigue sets in, Y might actually start to fall, although this will not affect the outcome below. The level of effort chosen by the entrepreneur, e_1, is given by the tangency between Y and the entrepreneur's indifference curve, U_1, and so it can be seen that the residual is below the maximum that could be generated.

Is this outcome consistent with the standard assumption that profits are maximised? That is, does the entrepreneur maximise the difference between revenue and all costs, including entrepreneurial services? Following Gravelle and Rees (1981) the curve U_0 passes through the origin and therefore shows the various effort–income combinations that yield the same utility as the alternative of supplying no effort to (and therefore receiving no income from) this activity. The alternative may be to become an employee, an entrepreneur elsewhere, or perhaps not to work at all. Whatever the case, for a given effort level the height of U_0 is the minimum income required to persuade E to engage in this activity. In other words, it depicts the opportunity cost in money terms of the entrepreneurial input. The profit-maximising effort level maximises the vertical distance between Y and U_0 and therefore only coincides with the actual level chosen, e_1, in the special case where U_0 and U_1 happen to be parallel at e_1.

This conclusion, however, can be shown to rest upon an implicit assumption that there is no market in entrepreneurial services. That is, E cannot buy in (or sell) units of 'coordination'. If, on the other hand, these services can be bought and sold on a market just like the other inputs then the *total* effort devoted to this product – by E and the outside supplier – will indeed be set at the profit-maximising level. This is illustrated in Figure 2.2, again following Gravelle and Rees, where the slope of OW and $W'W'$ is given by the price per unit of effort on the entrepreneurial labour market.

In the absence of the market, effort would be set at e_1 and E would receive utility U_1. But the ability to purchase inputs of effort will enable the entrepreneur to do better than this. The mechanism can be thought of as comprising two steps. First, E's effort is raised to e^* and gross income to Y^*. These are the profit-maximising levels, but if things were to stop here then utility would have been reduced. But the existence of the market now permits an exchange of effort for money, between E and the supplier,

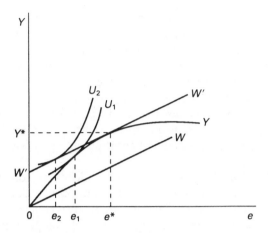

FIGURE 2.2 **Total effort devoted to the product**

along $W'W'$, and so the second step is to move along $W'W'$ until E attains the highest possible indifference curve. In the case depicted here this involves a leftward movement (buying-in effort) to the tangency with U_2. The market thus permits a separation between the amount of effort supplied by E and the total amount supplied to the product in question: the profit-maximising total of e^* is supplied with e_2 coming from E and the remainder purchased on the market. Similarly if the tangency happened to be to the right of e^* then E would supply e^* to this product and an additional amount to the market. The possibility that this market may not function perfectly is returned to in section 2.5.

2.3 RELATIONSHIP-SPECIFIC INVESTMENTS AND LONG-TERM CONTRACTS

In many instances production will require an individual to undertake some action that is *specific* to one of the other parties involved. For example, suppose that E initially has a wide choice of suppliers of raw material but each is located in a different country. The selection of a particular supplier, say S, may then dictate various investments to be undertaken by E. It may be necessary to gather information on the local legal system, export regulations, and available transport. Also, the optimal location of the factory to assemble the product may be sensitive to the choice of supplier. The point to note is that these investments are specific to S in the sense that they have no value (or more generally less value) if S were replaced by an alternative supplier. Thus, after the investment, E is to some degree *locked into* the relationship with S. Moreover, it may not be possible for the parties to write a contract regarding such investments due to the difficulties in, say, specifying and measuring the amount of effort put into gathering relevant information.

To examine the investment decision under these conditions we consider a two-period model which, for simplicity, makes the polar assumption that, after that investment, E has *no alternative* but to trade with S. Thus an *ex ante* situation of competition among suppliers is transformed into *ex post* bilateral monopoly.

At date 0, E undertakes some investment which can be thought of as effort, e. After this is completed, at date 1, the remaining inputs are supplied, production occurs, and E receives revenue $R(e)$ where $R'(e) > 0$ and $R''(e) < 0$ (investment increases the revenue, but at a decreasing rate). Suppose E and S negotiate a contract determining the price of the input at date 1; that is, after the investment has been made. With e being sunk, the amount to be divided between the two parties is $R(e) - k$, where k is the cost to S of supplying the input. Assume for simplicity that bargaining will result in an equal division. When deciding how much to invest at date 0, E will take into account this division and so set e to maximise

$$U = \frac{u(e, R(e) - k)}{2} \tag{2.2}$$

which results in an investment of e_0 and an income Y_0 in Figure 2.3 (there is no market for the type of effort required here due to the impossibility of writing contracts).

Now consider the alternative of writing a contract before the investment is made. Specifically, suppose at date 0 they fix the price, $\bar{p}$, at which the input will be supplied to E. Since this contract specifies an exchange to take place in the future it is termed a *long-term contract*. With the price fixed at $\bar{p}$, E will choose e to maximise

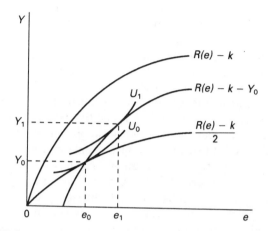

FIGURE 2.3 **Investment and income at date 0**

$$U = u(e, R(e) - \bar{p}) \qquad (2.3)$$

Under the previous arrangement each party received a net income of Y_0. Suppose that the long-term contract sets $\bar{p} = k + Y_0$ so that the welfare of S is unchanged. The entrepreneurial surplus is now $R(e) - k - Y_0$ and, as can be seen in Figure 2.3, the new equilibrium involves higher investment, e_1, higher income, Y_1, and higher utility, U_1, for E. Thus the long-run contract has generated a Pareto improvement. The explanation is that by transforming the price at which exchange occurs into a constant, E will, *at the margin*, receive the full benefit of additional investment. The actual price set determines the division of the benefit, but whatever its level – provided it does not generate a negative return to either party – investment will be efficient and hence overall benefit maximised.

There has been a considerable amount of empirical work in this area. For example, Joskow (1987) looked at contracts between coal suppliers and electric utilities in the USA. The specific investments in this case include plant location and the need to tailor the design of coal burning equipment to the particular type of coal being used. On the basis of a sample of 277 contracts that were in force in 1979, Joskow concludes that there is fairly strong support for the hypothesis that contracts tend to be longer the more important are relationship-specific investments.[1]

Notice that it is the simultaneous occurrence of actions that cannot be subject to contracts, and the shared residual claimant status emanating from specificity, that causes problems. If investment could be contracted on then, in the above example, E could simply agree to pay a penalty in the event of a deviation from the efficient level. Efficient investment is then ensured, revenue less k is split equally in the bargain at date 1, and the overall distribution of returns can be dealt with using a side-payment at date 0. Similarly, there would be an efficient outcome in the absence of the specificity property of investment which gave bargaining power, and hence a share of $R(e)$, to S. The general principle is therefore that, other things being equal, the rights to the residual should be given to the party taking the action in question. An example of this principle in operation in contained in Leffler and Rucker's (1991) study of timber harvesting contracts in North Carolina. Individuals wishing to sell their tracts of timber face a choice between hiring logging resources to fell the trees for them, or selling to a mill or logger the right to remove the standing timber. Some 200 cases were examined and without exception the owners chose to sell the rights to standing timber. The explanation offered by Leffler and Rucker is that efficiency in timber harvesting requires a certain amount of care in felling (for example, to protect neighbouring trees), and in minimising stump heights, but that such requirements are difficult to specify and monitor. The advantage of selling the standing timber is that it is transfers the status of residual claimant to the party doing the felling, and so gives them the incentive to exercise care.

2.4   THE OWNERSHIP OF PHYSICAL ASSETS

In the previous section it was demonstrated that a long-term contract may permit the efficient level of relationship-specific investment. But in practice there are many circumstances where a long-term contract would be impossible or prohibitively expensive to write or implement. Hart and Holmstrom (1987) identify four types of cost associated with contracting: (1) the cost of anticipating the various eventualities that may occur during the life of the relationship; (2) the cost of deciding and reaching agreement on how to deal with such eventualities; (3) the cost of writing the contract in a way that is sufficiently clear to be enforceable; and (4) the legal cost of enforcement. While these costs arise in contracts of any length, Hart and Holmstrom suggest that those in category (1) and perhaps (3) may be significantly higher for long-term contracts. In circumstances where relationship-specific investments are important but long-term contracts are ruled out, Grossman, Hart and Moore, in a series of papers, have shown that efficiency may be sensitive to who owns the physical assets that are used in production. The basic ideas can be illustrated by the following example taken from Hart and Moore (1990).[2]

There is one physical asset, a yacht. The agents comprise a chef, a skipper and a tycoon. The investment is the preparation of a meal by the chef for the tycoon. It is specific because it is assumed that there is only one tycoon – 'only he can afford to fly to these waters'. The yacht is also assumed to be 'indispensable' but there is competition among skippers. Suppose the investment, at date 0, costs the chef 100 and the resulting benefit to the tycoon at date 1 is 240. As in the previous section, the benefit is assumed to be split equally in the event of bargaining. The question is whether it matters who owns the yacht. The following table shows that it does.

	Chef's share of 240	Will chef invest?
Chef owns yacht	120	Yes
Skipper owns yacht	80	No
Tycoon owns yacht	120	Yes

The explanation is simple. If either the chef or the tycoon owns the yacht then only these two parties are involved in bargaining over the benefit from the chef's investment – remember there is competition among skippers. But if the skipper – or indeed anyone else – owns the yacht then there are three indispensable agents at date 1 and so the chef can expect to get only one-third of the benefit, which is not enough to cover the (sunk) investment cost. Two interesting directions in which Hart and Moore extend the analysis are, first, to have more than one agent investing and, second, to situations where production requires a number of assets. An important principle to emerge is that complementary assets should be owned together, but that economically independent assets should be owned separately.

Finally, notice that the essential idea underpinning the analysis is that the yacht must not be owned by an individual who would otherwise have no bargaining power – to maximise the incentive to invest, the pie must be divided into as few pieces as possible. The chef, like the entrepreneur of the previous section, is undertaking an investment which is specific to another party (the tycoon) and so, with a long-term contract ruled out, must share the surplus. The additional ingredient here is a further source of monopoly power (the yacht) which – to prevent a further dilution in investment incentives – should be owned by either the chef or tycoon. Thus, this model is not relevant for *any* physical assets that might be used in production, but only to those which confer bargaining power because they are scarce.

2.5   THE SEPARATION OF OWNERSHIP AND CONTROL

The modern corporation is typically characterised by a 'separation of ownership and control': shareholders are the owners but decision-making is in the hands of specialist management. Moreover, it is often argued, the managers will enjoy a degree of discretion in their actions (perhaps especially when shareholdings are widely dispersed), and therefore behaviour of the firm can be expected to reflect the objectives of managers as well as owners. These considerations lead, some thirty years ago, to the development of a number of *managerial theories of the firm*, the most well-known of which are Baumol (1959), Marris (1964) and Williamson (1964). Drawing upon work by organisational theorists, it was argued that managers derive satisfaction not only from salary but also from factors such as power, prestige, security and professional excellence. The approach then taken was not to model the interaction between managers and shareholders explicitly, but rather to seek to capture the outcome of managerial behaviour by an appropriate specification of the objective function of the firm and the constraints on its management. For example, Baumol suggested that the managerial utility function translates into a desire to maximise sales revenue, and that the assumption of profit maximisation should then be replaced by revenue maximisation subject to a minimum profit constraint. In Williamson's model the objective of the firm becomes the maximisation of a utility function comprising the number of staff, management emoluments (such as expense accounts and office furnishings) and the level of investment at the discretion of managers; and in Marris the objective is growth maximisation. For a detailed description and discussion of each of these models, and their resource implications, see Koutsoyiannis (1979) or Gravelle and Rees (1981). However, the fact that these models do not explicitly examine the relationship between owners and managers is a potential weakness, and it would seem sensible to consider the extent to which the manager can be constrained through an appropriate contract. This is the approach of the recent literature, to which we now turn.

There are various aspects of managerial behaviour that might constitute a potential source of conflict with owners. These include the choice of output level, the various categories of expenditure noted above, and also simply the level of effort expended by the manager. In each case there may be factors – notably complexity and uncertainty surrounding future events – which rule out a complete contract specifying precisely the action that the manager must take. Even so, any conflict could in principle be avoided by having the manager take on the role of owner. The manager would pay a fixed fee to the original owner and thus, as residual claimant, bear all the consequences of his or her actions. This works in exactly the same way as the fixed-price long-term contract, or the sale of the standing timber, in section 2.3. So if managerial discretion is to be an issue there must be something which prevents the concentration of the two roles into the hands of a single agent. One possibility is that there may be a time interval between the payments to input suppliers and the receipt of revenue. In such cases some initial finance is required and, if there are imperfections in the capital market, some initial wealth may be a necessary condition for residual claimant status. Alternatively, if we now admit some uncertainty into costs or revenue, and risk-aversion on the part of an individual manager, then it may be efficient for the role of residual claimant to be taken by a more risk-neutral body such as a group of shareholders with a diversified portfolio. These considerations may therefore impose some restriction on the supply of potential residual claimants, but is there any reason why they could not perform the managerial role? An obvious reason is that not everyone is equally endowed with managerial expertise. Also, if the residual claimant is a dispersed group of shareholders, then the alternative to a specialist manager is collective decision-making, and this may also be costly.

The following example considers the case where risk-aversion on the part of a manager, and inferior ability on the part of an owner, point towards a separation of roles, but they face the problem that the level of effort of the manager cannot be written into the contract.

A risk-neutral individual, A, faces a choice between acting as both residual claimant and manager, or delegating the managerial role to a specialist. Suppose that in the former case the residual from production may turn out to be either 5 or 20 with equal probability, and that the utility cost in money terms of acting as manager is 1. The expected profit is then 11.5. Now, A is aware that a specialist manager, M, could raise to 0.9 the probability of the net revenue (the residual before payment to the manager) being 20 *if she chose to work hard*; but if she chose to shirk, then the probability would remain 0.5. The manager is risk-averse with utility $U = u(s - d)$, where s denotes salary and d the disutility of effort in money terms. Suppose that $d = 1$ if she shirks and $d = 2$ if she works hard. Clearly if M is appointed there is a Pareto improvement if she chooses to work hard rather than shirk: the expected net revenue rises by 6 (from 12.5 to 18.5) at a cost of just 1 unit of utility. But can this be achieved?

If A offers a fixed salary then M will choose to shirk – the disutility of effort is lower and income is unaffected. But salary cannot be linked to effort because this is, by assumption, unobservable. Fortunately there is another alternative: a contract linking salary to the net revenue. Since working hard increases the probability of a high net revenue, a contract which pays more when net revenue turns out to be high may induce M to supply effort. Specifically, the differential will need to be high enough to satisfy the following *incentive compatibility constraint*:

$$(0.1).u(s_L - 2) + (0.9).u(s_H - 2) \geq (0.5).u(s_L - 1)$$
$$+ (0.5).u(s_H - 1) \tag{2.4}$$

where s_L denotes the salary if net revenue turns out to be 5 and s_H the salary if it is 20. That is, M's expected utility must be higher if she works hard than if she shirks.

Consider the particular utility function[3]

$$U = 11(s - d) - (s - d)^2 \qquad (2.5)$$

and suppose that the manager is offered a contract which pays a salary of 3 if the net revenue turns out to be 5, and 6 if it is 20. This generates an expected utility of 26.2 if she works hard but only 24 if she shirks, and so the incentive compatibility constraints is satisfied.   •

For the contract to be offered and signed there are two other constraints that must also be satisfied. First, it must be profitable for A. In the absence of this contract we saw that expected profit was 11.5. With the contract, profit is $(5 - 3)$ with probability 0.1 and $(20 - 6)$ with probability 0.9, giving an expected profit of 12.8. It is thus optimal for A to delegate the managerial role. Second, the utility received by the manager, 26.2, must at least equal the level that could be obtained elsewhere. If this is satisfied then the contract is feasible.

This example illustrates, first, that it can be optimal to have different individuals taking on the roles of residual claimant and manager even if there is the potential for discretionary behaviour due to some of the manager's actions being unobservable and, second, that it may be possible to design a contract that induces the manager to act in the interests of the residual claimant, even where the action is unobservable. However, unobservability does impose a cost: the expected salary bill is higher than otherwise. If effort could be observed then A could offer a fixed salary conditional upon working hard. From (2.5) it is straightforward to calculate that to generate a utility of 26.2 for the manager requires a fixed salary of 5.5 whereas the expected salary under unobservability was 5.7. The point to note here then is that due to risk-aversion on the part of M, the first-best contract would offer a fixed salary, but with unobservability some variability is required to induce effort.[4] Notice, however, that the cost of securing the lower effort level does not depend upon whether or not it is observable; the same flat wage will suffice. Thus a general message is that unobservability increases the additional cost necessary to induce higher effort, and therefore, in contrast to the above example, there will be situations where the equilibrium effort will be lower under unobservability than would be the case under observability.

The contract with shareholders may not be the only constraint on managerial discretion. A further possibility, that has been the focus of considerable research, is the takeover.[5] The argument is that a failure to maximise profit would depress the share price and so present an outsider – a 'corporate raider' – with the opportunity to purchase sufficient shares to acquire control, replace the incumbent management, revert to profit maximisation, and hence realise a profit in the form of an increase in the share price. This threat may be enough to dissuade a manager fearful of dismissal – perhaps because of the possibility of unemployment or at least an unwelcome entry on the curriculum vitae – from neglecting the interests of owners in the first place; and if not, then the discretionary behaviour would be transitory – lasting only until a takeover.

However, in practice there are a number of factors which limit the effectiveness of takeovers as a disciplining device. First, the process of takeover involves various costs. These include advertising, legal and brokerage fees and the tender offer premium (the excess of the offer price over the prevailing share price). Second, the incumbent managers have a variety of devices with which to attempt to fend off a predator. The most popular in the USA, according to Jarrell, Brickley and Netter (1988), is the *poison pill*. The idea here is that existing shareholders in the target company are given certain stock rights that are inactive unless triggered by a tender offer for control. For example, they may have the right to buy more shares at very attractive prices or to sell existing shares to the target, again at favourable prices. In either case the effect is to reduce the value of the target to the raider. Other tactics include initiating litigation against the raider – perhaps claiming antitrust or tender offer regulation violations – which at the very least delays the takeover; *greenmail* (the repurchase of the raider's shares at an inflated price); and *golden parachutes* (giving existing managers an entitlement to substantial compensation in the event of dismissal following a takeover).[6] The third problem with the takeover mechanism, identified by Grossman and Hart (1980) is that there may be an incentive to free-ride: in the event of a bid each individual shareholder in the target company has an incentive not to sell because they expect the shares to be worth more followi..₁ he takeover. How then can the existence of successful takeover bids be explained? One possibility is that the raider can accumulate shares quietly so that potential sellers are, at least in the early stages, not aware of a forthcoming takeover. Grossman and Hart (1980) also point to various ways in which the target shareholders can create an incentive for a raider (and hence discipline their management). For example, they might write a provision into the constitution enabling a successful raider to take a large salary, or to sell some of the targets assets to another of the raider's companies at a price below their value.

Given these imperfections in the takeover process an obvious question arises: why do we look to external agents at all – surely the existing shareholders have as much ability and incentive to remove managers who do not act in their interests? The answer lies in the difficulty of observing discretionary behaviour. It may, for example, be just by chance that it is an external agent who is the first to notice. Second, there is a class of agents who specialise in searching for situations of this sort. Of course they must also have expertise in dealing with the problem of discretionary behaviour itself – there is no point in replacing a manager if the new incumbent behaves just like the old. Finally, the raider may take on the role of manager as well as owner; opportunities for entrepreneurs can arise from the mismanagement of existing concerns as well as from new products and markets.

2.6 PRODUCT MARKET COMPETITION

An obvious omission from our analysis of production so far is a consideration of product market rivalry. The entrepreneur, chef and manager of previous sections have each taken their decisions without explicit reference to product market rivals, if they had any. One possible consequence of such competition is that it will serve to increase the amount of information available to contracting agents. In section 2.5 it was demonstrated that it may be appropriate to base a manager's salary on profit, despite the fact that this is subject to influences beyond the manager's control. But in general the outcome will not be a first best in these circumstances and it is desirable to remove the extraneous influences as far as possible. One technique, sometimes referred to as 'yardstick

competition', is to reward an individual on the basis of performance relative to that of agents in a similar situation, on the grounds
that this will take account of factors that are common to all. Product
market competition is therefore useful because it provides the
observations necessary for relative performance clauses in contracts.[7]

A second implication of product market rivalry is that it introduces the prospect of *strategic behaviour*. That is, when contem-
plating an action individuals may take account of the effect upon,
and response of, their competitors in the product market. Recent
research has demonstrated that a wide variety of actions may have
strategic consequences, and indeed some types of observed behaviour are difficult to rationalise in any other terms. The
framework for analysis is generally a two-stage game in which
some form of commitment is undertaken in the first stage, in the
knowledge that a Nash equilibrium will emerge in the product
market in the second. The following model, suggested by Vickers
(1985), is an interesting example of how strategic considerations
interact with intra-firm behaviour. It shows that it can be optimal
for a profit-maximising owner to provide a manager with an incentive to deviate from profit maximisation!

Consider a homogeneous product duopoly with linear demand,
constant marginal costs of production, c, and Cournot competition. Under standard profit-maximising assumptions output will be
set to

$$\max \Pi_i = pq_i - cq_i, \qquad i = 1,2 \tag{2.6}$$

$$\text{subject to } p = a - bQ, \qquad a, b > 0 \tag{2.7}$$

where Π_i is the level of profit for firm i, p is the market price and
$Q = q_1 + q_2$ is the total output in the industry. This yields a pair of
Cournot reaction functions:

$$q_i = \frac{a - c - bq_j}{2a} \tag{2.8}$$

Now consider the alternative situation where the production of
firm 1 is under the control of a specialist manager who seeks not to
maximise profit, but rather:

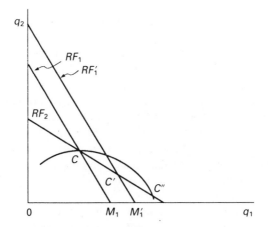

FIGURE 2.4   Equilibrium with an output incentive

$$M_1 = \Pi_1 + \theta q_1 \qquad \theta > 0 \qquad\qquad (2.9)$$

This alternative objective function for the firm may reflect the fact that output is an argument in the manager's utility function, or that the owner – for reasons that will become apparent – has chosen to base salary on output as well as profit. The higher is θ the greater the extent to which the manager will increase output at the expense of profit. The Cournot reaction function now becomes:

$$q_1 = \frac{a - c + \theta - bq_2}{2b} \qquad\qquad (2.10)$$

Comparing (2.10) with (2.8), it can be seen that the introduction of θ induces a larger output from firm 1 for any given q_2. Diagrammatically, the effect is to shift the reaction function from RF_1 outwards to RF_1' (Figure 2.4). Thus as θ increases from zero, the equilibrium moves rightwards along RF_2 from C to C'. As a result, provided that θ is not so large as to produce a shift beyond point C'' (where the iso-profit curve passing through C intersects with RF_2), firm 1's profit will increase.[8] The underlying reason is that, given the downward-sloping Cournot reaction function RF_2, the rightward shift in firm 1's own reaction function induces a *reduction* in

q_2. Market structure here is thus crucial, and we note, in particular that under monopoly there would of course be no such rival's response and so, with the equilibrium moving along the horizontal axis from M_1 to M_1', firm 1's profit would fall.

These product market interactions bring with them the prospect of prior strategic behaviour: given that a Cournot equilibrium will ensue (in the second period), the owner of firm 1 has an incentive to make a prior (first-period) commitment to cede control to a manager to will maximise (2.9) rather than just profit. This could be achieved by basing salary partly on output and partly on profit. Alternatively, salary may be based only on profit, but the owner selects a manager who is known to be prepared to sacrifice income in favour of the prestige associated with size (output). Discretionary behaviour is therefore not necessarily undesirable from the owner's point of view. However, if we were to extend the model so that both firms could make such a first-period commitment the situation changes. The game would have the structure of the prisoner's dilemma in that both would make the commitment yet the resulting Cournot equilibrium would involve lower profit than at C (because the output of *both* firms would be higher). Finally, we briefly note that delegation to a manager is not the only element of organisational design that may have strategic implications. Others include the adoption of a multidivisional structure (Schwartz and Thompson, 1986) and profit-sharing with employees (Stewart, 1989).[9]

2.7 SUMMARY AND CONCLUSIONS

This chapter has examined the organisation of production, taking the individual agent as the basic unit of analysis. A main focus was the issue of providing incentives when – as is often the case – an input is difficult to measure or specify in a contract. A general principle to emerge is that, wherever possible, the status of residual claimant should be assigned to the individual in question, thereby ensuring that they receive the full benefit, at the margin, generated by their input. Where specific investments are involved this may require a long-term contract to be written; and if there are essential physical assets these should not be held by individuals who would otherwise not have any claim on the residual. But the status of residual claimant may carry with it an exposure to risk. In this situation we saw that insurance considerations can make it optimal to allocate a entitlement to a share of the residual to another party, even though the incentive to supply the input may thereby be diluted.

Incentives and insurance are not the only factors determining organisation. We demonstrated that in oligopolistic product markets there can be strategic effects to take into account. Other considerations – that we have not had space to explore here – include the need to have decisions taken by individuals with information, and the possibility that individual incentives may need to be dampened to encourage cooperation. For an excellent discussion of these and many other issues concerning firm organisation see Milgrom and Roberts (1992), and for a detailed treatment of participatory and labour-managed firms see Chapter 3 by Estrin in this volume.

3 Alternative Forms of Productive Enterprise

SAUL ESTRIN

3.1 INTRODUCTION

The literature of industrial economics is overwhelmingly addressed to the behaviour of privately owned firms, which are assumed to choose level of inputs and output so as to maximise profits. In most Western economies there is however a small but rapidly growing sector of labour-managed and participatory firms, owned and controlled in various ways and to varying degrees by workers. The behaviour and performance of such firms may be expected to differ from that of the traditional firm. Research has concentrated on output and employment decisions, x-inefficiency issues and financial questions. Interestingly, theoretical attention has concentrated on price responsiveness, an area in which labour-managed firms are alleged to perform poorly, while empirical work has been primarily directed to investigating productivity differentials, an area in which such organisations appear to do well (see Ireland and Law, 1982; Bonin and Putterman, 1987 for surveys).

The 'alternative' production sector is in fact quite large. Even producer cooperatives, where workers hire capital and control the firm via a democratic 'one member, one vote' system, are not uncommon in Western Europe (see Ben-Ner, 1988), with nearly 1/2 million employees in 1981, primarily in Italy (350,000), France (50,000), Spain (30,000) and Britain (10,000), though even in Italy the sector only accounts for less than 1 per cent of GNP. There are also examples of very large employee controlled firms which are owned by trusts, most notably in Britain the John Lewis Partnership which has 30,000 employees and turnover in excess of £1.3 billion (see Bradley, Estrin and Taylor, 1990). 'Participative organisations' involving partial ownership and control are more numerous still and their numbers are also growing rapidly. For example, since 1976 around 5,000 firms with an estimated 7 million workers in the United States have become partially owned by their labour forces through employee stock ownership plans (ESOPs). The first ESOP was formed in Britain in 1987 and there are now sixteen such organisations. Turning to participation, the West Germany economy has functioned efficiently for many years on the basis of worker–owner 'co-determination', with employee representatives sitting on supervisory boards, and the system has been examined by both the British and the French. Until the country's disintegration, Yugoslav firms were all managed by their workers in a unique system of workers' self-management. Final examples can be drawn from Israel where, in addition to numerous Kibbutzim in which groups of individuals make collective, democratic decisions about consumption as well as production, Koor firms – enterprises owned and run by the trade and union movement – made up 10 per cent of industrial employment in 1981 (see Ben-Ner and Estrin, 1991). The existence and growth of this 'alternative' production sector has generated a substantial theoretical and empirical literature.

The behaviour of labour-managed firms, and the ways that they differ from traditional capitalist ones, depends on the nature of both the ownership and the control structures. One can conceive of a taxonomy in which firms are controlled either exclusively by workers through a democratic mechanism – labour-managed – or jointly by workers' representatives and conventional owner/managers – participatory firms. In either, ownership is assumed to be external. If one combines workers' control with social ownership along Yugoslav lines (see Estrin, 1983), the enterprise is referred to as self-managed. Finally, there are organisations in which employee ownership takes the form of tradeable equity shares. If only workers are entitled to own shares, such firms are referred to as worker-partnerships. In ESOPs, ownership is partially in the hands of employee shareholders.[1]

In section 3.2, we analyse output and employment decisions in the labour-managed firm. Section 3.3 is devoted to economic issues raised by more realistic assumptions concerning ownership, efficiency and investment. The behaviour of the participatory firm is addressed in section 3.4, and the subject matter is reviewed in the conclusions, section 3.5.

3.2   OUTPUT AND EMPLOYMENT IN THE LABOUR-MANAGED FIRM

Enterprise objectives

Benjamin Ward in his seminal (1958) paper proposed that labour-managed firms should be assumed to maximise average earnings per head. In capitalist firms, owners want to maximise their profits (π). If output decisions are not affected by the number of owners, profit per entrepreneur is maximised by maximising absolute profits. However, in the labour-managed firm, the entrepreneurs are workers and there is a monotonic relationship between their numbers and output, so profits per head and profit maximisation can lead to different output and factor input decisions.

Consider a capitalist firm producing a single output (X), to be sold at P, using two inputs, a homogeneous force (L) and the capital stock (K). We henceforth always assume that the labour-managed firm operates on *competitive* product markets (see Ireland and Law, 1982 for results under imperfect competition). Capital is rented from a perfect capital market at marginal cost, r, and workers are paid a fixed wage, w. Profits are therefore,

$$\pi = pX - rK - wL \tag{3.1}$$

so if surplus is distributed equally, profits per head are

$$\frac{\pi}{L} = \frac{pX - rK}{L} - w \tag{3.2}$$

Then we can define average earnings per worker (y) to be the amount paid to workers in a labour-managed firm, comprising the nominal wage and the share of profit,

$$y = w + \frac{\pi}{L} = \frac{pX - rK}{L} \tag{3.3}$$

Equation (3.3) is the objective function of the labour-managed firm.

Output and employment in the short run

The labour-managed firm is assumed to maximise objective function (3.3) subject to a well-behaved production function which is twice differentiable and concave ($\partial X/\partial L$, $\partial X/\partial K > 0$; $\partial^2 X/\partial^2 L$, $\partial^2 X/\partial^2 K < 0$),

$$X = f(L, K) \tag{3.4}$$

The first-order conditions are

$$\frac{\partial y}{\partial L} = \frac{1}{L}[p\partial X/\partial L - y] = 0 \tag{3.5}$$

$$\frac{\partial y}{\partial K} = \frac{1}{L}\left(p\frac{\partial X}{\partial K} - r \right) = 0 \tag{3.6}$$

Equation (3.5) states that in short-run equilibrium, the labour-managed firm hires workers until their marginal revenue product equals average earnings. This appears identical to the capitalist case in which the marginal revenue product of labour must equal the wage. However, the resulting equilibria are not necessarily the same, because under labour-management average earnings are a choice variable whereas under capitalism the wage is assumed to be exogenous. In contrast, equation (3.6) is satisfied when the marginal revenue product of capital equals its cost, exactly the same capital rule as pertains in profit-maximising firms. The first order conditions therefore imply that average earnings maximisation affects the choice of employment but not capital, provided the firm is able to finance itself using funds borrowed from a perfect capital market.

To focus on employment, we initially concentrate on the short run, when the capital stock is fixed at K_0. Hence the first order condition is

$$\frac{\partial y}{\partial L} = \frac{1}{L^2} \left(Lp\frac{\partial X}{\partial L} - pX + rK_0 \right) = 0 \tag{3.7}$$

which implies $pdX/dL = y$.

To understand equation (3.7), consider how average earnings vary with employment. Equation (3.3) can be rearranged to contain two expressions; average revenue per head, which is assumed to be declining as a result of diminishing returns to a factor, and fixed costs per head, which in the short run take the shape of a rectangular hyperbola. The two are plotted in Figure 3.1a. The difference between them, which gives average earnings per head, is plotted in Figure 3.1b and has a characteristic inverse-U shape with a maximum at L_m. The marginal revenue product of labour in Figure 3.1b is downward-sloping and, we know from equation (3.7), passes through the average earnings curve at its maximum.

The major results of the short-run literature can be summarised as follows (see Ward, 1958; Vanek, 1970):

(1)   The labour-managed firm will be smaller than the capitalist firm when profits are positive.

To see this, consider a capitalist firm with positive profits which is instantaneously turned into a labour-managed organisation. Even without any adjustment of output and employment, from equation (3.3), $\pi > 0$ implies $y > w$ at the initial level of employment. But we know that the capitalist firm hires workers up to the point where the wage equals the marginal revenue product of labour. Hence, at the initial level of employment, average earnings must exceed the marginal revenue product of labour for the labour-managed firm. But our previous discussion has established that average earnings lie above the marginal product only to the right of the maximum of average earnings. The labour-managed firm will seek to increase earnings to their equilibrium by reducing employment and therefore output. The equilibria are illustrated in Figure 3.1b, with the capitalist outcome subscripted by C.

When labour management is introduced into a loss-making firm, by converse reasoning, employment will be increased. This suggests a role for labour-managed organisations in declining sectors or regions where issues of employment maintenance are paramount in the short run.[2]

(2)   The firm responds 'perversely' to a change in price in the short run.

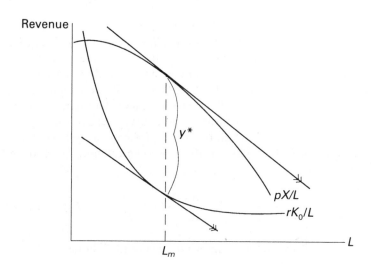

FIGURE 3.1(a)   Average revenue and fixed costs per head

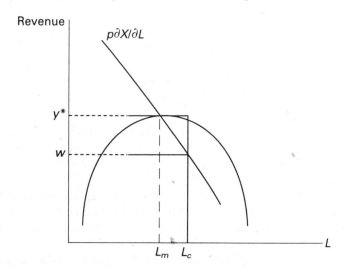

FIGURE 3.1(b)   Equilibrium for labour-managed and capitalist firms

We start at the initial equilibrium y_1^*, L_1^* in Figure 3.2, satisfying first order condition (3.7). An increase in price from p_1 to p_2 raises both the marginal revenue product, by $\partial X/\partial L$, and average earnings by X/L (given equation (3.7)). But this implies that earnings must increase by more than the marginal revenue product because with diminishing returns to a factor X/L exceeds $\partial X/\partial L$. Hence at the initial equilibrium we must be to the right of the maximum of the new earnings curve y_2. Therefore the firm will reduce employment to increase earnings further, to reach its new equilibrium, L_2^*, y_2^*. Since, in the short run, employment determines output, this result implies that the firm's supply curve is backward-sloping.

This important result can be derived formally as follows. Starting with first order condition (3.7), we can differentiate with respect to price.

$$\frac{\partial X}{\partial L} + p \frac{\partial^2 X}{\partial L^2} \frac{\partial L}{\partial p} - \frac{1}{L} \left[\left(p \frac{\partial X}{\partial L} - y(\cdot) \right) \frac{\partial L}{\partial p} + X(L) \right] = 0 \quad (3.8)$$

Evaluated at the initial equilibrium, where (3.7) holds,

$$\frac{\partial L}{\partial p} = \frac{(X/L - \partial X/\partial L)}{p \partial^2 X/\partial L^2} < 0 \quad (3.9)$$

The output response is derived from,

$$\frac{\partial X}{\partial p} = \frac{\partial X}{\partial L} \frac{\partial L}{\partial p} = \frac{\partial X}{\partial L} \left[\frac{X/L - \partial X/\partial L}{p \partial^2 X/\partial L^2} \right] < 0 \quad (3.10)$$

Supply perversity means that labour management may undermine the market mechanism itself; market equilibria will be unstable if the (negative) elasticity of supply is greater than that of demand.

(3)   Output and employment in labour-managed firms respond positively in the short run to an increase in fixed costs. This is in contrast to profit-maximising firms, which do not respond to changes in fixed costs in the short run.

An increase in fixed costs alters the short-run first order condition (3.7) by reducing earnings while leaving the marginal revenue product of labour unchanged. The situation is also illustrated in Figure 3.2, where now (y_1^*, L_1^*) and (y_3^*, L_3^*) represent the initial and final equilibrium, respectively. At the initial equilibrium employment, we find earnings after the cost change, y', to be less than the marginal revenue product. This implies that we must be to the left of the new (lower) earnings curve.

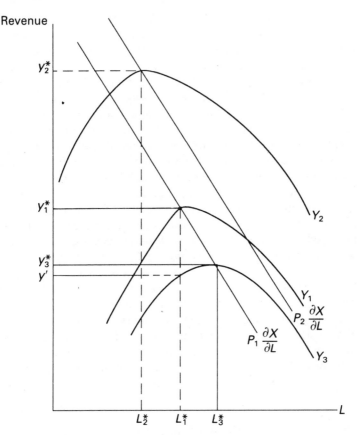

FIGURE 3.2 Initial equilibrium L_1^*, y_1^*

(4) The allocation of labour between alternative employments is inefficient in the short run when profits are positive.

Pareto efficiency requires the equalisation of marginal products across uses. Suppose that, in a two-sector world of identical firms, price increases in one sector (X) and falls in the other (Y). The initial effect, prior to changes in employment, is for marginal products in X to exceed these in Y and for earnings in X to exceed marginal products in both X and Y, and earnings in Y. We have seen that labour-managed firms equalise earnings and marginal products within each sector by a transfer of labour from the high- to the low-value added use. At the new short-run equilibrium, earnings equal marginal products within each sector, but are not equal between sectors. Meade (1972) has stressed that, as a consequence of this short-run reaction, the labour-managed economy must rely disproportionately on entry and exit of firms to restore Pareto efficiency after exogenous perturbations.

The Pareto inefficiency occurs because labour management prevents the labour market from clearing. If firms were maximising profits, the income differences would induce workers in sector Y firms to move to sector X. They would offer to work for more than they were currently earning in X, though less than was paid in Y. Firms in sector X would always accept such offers because they could thereby raise profits (provided the offered wage was less than the marginal revenue product of labour). However, labour-managed firms will *not* accept such offers because, on the terms whereby additional workers could be admitted to the membership, namely an equal share of the surplus, everyone else's average earnings would be reduced by permitting the new workers to join. This suggests that the efficiency problems could be eradicated by allowing discrimination between members according to seniority. New workers could be recruited on less favourable terms than those enjoyed by existing members (see Meade, 1972). But such an approach is probably not consistent with the democratic ethos of such organisations.

Output and employment in the long run

The short-run results are the best known in the theoretical literature, and have motivated substantial research. But they draw on the assumption that the firm adjusts employment but not capital in response to a change in product price. This assumption is innocuous for the capitalist firm because labour and capital demand are both positively related to product price. Output adjusts in the same direction in both the short and long run. However we have seen in labour-managed firms that capital and labour must respond in opposite directions to price changes. Output results for the long run are not so clear-cut. Our exposition follows Estrin (1982).[3]

If we substitute equations (3.5) and (3.6) into (3.3), divide by price and rearrange terms, we can derive,

$$0 = X - L \frac{\partial X}{\partial L} - K \frac{\partial X}{\partial K} \qquad (3.11)$$

which is Euler's theorem. It tells us that equilibrium for labour-managed firms is necessarily characterised by constant returns to scale. Hence if, for example, the production function (3.4) was homogeneous, equilibrium could be achieved only if the function were linearly homogeneous. If instead the labour-managed firms' technology displayed first increasing and later decreasing returns (generating a U-shaped long-run average cost curve for profit maximisers), equation (3.11) tells us that labour-managed firm always attains cost efficiency; i.e. it always produces at the level of output at which long-run average costs would be minimised.

We can define returns to scale as

$$\lambda = L \frac{\partial X}{\partial L} + K \frac{\partial X}{\partial K} \qquad (3.12)$$

and equation (3.11) implies that in equilibrium returns to scale equal unity.

The intuition behind this important result is as follows. The competitive labour-managed firm always exhausts the surplus, because all profits are distributed to workers as income (see equation (3.3)). However, income maximisation also leads the firm to pay factors their marginal products. Only with constant returns to scale can zero residual surplus be achieved simultaneously with payments to factors of their marginal products.

Returns to scale are normally defined with respect to output assuming constant factor proportions. However to understand the nature of the firms' adjustment to product prices under labour management, it is useful to consider in addition two further parameters of the returns to scale function. These are λ_x, the change in returns to scale as output varies, holding employment constant, and λ_L, the change in returns to scale as employment varies for a given level of output around an isoquant. If we assume $\lambda_x < 0$, then it can be shown that,

$$\frac{\partial X}{\partial p} \begin{array}{c} > \\ < \end{array} 0 \text{ as } \lambda_L \begin{array}{c} < \\ > \end{array} 0 \qquad (3.13)$$

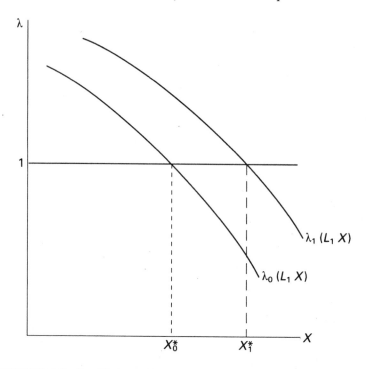

FIGURE 3.3 **Equilibrium when returns to scale equal unity**

By way of illustration, assume the production function displays increasing then decreasing returns to scale and is homothetic.[4] The firm faces an initial price p_0, and capital cost r_0, and output is given by technology at the point where returns to scale equal unity. With returns to scale function λ_0, the equilibrium is represented as X_0^*, in Figure 3.3.

We can represent average earnings by an 'iso-earnings curve' in capital–labour space, the equation of which is derived from equation (3.3) when output, price and capital costs are given,

$$K = \frac{p_0 X_0^*}{r_0} - \frac{y}{r_0} L \qquad (3.14)$$

Given the iso-quant X_0^* in Figure 3.4, and the intercept $p_0 X_0^*/r_0$, the firm chooses the capital–labour ratio to maximise average earn-

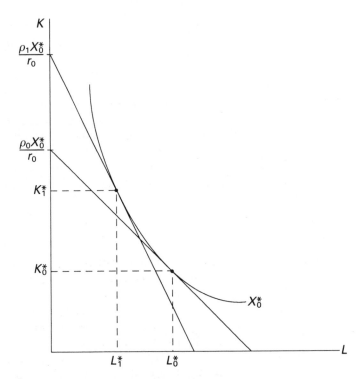

FIGURE 3.4   Optimum capital intensity

ings, which given equation (3.14) implies choosing the tangency from the intercept $p_0 X_0^* / r_0$ to the iso-quant. In Figure 3.4, the firm therefore chooses (K_0^*, L_0^*).

If product price increases to p_1, so the intercept rises to $p_1 X_0^* / r_0$ in Figure 3.4, the firm chooses a more capital-intensive technique of production, (K_1^*, L_1^*). In labour-managed firms, product price changes affect the choice of technique directly by increasing the cost of labour. The firm responds by substituting capital for labour.

What about the long-run supply response? It was assumed in Figure 3.4 that returns to scale equals unity only at output X_0^*. This returns to scale constraint continues to be satisfied at the new capital–labour ratio, K_1^* / L_1^*. Hence if returns to scale do not alter with employment while output remains constant around iso-quant

X_0^*, the labour-managed firm will not alter output in response to a change in product price; the long-run supply curve is perfectly elastic. This is consistent with the equality in equation (3.13).

Suppose instead that because of factor substitution the decline in employment from L_0^* to L_1^* caused returns of scale to increase ($\lambda_L < 0$). Since we have assumed that returns to scale diminish with output, the firm must increase output in order to restore constant returns. If we denote the new returns to scale function at K_1^*/L_1^* to be the function $\lambda_1 > 0$ as in Figure 3.4, then output will be increased to X_1^* to restore constant returns.[5] Thus, as equation (3.13) states, the firm will increase output when $\lambda_L < 0$. A converse argument applies when $\lambda_L > 0$.

Extensions

The supply perversity result has attracted particularly extensive attention in the literature, largely devoted to investigating its robustness. Effort has been concentrated on technical assumptions of the model and the assumed objectives of the organisation.[6]

Ward's original supply perversity result was derived on very restrictive assumptions, namely a single product firm using only one input in the short run. Domar (1966), Pfouts and Rosefelde (1986) and Bonin and Fukuda (1986) establish that supply perversity does not necessarily hold in the multiple input, multiple output case; the sign of the output response is in general ambiguous. Domar (1966) concludes that income maximisation will however lead supply curves to be less elastic in the labour-managed economy than in an equivalent capitalist one. For example in a multiproduct firm an increase in price leads to substitution towards that product but *away* from other products; the total demand for labour may still respond perversely. Employment restrictiveness relative to capitalist firms also frequently carries over to the multiple input and output case. For example, homogeneous production functions always display a perverse response of output and employment to changes in product price.[7] The assumption of certainty also proves to be important. Uncertainty acts to increase output in the labour-managed firm, but to decrease it in the profit-maximising one (see e.g. Bonin and Putterman, 1987).

Another strand of the literature starts from the premise that a democratically run organisation would never actually sack members (see Robinson, 1967). The concern about employment can be modelled directly by assuming the firm to maximise a utility function in both earnings and employment, $U = U(y, L)$. However, even in this case the firm can only be guaranteed to increase employment with product price when the utility function places 'more weight' to employment; for example in a Stone-Geary utility function a larger coefficient attached to employment than earnings. (see Ireland and Law, 1982).

Alternative ownership arrangements have also proved a fruitful line of enquiry. Supply perversity does not occur in worker partnerships, because workers can trade their ownership rights in the company. Sertel (1982) has convincingly argued that workers in such companies will seek to maximise the expected value of their shareholding, and that this is best achieved by the maximisation of enterprise expected future returns, or profits. Hence worker partnerships make the same choices with respect to inputs and outputs as equivalent capitalist firms.

Another organisational form which has a significant degree of employee control but is not supply perverse is the labour-managed firm which uses hired workers. Let us suppose that the labour force is now composed of two types of workers; members (denoted M) who receive the surplus net of all costs, and hired workers (H), who receive a wage (w). We assume that hired workers and members make an identical contribution on the margin to output.

The members now maximise earnings per member net of hired labour costs, i.e. $y = (pX - rK - wH)/M$, subject to the production function (3.4). We assume that member's earnings exceed the external wage, in which case the firm always chooses to use hired workers. The number of members can then be treated as constant, with marginal employment decisions always falling on hired workers. The first order condition with respect to employment is

$$\frac{\partial y}{\partial L} = \frac{1}{M} \left[P \frac{\partial X}{\partial L} - w \right] = 0 \tag{3.15}$$

Members hire labourers until their marginal product equals their wage, exactly as profit maximisers would do in the same circumstances. This result has particular significance for empirical work, because most observed labour-managed firms have a significant number of hired workers. The weak evidence on supply perversity brings into question the relevance of much of the literature, but not necessarily its accuracy.

This theoretical literature has been primarily driven by striking and counter-intuitive short-run results, and has been little motivated by empirical findings. A paper by Bartlett *et al.* (1992) in fact finds few differences in levels of employment and output in a matched sample of small private firms and producer cooperatives in Italy. There have also been surprisingly few attempts to test the output and employment predictions. An exception is Berman and Berman (1989) who used a sample of 37 plants in the American plywood industry (17 producer cooperatives and 20 privately owned firms) over six data points between 1958 and 1977. This gave them an unbalanced panel of 144 observations. The test for supply perversity involved regressing the mean coop capacity utilisation rate on the average rate for capitalist firms over the entire period. A negative relationship would indicate supply perversity because capacity rates in the two forms of organisation must be moving in opposite directions. Unfortunately the estimates are rather imprecise, but they suggest that the supply curve under labour management is less elastic than in the capitalist firms, though not necessarily backward-sloping.

3.3   THE CONSEQUENCES OF EMPLOYEE OWNERSHIP

The income-maximising framework suggests that, while labour-managed firms may be a source of allocative inefficiency in the short run, they are no less viable as an organisational form than their capitalist counterpart. Vanek (1970) and Drèze (1976) have established formally that an economy composed entirely of labour-managed firms can sustain exactly the same Pareto-efficient general equilibrium as a capitalist economy, provided that there is free entry and exit of firms. Yet we see relatively few labour-managed firms in capitalist economies, and this had led to a widespread but not universally held perception that they must be prone to inherent deficiencies. These, it is alleged, are that labour-managed firms are badly run and in practice tend to extract surpluses as wages rather than invest them. In contrast, a substantial empirical literature is emerging to suggest that employee ownership and participation may enhance company performance. We deal with each issue briefly in this section.

Productivity differentials

There is a long tradition of questioning workers' ability to manage firms democratically (see, for example, Webb and Webb, 1920). This pessimistic view has been formalised by Alchian and Demsetz (1972) who stress that organisations require an agent to monitor the level of effort supplied by each individual worker, to prevent or reduce shirking. This agent is best motivated if made the residual claimant. Participative organisations in which the residual is shared by all members will offer more diffuse motivation to monitor and therefore be less efficient than those in which a single agent is residual claimant. Organisational deficiencies are also cited as a basis for differences in efficiency. Factors include the view that democratic decision-making will necessarily be slow or inefficient, that management will be unable to supervise workers whom they cannot discipline or fire and that workers ar more risk-averse than managers.

However, there are also strong arguments to suggest that employee ownership, participation and residual sharing will have positive motivational effects. One line of argument has been the potential role of workers' participation as an institutional mechanism for channelling the antagonistic relations between workers and management towards greater cooperation and productivity. Cable (1984) has formalised this by viewing the conflict between management and workers in the form of a prisoner's dilemma game, in which each side has the choice between cooperating and conflicting in the production process. The optimal outcome is for mutual cooperation but in the conventional hierarchical organisational structure each side believes it can do better by choosing an antagonistic posture. One solution to this dilemma is to establish long-term institutional arrangements trusted by both sides in which the optimal outcome can be chosen. Employee ownership and participation are examples of such arrangements. Mechanisms for the way that participation might increase workers' efficiency, include a reduction of strikes and absenteeism; an increase in firm-specific capital that can result from lower labour turnover rates; and an increase in shop floor effort and even innovation resulting from the sharpening via residual sharing of performance-related incentives throughout the organisation (see Estrin, Grout and Wadhwani, 1986).

Empirical attention on alternative organisational forms has been focused on these productivity issues (see Blinder, 1990 for a survey). Numerous case studies attest to the productivity enhancement associated with the introduction of employee ownership or control (see Estrin, 1986). Three examples will suffice. Bartlett *et al.* (1991) find labour productivity in a small sample of Italian producer cooperatives to be significantly higher than in a matched sample of private firms. The Mondragon cooperative sector, in Spain, has shown for more than thirty years an ability to achieve higher levels and rates of growth of productivity than Spanish industry as a whole (see e.g. Bradley and Gelb, 1980). Finally, Bradley, Estrin and Taylor (1991) find growth, profitability and productivity in the John Lewis Partnership since the late 1950s to be exceptionally high by the standards of the British retail sector, and offer an explanation in terms of the firm's employee ownership and profit-sharing arrangements.

Econometric work typically involves the estimation of augmented production functions of the form $X = f(L, K, Z)$ where Z represents a proxy for organisational form. When researchers have used data sets containing information only on employee controlled firms, Z represents the degree of worker participation in ownership, decision-making and profits. The most exhaustive study of this latter sort is Estrin, Jones and Svejnar (1987) which summarises results for cooperatives in Italy (1975–80), France (1978–9) and Britain (1948–68). This study uses alternative specifications of technology (Cobb–Douglas, CES and translog) together with numerous indicators of workers' participation, most notably the proportion of workers who were members of the cooperative (as distinct from hired hands) and therefore participated in decision-making; the profits shared between workers; and the ratio of individually owned to total assets. A positive significant effect on productivity is established from profit-sharing for all countries, and from participation or equity in some.

This work suggests that, in firms which are already democratically run, increased employee participation raises efficiency. But are labour-managed firms less efficient than their capitalist counterparts? Estrin (1991) and Lee (1988) use data on both types of firms, and their results are not entirely consistent. Estrin (1991) finds that there is no significant difference of productive efficiency in the small matched sample of private firms and producer cooperatives in Italy. In Lee's sample of Swedish employee owned and private firms, however, total factor productivity is slightly lower, on average, in employee owned firms, though productivity is still positively associated with indicators of the degree of participation. Highly participatory firms can thus in principle be more efficient than their profit-maximising competitors. The findings in part reflect sample selection; the cooperative sector is strong in Italy and very weak in Sweden.

The empirical work on productivity suggests that employee ownership and participation probably does not impair company performance, and in certain circumstances, for example immediately after its introduction or via profit-sharing, may enhance it. These findings are clearly sensitive to the initial situation of the firm, and the type of employee participation being introduced.

'Underinvestment'

We have seen when the labour-managed firm faces a perfectly elastic supply of funds, investment decisions will be on the same basis as in profit-maximising firms. This tells us that any differences in investment behaviour between the two types of organisation must stem from capital market imperfections, either in the market itself or arising from the firm's ownership. The argument that labour-managed firms will invest less than capitalist ones is deduced on the assumptions that capital is financed solely through internal investment and that worker members do not have any personal equity stake in the organisation.

The 'property rights' school, most notably Furubotn and Pejovich (1970) regard the attenuation of individual ownership rights as the source of underinvestment. Investment is financed by enterprise savings from the residual surplus, but if there is no individual basis to the property rights, workers have a claim to the returns from the assets only for the duration of their membership of the firm. As a consequence, the return to each worker from an internally-funded investment project must be large enough to compensate for the *principal* invested as well as the interest foregone, and this total return must be paid during the worker's tenure with the organisation. Formally, we assume that each (identical) worker i has a savings function $S_i(\cdot)$ which depends on the interest rate, so that total savings in the firm, $\Sigma_i S_i$, are,

$$S = \sum_i S_i = S(r), \frac{\partial S}{\partial r} > 0 \tag{3.16}$$

Workers can either save with outside financial institutions, in which case they receive the market rate of interest, r^* or invest in their own firm. Clearly, if the ownership rights over the funds saved are individual, then workers will invest in the firm provided that the return exceeds r*. The worker partnership therefore has an identical capital demand to the capitalist firm, even if it is internally financed, and therefore does not suffer from under-investment.

When ownership rights are collective, and both principal and interest cannot be recovered, however, Furubotn and Pejovic (1970) show that workers will invest until the marginal product of capital equals

$$\ddot{\partial}^* = \frac{r^*(1 + r^*)^T}{(1 + r^*)^{T-1}} \tag{3.17}$$

where T is the expected employment duration of current workers. Since T is finite, $\partial^* > r^*$. Assuming that capital demand curves slope down $(\partial^2 X/\partial K^2 < 0)$, investment will be less in collectively owned, participative firms than in their capitalist (and worker partnership) counterparts. Moreover the shorter the expected tenure of workers, the greater will be the degree of 'underinvestment'.

Attempts to test the underinvestment hypothesis empirically have supported the relevance of the distinction between collective and individual ownership. The most significant example of worker partnerships – the Mondragon group of cooperatives – appear to invest at least as much as their capitalist counterparts (see Bradley and Gelb, 1983). On the other hand, Estrin, Jones and Svejnar (1987) reveal low levels of capitalisation for producer cooperatives in Western Europe, a view confirmed by case study evidence (see for example Russell, 1985).

In their direct comparison of small private firms and producer cooperatives in Italy, Bartlett *et al.* (1991) find no significant differences in the criteria used for project evaluation or the time horizon over which investments are evaluated in the two sorts of organisation. Moreover, the sources of investment finance were very similar, with coops financing 48 per cent of investment internally and borrowing 40 per cent from banks, as against 50 per cent and 32 per cent respectively for private firms. However, there were significant differences in the capital–labour ratio; fixed assets per head were around 50 per cent greater in privately owned firms.

The only formal econometric work on investment analyses a large balanced panel of 2700 observations of French producer cooperatives, (see Estrin and Jones, 1991). The paper estimates a neo-classical investment functions augmented by variables to pick up underinvestment effects, notably the proportion of assets which are collectively owned, the share of external funding in total investment and the degree of workers' participation in ownership and decision-making. Investment in French producer cooperatives was explained by the same factors as proved relevant for capitalist firms, most notably expected future demand and external capital constraints.

While *a priori* reasoning has given us several reasons for concern about the likely performance of labour-managed firms, the evidence suggests that such organisations have usually been set up in practice in ways that minimise these deficiencies while facilitating the exploitation of enhanced employee motivation. This leaves open the question of why the labour-managed sector is so small. Ben-Ner (1984) has put forward the interesting hypothesis that the problems are of degeneration, not viability. His model assumes that cooperatives use hired workers. They are founded in recessions to preserve employment. We saw in Figure 3.2 that labour management allows workers to maintain (or increase) employment in situations when profit-maximising firms would close. When founded, all workers are members because average earnings are less than the market wage but as conditions improve, earnings exceed the wage (i.e. a private firm would be profitable). Ben-Ner shows that once this occurs, optimal membership in the cooperative is one. Hence, whenever members leave, they will be replaced by hired workers and the firm will gradually degenerate back to the capitalist form. His argument is consistent with the evidence in so far as cooperatives have been founded in waves inversely associated with the trade cycle. In Western Europe, there is rather less evidence of degeneration back to the capitalist form, however (see Estrin and Jones, 1988).

3.4   THE PARTICIPATORY FIRM

In the previous sections, we have contrasted the behaviour of firms in which capital hires labour with those in which labour hires capital. Between there lies a spectrum of participatory organisations, differentiated according to the proportion of ownership or control in the hands of labour and management. Over this range, one might expect the objectives of the organisation to be broadened to take account of the preferences of the labour force.

The pathbreaking work on participatory firms was done by Svejnar (1982), though the approach draws on models of collective bargaining between managers and unions (see e.g. McDonald and Solow, 1981). In Nash bargaining equilibrium, the two parties cooperate to achieve the highest joint reward and then divide the surplus between themselves according to their relative bargaining power. 'Reward' refers to gain relative to 'threat points'; payments each party would receive in the absence of agreement between them. When applied to participatory firms, owners are assumed to obtain their satisfaction from profits, with the minimum acceptable level of profit denoted π_{min}. Workers maximise a utility function, U^w, of the form

$$U^w = U^w(w, L) \tag{3.18}$$

where wages (w) are not necessarily equal to the market wage, w_a. If the labour force as a whole refuse to work for the organisation, they earn an outside level of utility, assumed to be less than that available inside the firm because of the existence of firm-specific rents (U^w_{min}).

We can represent the relative bargaining power of the firm as against the union by the parameter, μ. The two sides in the participatory firm will choose employment and wages to maximise the Nash product

$$N = [\pi - \pi_{min}]^\mu [U^w(w, L) - U^w_{min}] \tag{3.19}$$

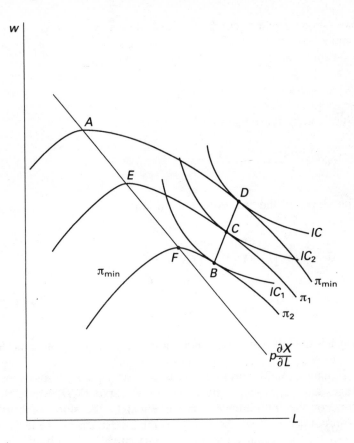

FIGURE 3.5 Pareto efficient wage-employment combinations *BCD*

The two first-order conditions to this maximisation problem can be rearranged to yield

$$\frac{1}{L}\left[p\frac{\partial X}{\partial L} - w\right] = \frac{-\partial U^w/\partial L}{\partial U^w/\partial w} \tag{3.20}$$

which plots out a contract curve *BCD* in wage–employment space (see Figure 3.5). Here, indifference curves IC_1, IC_2, IC_3 illustrate the workers' tradeoff between wages and employment, and have the slope $(\partial U^w/\partial L)/(\partial U^w/\partial w)$. The firm's marginal revenue product curve is its labour-demand curve $p\partial X/\partial L$. For each point on the labour-demand curve, we can derive a locus of wage–employment combinations which yield the same level of profits; an 'iso-profit' curve. For a given level of profits, Π,

$$\Pi = pX - rK - wL \tag{3.21}$$

which can be rearranged as

$$w = \frac{pX - rK - \Pi}{L} \tag{3.22}$$

The slope of the iso-profit line in wage–employment space is therefore,

$$\frac{\partial w}{\partial L} = \frac{1}{L^2} \left[Lp \partial X / \partial L - (pX - rK - \Pi) \right]$$

$$= \frac{1}{L} \left[p \frac{\partial X}{\partial L} - w \right] \tag{3.23}$$

which is the left-hand side of equation (3.20). A family of iso-profit curves, π_{min}, π_1, π_2, are drawn in Figure 3.5.

Equation (3.22) therefore tells us that participatory firms choose wages and employment on the contract curve *BCD*, where the slope of the indifference curve is equal to the slope of firm's iso-profit curve. If we assume IC_1 is the lowest acceptable level of utility for the labour force, the contract curve is given by the line *BD*.[8] Actual outcomes depend on μ. If workers cannot raise their utility level above IC_1, the outcome will be at *B*, on the labour-demand curve. In all other cases, employee participation leads to higher levels of employment than would pertain at that wage rate if the choice were left solely to management. If workers are powerful enough to push owners to their threat point, the outcome lies at *D*. Intermediate cases, where both parties have some bargaining power, lie, for example, at *C*.

How does this result compare with the outcome under labour-management? Profits are zero in the labour-managed firm, so the average earnings curve is in fact the same curve as the iso-profit curve π_{min} in Figure 3.5 if $\pi_{min} = 0$. In section 3.2, we assumed that workers received utility from income but not employment. Hence, they choose the *maximum* of that iso-profit (earnings) curve, at point A. If workers in the participatory firm are also assumed to maximise only earnings, rather than a utility function in wages and employment, their indifference curves become horizontal and workers' representatives choose points at the maximum of the iso-profit curve. These always lie on the labour-demand curve, $p\partial X/\partial L$ so the contract curve now lies between points A and F.

Workers' participation therefore leads to a sharing of firm-specific rents between workers and owners according to their relative bargaining power. Provided workers' bargaining power takes them above their threat point, employee participation reduces the returns to private owners to the benefit of employees. The way that workers will use their share of profits depends on their objectives. If they relate solely to income, workers will take their share of the residual in higher pay. Output and employment will be lower than in the non-participatory firm as a consequence. If, on the other hand, they gain satisfaction from employment as well as wages, they may also hire extra workers, instead increasing output and employment.

The participatory model has also been subjected to econometric test, most notably by Ben-Ner and Estrin (1991). Using a sample of private and union controlled firms in Israel, they found strong evidence that employee participation did force firms off their labour-demand curves, and that this led to employment as well as income enhancement. They concluded that Israeli workers were surprisingly powerful in the bargaining process, and that they attached almost equal weight in their preferences to wages and employment. They also found strong evidence that the participatory organisations were more productive than non-participatory ones, so increased employee power did not necessarily reduce absolute profit levels. Cable and Fitzroy (1980), in a study on West Germany, also found higher productivity in participatory organisations.

3.5 CONCLUSIONS

The reader will have been struck by the sharp disjunction between theory and empirical work in this area. The former is obsessed with the ramifications of average earnings maximisation on output and employment decisions, usually assuming perfect capital markets and invariant productivity between organisational forms. An enormous literature, summarised, for example, in Bonin and Putterman (1987), extends this framework to different market structures and situations. The empirical literature asks whether the differences in organisational structure affect x-efficiency, investment and survival. The results of the former literature are for the most part pessimistic about the potential impact of employee participation; the findings of the latter are frequently optimistic. So what is our conclusion about these alternative organisational forms?

The matter can in part be resolved by further empirical work. The favourable empirical work on cooperatives is based on relatively few studies and, Ben-Ner's (1984) degeneration argument notwithstanding, fly in the face of the evidence concerning the scale and scope of the participatory sector in most market economies. We have also noted that the average earnings-maximisation literature has rarely been subjected to empirical verification. Large data sets like that used by Bartlett *et al.* (1991) with matched samples of private and labour managed firms are needed.

In the interim, there are two possible ways to resolve the question. One might conclude, when comparing the labour-managed and capitalist economy, that the former will suffer relatively more from allocative inefficiency while the latter may face more serious problems of x-inefficiency, at least in the area of employee motivation. The problem here is that successful labour-managed sectors such as in Mondragon or Italy have typically adopted ownership structures and institutional arrangements which avoid the inefficiencies stressed in the theoretical literature, e.g. using individualised ownership and hired workers. Most of the perversities discussed in section 3.2 are therefore of considerable conceptual interest, but of limited practical relevance. This leaves the way open for a relatively optimistic conclusion about the prospects for alternative organisational structures, with the proviso that this is not yet convincingly established and could be overturned by further empirical work.

4 Conjectural Variations

C. D. FRASER

4.1 INTRODUCTION

The conjectural variations (CV) approach to oligopoly equilibrium represents a way of unifying the many disparate models of oligopoly behaviour and suppliers' underlying beliefs about the nature of rivalry which are possible. In this chapter we will first outline the conventional, static CV framework for a homogeneous goods market, where firms regard output choices as their strategic variable. Within this framework, we argue that it is possible to accommodate all the popular static models of oligopoly behaviour, including the Cournot, Stackelberg, and the collusive or market-sharing models. We then consider situations where firms consider price as their decision variable with differentiated products. These include Chamberlin's and Sweezy–Stigler's kinked demand curve models.

While CVs are useful in allowing a taxonomy of the possible static models and outcomes in oligopolistic scenarios, their uses extend far beyond this. In particular, the CV approach has proven especially valuable in the theoretical specification of structure–conduct–performance (SCP) relationships, for long the dominant empirically-driven paradigmatic approach to industrial economics. This specification can be extended to include consideration of oligopolistic equilibria involving advertising and technological competition, as well as of the distributional outcomes of such equilibria.

Faced with a multiplicity of possible oligopoly models and their underlying CVs, we confront an obvious problem: how do we choose between the contenders? We outline one approach which has been advanced for handling this model selection problem: the idea of consistent or rational conjectures. This idea, akin to the concept of rational expectations in macroeconomics, follows from the observation that a number of the popular oligopoly models are based on firms having, and acting upon, conjectures about their rivals which are patently falsified by their rivals' behaviour. Given this observation, it seems reasonable to require that conjectures which are held satisfy some criteria of plausibility – such as that they coincide with rivals' actual behaviour, at least in the neighbourhood of equilibrium. It will be shown that while this requirement limits the possible oligopoly equilibria in some special cases, in general the number of possible equilibria still remains embarrassingly large.

While the consistent conjectures idea represents, in principle, a reasonable route to take in selecting between the alternative oligopoly models at the theoretical level, an equally natural route would seem to lie in confronting the theory with data. If oligopolists behave according to their conjectures, these conjectures should be implicit in the data derived from their equilibrium behaviour. Accordingly, we will review some of the attempts to estimate actual conjectures on this basis.

Finally, we include also some criticisms of the CV approach. The major criticism derives from the fact that it is a static equilibrium approach, while oligopolistic interactions are inherently dynamic. It thus seems more natural to model oligopoly equilibria via multiperiod game theory. However, not only does adopting the latter route not serve to eliminate the multiplicity of possible equilibria, but also, and more importantly, some ostensibly simplistic oligopoly solutions can be shown to derive from much more complicated game-theoretic scenarios. Moreover, as we stress, a primary motivation for the development of the CV approach was to provide a satisfactory theoretical basis for the early empirical work on the SCP paradigm. Leading proponents of the 'new' Industrial Organisation concede, sometimes grudgingly, the value of CVs in this area.

4.2 CONJECTURAL VARIATIONS IN OLIGOPOLY THEORY

Non-differentiated products

To illustrate the basic idea, we will consider initially an oligopoly situation with n suppliers of a homogeneous commodity. These suppliers confront collectively an inverse market demand function for the commodity given by the relationship $p = p(Q)$ with $p' < 0$, by assumption. Here, p is the common price and Q is the market output, satisfying $Q = \Sigma_i q_i$, where q_i, $i = 1, \ldots, n$, is the output of the ith supplier. Suppose the arbitrary ith supplier has total cost function $c_i(q_i)$ and seeks to maximise its profits given by

$$\Pi_i = q_i p(Q) - c_i(q_i) \tag{4.1}$$

If this profit function is concave in q_i (thus the second-order condition for the maximisation is satisfied), the first order condition for the solution to this problem requires:

$$d\Pi_i/dq_i = p + q_i p'(Q)dQ/dq_i - c_i' = 0 \tag{4.2}$$

Here, $dQ/dq_i = 1 + dQ_{-i}/dq_i \equiv 1 + \lambda_i$, where Q_{-i} is the total output of all firms excluding the ith and $\lambda_i \equiv dQ_{-i}/dq_i$ is the ith firm's *conjectural variation* – i.e. its belief about how its rivals in aggregate will vary their output in response to its own output variation.

Using these notational conventions, (4.2) can be rearranged thus:

$$(p - c_i')/p = s_i(1 + \lambda_i)/\varepsilon \tag{4.3}$$

Here, $(p - c_i')/p \equiv L_i$, or Lerner's (1934) index for monopoly power for firm i, gives its proportional markup on the marginal cost pricing which would occur under competition; $s_i \equiv q_i/Q$ is oligopolist i's equilibrium market share and $\varepsilon \equiv -(dQ/dp)p/Q$ is the absolute value of the price elasticity of market demand at equilibrium output.

If all oligopolists behave the same way, (4.3) can be aggregated to give the market equilibrium relationship:[1]

$$(\textstyle\sum_i pq_i - \sum_i c_i' q_i)/pQ = \sum_i s_i^2 (1 + \lambda_i)/\varepsilon \equiv H(1 + \lambda)/\varepsilon \quad (4.4)$$

$H \equiv \Sigma_i s_i^2$ is the Herfindahl–Hirschman index of concentration, theoretically perhaps the most satisfactory measure of market structure, and $\lambda \equiv \Sigma_i s_i^2 \lambda_i / H$ is a market shares-weighted average conjectural variation for the oligopolists. When marginal costs equal average variable costs (i.e. in the constant returns case), and letting R, F and Π denote industry aggregate revenues, fixed costs and profits respectively, (4.4) simplifies to

$$(\Pi + F)/R = H(1 + \lambda)/\varepsilon \qquad\qquad (4.5)$$

As we will discuss below, (4.4) and (4.5) play an important role in the theoretical specification of industry-wide SCP relationships and as a guide to empirical work.

The various static oligopoly models can now be derived from (4.3) and (4.4) or (4.5) by an appropriate specification of the CV term. We will consider the Cournot, Stackelberg and the collusive models in turn.

(i) *Cournot*

Cournot (1863) provides what is indubitably the simplest oligopoly model. It assumes, seemingly implausibly, $\lambda_i = 0$ for all i. (4.3) then becomes

$$(p - c_i')/p = s_i/\varepsilon \qquad\qquad (4.6)$$

Comparing (4.6) with the equivalent condition for a profit-maximising monopolist (i.e. $[(p - c')/p = 1/\varepsilon]$), it is apparent that the Cournot oligopolist acts like a monopolist with respect to the *residual demand curve*, $p = f(q_i) \equiv p(q_i + \bar{Q}_{-i})$, which it faces, assuming its rivals pre-empt sales of $\bar{Q}_{-i}$.

Equation (4.6), and the marginal-revenue-equals-marginal-cost condition which underlies it, define a *reaction function* for firm i. This specifies the optimal output for i as a function of its rivals' output, $\bar{Q}_{-i}$, and will be denoted $\phi_i(Q_{-i})$. In the duopoly case, the rivals' reaction functions can be depicted in two-dimensional output space, as in Figure 4.1.

In the case where the rivals' outputs are *strategic substitutes*,[2] the

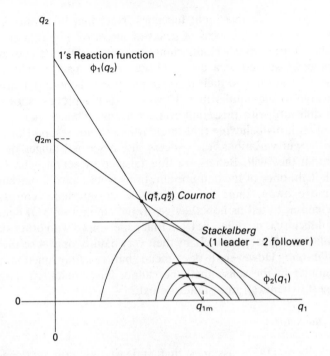

FIGURE 4.1 Rivals' reaction functions

reaction functions are downward-sloping, as drawn.[3] The pair of outputs q_1^* and q_2^* where they intersect locates the so-called Cournot, or Cournot–Nash, equilibrium.[4] This has the feature that each firm is maximising profits given its rival's output and given its conjecture about its rival's behaviour. The generalisation to the case $n > 2$ is straightforward, as is that to where reaction functions are non-linear and have multiple intersections.

The intersection of a given firm's reaction function with the firm's own output axis (involving zero output by its rivals) indicates that firm's pure monopoly output. This is obviously the best that that firm can do, and moves away from that point in output space involve output configurations yielding the given firm less profits. *Iso-profit contours*, the loci of output combinations corresponding to given profit levels for a particular firm, can be drawn in this space. They ripple from the firm's monopoly point, as

indicated, for suitable profit functions. Note that the Cournot reaction function is the locus of peaks of successive iso-profit curves.

The Cournot–Nash equilibrium depicted is stable in the sense
that, if we started at a disequilibrium output pair, and if firms
behaved according to their reaction functions, then outputs would
converge to the equilibrium. However, such a process shows up
one difficulty with this equilibrium concept. Though it is predicated on firms believing that their rivals will *not* respond to their
own output variations, the process just described hinges on the
fact that they will. Beliefs are thus falsified by actual behaviour.
Although, once at the equilibrium, firms would have no incentive
to move away, there is no plausible or internally consistent
mechanism to tell us how they *get* to the equilibrium. Of course,
this difficulty is no different from that experienced with other static
equilibrium concepts which, by their very nature, only describe the
equilibrium. However, it does mean that 'reaction function' is a
misnomer in the sense that one cannot have 'reactions' (which
suggest dynamics), in a static context.[5]

(ii) *Stackelberg*

Stackelberg (1952) assumes that at least one firm (a 'leader')
recognises that its rivals (termed 'followers') will not hold output
constant in response to its own output variation but, instead, will
behave optimally as specified by their reaction functions, *given* the
leader's behaviour.[6] The leader, i, thus incorporate this behaviour
by its rivals into its own maximisation, giving it the following
profit-maximisation problem:[7]

$$\max_{q_i} q_i p[q_i + \textstyle\sum_j \phi_j(Q_{-j})] - c_i(q_i) \tag{4.7}$$

In the duopoly case, (4.7) reduces to the much simpler problem

$$\max_{q_i} q_i p[q_i + \phi_j(q_i)] - c_i(q_i) \tag{4.7'}$$

The first-order condition for (4.7′) is

$$p + q_i p'.[1 + \phi_j'(q_i)] - c_i' = 0 \tag{4.8}$$

Clearly, comparing (4.8) and (4.2), the leader's conjectural variation is simply the slope of the follower's reaction function. (This means, anticipating somewhat developments below, that the Stackelberg leader–follower equilibrium is a *consistent conjectures equilibrium*.) Geometrically, the solution to (4.7′), and hence also to (4.8), occurs where a leader's iso-profit schedule is tangential to the follower's reaction function. This will usually give the leader greater profits than at the Cournot–Nash equilibrium, but lower profits to the follower.

Although arguably a step in the direction of reality by allowing at least one oligopolist to recognise that interdependence means that its rivals will respond to its own output variation, Stackelberg's theory has been criticised because it contains no mechanism for determining which firm(s) will act as leader(s). (See e.g. Hay and Morris, 1991.) Also, if more than one firm attempts to act as leader, then 'Stackelberg warfare' ensues, and the eventual outcome is indeterminate.

(iii) *Collusion*

The possibility of the oligopolists colluding to organise the supply side of the industry as a multiplant, joint profit-maximising monopoly (i.e. a cartel) has received much attention in both static and dynamic models (see e.g. Stigler, 1964; Friedman, 1971). Indeed, as Cubbin (1983) reminds us, Stigler (1964) regards this as the only rational outcome for the oligopolists. For them to behave otherwise means that, in principle, they could obtain greater profits than they do. Thus, neglecting the obvious coordination problems, if Kamien and Schwartz (1983) are right in their contention that 'just as nature is thought to abhor a vacuum, so a market might be thought to abhor an unexploited profit opportunity', models of oligopoly which presuppose non-collusive behaviour presume suboptimal behaviour by the oligopolists.

When the oligopolists collude, it is usual to assume they conjecture that their rivals would vary their outputs exactly in proportion to their own output variation to preserve market shares. The basis for this belief is not well founded in a static model as the implied behaviour need not be optimal (but see Osborne, 1976; Jacquemin and Slade, 1988). However, it can be rationalised in a dynamic context when meeting rivals' output expansions is a 'punishment' strategy which might induce them to adhere to the joint profit-maximising output configuration (Osborne, 1976). Be that as it may, if behaviour *is* of this form, the conjectural variation terms now take the form $\lambda_i = (1 - s_i)/s_i$. Substituting into (4.3) and (4.5) yields (4.9) and (4.10), respectively:

$$L_i = (p - c_i')/p = 1/\varepsilon; \tag{4.9}$$

$$(\Pi + F)/R = 1/\varepsilon. \tag{4.10}$$

Since the Lerner index now corresponds to that of monopoly at both the firm and industry levels, the effect of firms acting according to these conjectures is to achieve joint profit maximisation.

Strictly speaking (4.3) and (4.9) hold only if i has non-zero output within the cartel. However, if i's technology is relatively inefficient compared with its rivals', it is quite possible that it will be allocated a quota of zero output. In that event, if it could make positive profits by producing positive output acting outside the group, side-payments will generally be required to ensure its compliance within the cartel.

Several authors (e.g. Cubbin, 1983; Clarke and Davies, 1982; Dixit and Stern, 1982; Daskin, 1991) have achieved a significant generalisation of the collusive model by assuming that firms have conjectural variations proportional (but not necessarily equal) to relative market shares. We will defer discussion of Cubbin's model as it is somewhat more subtle than the others and also deals with differentiated products. Of the rest, Daskin's empirically-driven model achieves a slight advance on Clarke and Davies and Dixit and Stern as he allows the proportional conjectural variation term to differ between firms, unlike those authors. Thus, we will consider his model.

Suppose, following Daskin, we assume oligopolist i has a CV of $\lambda_i = \alpha_i(1 - s_i)/s_i$. This is simply α_i times the fully collusive CV just considered and, by allowing α_i to range between 0 and 1, we range from the Cournot–Nash to the fully collusive solution. The Lerner indices at the firm and industry levels now become, respectively (cf. Daskin, 1991, p. 16),

$$L_i = [s_i + (1 - s_i)\alpha_i]/\varepsilon \tag{4.11}$$

$$(\Pi + F)/R = [H + \sum_i \alpha_i s_i(1 - s_i)]/\varepsilon \tag{4.12}$$

In (4.11) and (4.12), respectively, $\alpha_i(1 - s_i)/\varepsilon$ and $\Sigma_i\alpha_is_i(1 - s_i)/\varepsilon$, in turn, show the gains at the firm and industry level from this anticipated output-matching behaviour relative to the Cournot equilibrium. However, as Daskin notes, the principal advantage of his generalisation is that it allows firms' price–cost margins (L_i) to be non-monotonic with respect to their market shares. This accords with the empirical fact that the largest firms are not always the most efficient. Moreover, (4.11) indicates that, other things equal, the less aggressively a firm believes its rivals will respond to its own output variation, the greater will be its output, and hence its market share.

Differentiated products

With an homogeneous product, it is natural to assume that firms use output as their strategic variable, given that the outcome with price competition in these circumstances would be the competitive one (provided that firms have identical marginal costs and sufficient capacity to supply the demand arising with marginal cost pricing). This was Bertrand's (1883) unique insight. With a differentiated product, however, it is possible for firms to compete in price (and advertising and quality). This is because the fact of differentiation means each firm confronts its own downward-sloping demand schedule which, however, will depend on its rivals' prices as well. Cubbin (1983, p. 156) notes that in many markets firms 'do choose price while consumers choose quantities'.

In the case of price-setting, the CV involves conjectured price responses to price changes. Cubbin's (1983) model is of particular interest, as it demonstrates a formal equivalence between, on the one hand, outcomes from assumptions of a 'mechanical' CV and, on the other hand, the outcomes from firms trying to sustain a collusive equilibrium by finding the set of prices (and advertising intensities, depending on the context) from which no deviation increases expected profits for any firm. Essentially, he adopts the Stiglerian viewpoint that the collusive oligopoly problem is one of enforcement. His model also incorporates a mild form of 'punishment strategy' ('tit-for-tat') of the type used to support tacit collusion in the game-theoretic approach.[8]

Suppose, following Cubbin, oligopolist i's demand function is

$$q_i = f_i(p_i, p_{-i}) \tag{4.13}$$

p_{-i} being the vector of its rivals' prices. Now, the impact on i's sales when it varies its price depends on whether or not its change is followed by its rivals. (Throughout, Cubbin talks of price cuts although it is not obvious that the deviating firm necessarily always wishes to cut price.) In the case where the price change is followed, i will move along the 'industry' demand curve (Chamberlin's DD' curve), which is less elastic than the 'firm' demand curve (Chamberlin's dd') in the case where price changes have not been followed. Denote these elasticities (which will, in general, depend on the set of prices at which they are being evaluated) by ε_i^l and ε_i^f, respectively. They correspond, respectively, to the cases where i conjectures a reaction 'as if' firms are colluding and one where a Cournot conjecture in prices is appropriate.

Whichever regime i believes itself to be in, the impact on profit of a change in its price takes the general form

$$d\Pi_i/dp_i = p_i(dq_i/dp_i) + q_i - c_i'dq_i/dp_i = -q_iL_i\varepsilon_i + q_i \qquad (4.14)$$

Here, ε_i has value ε_i^l or ε_i^f, respectively, according to whether or not a price change is detected and met. Suppose ϑ_i is the probability that the change is met and $(1 - \vartheta_i)$ is the probability that it is not. The expected change in profits arising from i's price cut is then

$$E(d\Pi_i/dp_i) = \vartheta_i(-q_iL_i\varepsilon_i^l + q_i) + (1 - \vartheta_i)(-q_iL_i\varepsilon_i^f + q_i) \qquad (4.15)$$

$$= -q_iL_i[\vartheta_i\,\varepsilon_i^l + (1 - \vartheta_i)\varepsilon_i^f] + q_i \qquad (4.16)$$

It is optimal for i not to change any given price if that price change reduces expected profits. At the highest price for which this is so, a marginal raising or lowering of price will have no impact on profits – i.e. the expected change in profits from a price change will be zero. At that price we have, on rearranging (4.16),

$$L_i = [\vartheta_i\,\varepsilon_i^l + (1 - \vartheta_i)\varepsilon_i^f]^{-1} \qquad (4.17)$$

Cubbin identifies $\vartheta_i = 1$ as the perfectly collusive case, since (4.17) then reduces to the standard monopoly condition: $L_i = 1/\varepsilon_i^l$.[9] $\vartheta_i = 0$ is then the totally non-collusive solution and, more generally, $0 \leq \vartheta_i \leq 1$ can be regarded as a suitable index of the degree of collusion. However, 'to allow for the possibility that other kinds of oligopoly behaviour have produced a given price–cost margin' (1983, p. 159), Cubbin regards ϑ_i as the degree of *apparent* collusion. ϑ_i can be estimated given knowledge of L_i, ε_i^l and ε_i^f.

Cubbin proceeds to derive further results, as follows.

(i) If detection and/or retaliation are not instantaneous, and if profits depend only on current prices, then the set of stable prices satisfies

$$L_i = -[e^{-rt} \varepsilon_i^l + (1 - e^{-rt})\varepsilon_i^f]^{-1} \tag{4.18}$$

Here, t is the retaliation lag and r is the discount rate. (4.18) is identical in form to (4.17), with e^{-rt} *playing the role of* ϑ_i. The highest stable price then varies inversely with the retaliation lag.

(ii) Likewise, when there is a conditional probability of detection and retaliation at any given time, g, the highest stable price–cost margin is then given by

$$L_i = - \left[\frac{g}{g + r}\varepsilon_i^l + \frac{r}{g + r}\varepsilon_i^f \right]^{-1} \tag{4.19}$$

Thus the degree of apparent collusion is now higher, the larger is the conditional probability of a price cut being detected and punished at any moment, relative to the discount rate.

(iii) When there is competition via advertising, denoted A, if the probability of instantaneous retaliation to i via advertising is β_i, then i's optimal advertising intensity, A_i/p_iq_i, is given by

$$\frac{A_i}{p_iq_i} = \frac{\beta_i\mu_i^l + (1 - \beta_i)\mu_i^f}{\vartheta_i\varepsilon_i^l + (1 - \vartheta_i)\varepsilon_i^f} \tag{4.20}$$

Hence, an increase in the degree of apparent collusion over advertising (β_i) lowers advertising intensity, other things equal.

(iv) Most importantly, Cubbin shows the following. Starting with a differentiated demand structure satisfying (4.13) above, and with p_{-i} now representing a suitable index of i's rivals' prices, let ε_i^f and ε_i^l represent i's demand elasticities when, respectively, only i changes price and when i conjectures that the elasticity of his rivals' price response to his own price variation is unity (i.e. all prices move in unison). If i then conjectures an elasticity of rivals' price response of α_i', i has a generalised demand elasticity, ε_i^G, defined by

$$\varepsilon_i^G = \alpha_i'\varepsilon_i^I + (1 - \alpha_i')\varepsilon_i^f \qquad (4.21)$$

Using this elasticity, i's Lerner index under a CV approach becomes

$$L_i = -[\alpha_i'\varepsilon_i^I + (1 - \alpha_i')\varepsilon_i^f]^{-1} \qquad (4.22)$$

This is identical in form to the Lerner indices derived from apparently collusive behaviour (i.e. as in (4.17)) despite being, in Cubbin's terms, based on 'a mechanical rule without justification' (1983, p. 162). Thus a model based on the CV is formally equivalent to others which can be justified on theoretically more satisfactory grounds. Moreover, it is relatively easy to demonstrate, as Cubbin argues (and Waterson, 1984, shows) that other familiar models, such as Sweezy–Stigler's 'kinked demand curve theory', can be put within the CV framework if we allow discontinuous or non-differentiable CV functions of prices.

4.3 REFINEMENTS OF CONJECTURAL VARIATIONS

We have now seen that a large number of oligopoly models, for both homogeneous and differentiated product markets, can be accommodated within the static CV approach. From an empiricist's standpoint, this catholicity can be regarded as desirable because it enables us to encompass a large number of the possibilities in the admittedly diverse real world within one model. From the standpoint of the theorist striving for precision, however, the situation is rather frustrating for it indicates that, in principle, any outcome can be generated at the theoretical level unless we impose further restrictions.

Three responses to this indeterminacy suggest themselves: (i) refine the CV notion by incorporating criteria of reasonableness which CVs have to satisfy to be admissable, at least to the theorist. This is the approach of *rational* or *consistent conjectures*. (ii) recognise the shortcomings of analysing an inherently dynamic interaction within a static model and proceed to an explicitly dynamic analysis; (iii) use empirical data to try to distinguish between the competing theories, if possible. We consider (i) and (ii) here, and (iii) in section 4.4.

(i) *Rational or consistent conjectures*

Consistent conjectures are CVs which have the property that, if held and acted upon by the oligopolists, they will yield behaviour in equilibrium which confirms or validates the conjectures. This usually translates to meaning that the slopes of the oligopolists' reactions functions in equilibrium should coincide with their rivals' conjectures about those slopes. Breshnahan (1981), Perry (1982), Laitner (1980) and Kamien and Schwartz (1983) are perhaps the most quoted papers in this area. However, to express the basic idea formally, we will follow initially the exposition of Boyer and Moreaux (1983). Subsequently, as the issues in the development of the basic model are somewhat complex, we will confine ourselves to a narrative outline.

Boyer and Moreaux ask: given the demand and cost functions, what conjectures giving linear CVs are consistent with the production levels observed on the market? They consider a homogeneous good duopoly with essentially the same assumptions as we employed initially. Let i, j, $(i, j = 1, 2)$ index these duopolists and suppose they have common constant marginal and average costs, c. The restriction to linear conjectures mean their CVs, λ_i, λ_j, are scalars.

Profit maximisation by the duopolists now yields FOCs (versions of (4.2)):

$$\psi^i(q_i, q_j) \equiv p(Q) - c + q_i p'[1 + \lambda_i] = 0 \qquad (4.23)$$

$$\psi^j(q_i, q_j) \equiv p(Q) - c + q_j p'[1 + \lambda_j] = 0 \qquad (4.24)$$

Given satisfaction of the second-order conditions, any feasible pair of outputs can be derived by solving these FOCs for different values of λ_i, λ_j: $\lambda_i = \lambda_j = 0$ gives the Cournot outcome; $\lambda_i = \lambda_j = -1$ gives the competitive (price-taking) outcome; $\lambda_i = \lambda_j = +1$ gives the collusive outcome; $\lambda_i = 1$, $\lambda_j = 0$ also gives the competitive outcome. To see which of these outcomes is consistent, we implicitly differentiate (4.23) and (4.24) and rearrange to obtain the profit-maximising response of each firm to its rival's output behaviour in the neighbourhood of equilibrium:

$$dq_i/dq_j \mid_{\psi i} = - [p' + p''q_i(1 + \lambda_i)][p'(2 + \lambda_i)$$
$$+ p''q_i(1 + \lambda_i)]^{-1} \qquad (4.25)$$

$$dq_j/dq_i \mid_{\psi j} = - [p' + p''q_j(1 + \lambda_j)][p'(2 + \lambda_j)$$
$$+ p''q_j(1 + \lambda_j)]^{-1} \qquad (4.26)$$

Now, for conjectures to be consistent, $dq_j/dq_i \mid_{\psi j} = \lambda_i$ and $dq_i/dq_j \mid_{\psi i} = \lambda_j$; i.e. *actual* output variations equal *conjectured* output variations. For linear demand ($p'' = 0$) it is easy to see that, if Cournot conjectures are held, $dq_i/dq_j \mid_{\psi i} = -1/2 \neq \lambda_j = 0, i, j, = 1, 2$. Thus, as we know already, Cournot conjectures are inconsistent. For general demand functions and a symmetric solution with symmetric conjectures ($q_i = q_j \equiv q$, $\lambda_j = \lambda_i \equiv \bar{\lambda}$), the only consistent case is obtained when $\lambda_j = \lambda_i \equiv \bar{\lambda} = -1$ (i.e. the competitive case, which is also sometimes referred to as the Bertrand case). This can be seen by substituting $\lambda_j = \lambda_i \equiv \bar{\lambda}$ and $q_i = q_j \equiv q$ into the consistency conditions to obtain

$$\bar{\lambda} = -[p' + p''q(1 + \bar{\lambda})][p'(2 + \bar{\lambda}) + p''q(1 + \bar{\lambda})]^{-1} \qquad (4.27)$$

or $(p' + qp'')(\bar{\lambda}^2 + 2\bar{\lambda} + 1) = 0$. Thus, if $(p' + qp'') \neq 0, \bar{\lambda} = -1$ is the only solution. If $(p' + qp'') = 0$, *any* $\bar{\lambda}$ is consistent. This will be the case if the demand function in the neighbourhood of equilibrium is of the form $p(Q) = a + bQ^{-1}$.

Boyer and Moreaux go on to show that: (a) 'any sustainable pair of production levels can be obtained as a locally [consistent] conjectural equilibrium for appropriately chosen linear conjectural functions for the duopolists [i.e. for conjectural variations which are linear functions of the output levels of the duopolists]' (p. 13); (b) these exist linear conjectural variation functions which make the Cournot outcome a locally consistent conjectural equilibrium, these functions taking the value of zero at the Cournot equilibrium (but not necessarily elsewhere). These results are obtained under conditions allowing U-shaped average cost functions. They generalise Breshnahan's (1981) results, which restricts attention to linear demand and quadratic costs. However, Breshnahan is able to show that, under these more restrictive assumptions, the consistent conjectures equilibrium exists and is unique in the class of polynomial conjectural functions, where the conjectural variation function of i is required to have identical slope as the reaction function of j at the equilibrium. (This seems a strong result, given that *any* conjectural function can be approximated arbitrarily closely by a polynomial of sufficiently high degree.) Perry (1982) also obtains a uniqueness result for an n-firm oligopoly while, like Boyer and Moreaux, Laitner (1980) indicated the multiplicity of consistency CVs.

Before considering how to reconcile the Breshnahan and Perry uniqueness results with the Boyer–Moreaux and Laitner results, it is worth discussing Kamien and Schwartz (1983). Despite making the restrictive assumption that firms have common constant average and marginal costs, and confining attention mainly to symmetric solutions, this paper presents in many respects the most comprehensive treatment of CVs. It considers homogeneous and differentiated product markets, CVs with respect to both prices and quantities, consistent conjectures equilibria in both, and the relationship between consistent conjectures in prices and in quantities.

On the relationship between price and quantity CVs, Kamien and Schwartz note that if the CV in quantity is zero (so that each firm believes that its rivals will not change output in response to an increase in its own sales) then each firm must assume implicitly that its rivals will lower price to maintain their sales in the face of its own price reduction which must accompany its planned increase in sales. Thus, any CV in quantity (or price) implicitly implies a corresponding equivalent CV in price (or quantity) that yields the same symmetric price and quantity. To see this, consider the case of zero CVs again. If we have zero CVs in quantities, as i expects its rivals to keep their own output constant in response to its output increase, it must be assuming that others will change price in the same direction as it changes its own (downwards) – i.e. $dq_j/dq_i = 0 \Rightarrow dp_j/dp_i > 0$. These authors show further that, in the linear demand symmetric case, the constant consistent CVs in quantity and in price lead to the same equilibrium output and thus the same equilibrium market price. However, these constant consistent CVs are of equal magnitude but opposite signs (the price conjecture being positive).

In a deep paper, Ulph (1983) attempts a reconciliation of, on the one hand, the results of Breshnahan and of Perry showing uniqueness, and on the other hand, those of Boyer–Moreaux and of Laitner indicating a possible infinity of consistent conjectures equilibria. He argues that Boyer–Moreaux's and Laitner's concept of consistent conjectures requires the following. At a consistent conjectures equilibrium, what i conjectures j will do in response to i's output choice, starting from any initial output pair, must lead to greater profits for j than would any other output for j, given j's conjecture about what i's response will be if j chose this other output. This is the only way for i's conjectures to turn out correct because it is the only way for j to remain where i conjectures j will be in response to i's output variation. Inherent in this definition is the idea of conjectures being verified by firms seeing what the consequences of any deviation from the candidate consistent conjectures equilibrium happen to be (although Laitner regarded such experimentation as irrational and inconsistent with the underlying model). Ulph argues that, unfortunately, this concept of consistency is too weak to limit the set of equilibria, given a set of axioms which he regards as reasonable. In particular, the above condition for consistency does not specify how firm i thinks j's response to a small change in i's output depends on the starting point from which i's change in output occurs. This dependence would require firms' beliefs to be based on experience. They would have to have conjectures for all possible pairs of outputs which could form the starting point for output variations. In turn, this would require additional rationality criteria, or tests, to be satisfied if conjectures relating to output changes from non-equilibrium points relative to given beliefs are to be correct.[10] Ulph states that these rationality tests are impossible to construct in general, thus firms will not know on the basis of any experience how rivals' responses will differ according to the point from which changes occur. If it is then assumed that firms assume that rivals will respond to a given change in their own output in the same way irrespective of the starting point (if the starting point is interior, i.e. involving positive outputs for all), then conjectures are linear in output changes and the uniqueness results of Breshnahan and of Perry can be resurrected.[11]

In a set-theoretic analysis attempting to elucidate rational conjectures, Makowski (1987) partly picks up Ulph's theme. In particular, he notes that any reasonable definition of consistent conjectures would need to specify how firms are induced to move from any status quo point to a candidate consistent conjectures equilibrium. This, he notes, can generally be achieved only by resort to a *deus ex machina* or contrivance outwith a particular model's internal logic. While firm i might wish to remain at such an equilibrium were it to find itself there, the move to such a position is not required to be an optimising move, given i's conjecture, and generally will not be. The essentially simple argument can be illustrated by Makowski's demonstration that, contrary to everything which we have said above, following the quoted authors, the Bertrand or competitive solution $\lambda_j = \lambda_i = -1$ is not consistent if we require, additionally, that a consistent conjectures equilibrium should have the feature that the response which i anticipates from j when i deviates to q_i from (q_i^*, q_j^*) is the response which j perceives to be desirable when j finds itself at the new status quo (q_i, q_j^*). Suppose i decreases its output by Δq_i when at an output pair where price, p, equals common average and marginal cost, c. Then j will not want to increase its output by an amount equal to Δq_i, as i conjectures. Instead, noting that i's decrease in output means that, without j changing its output, price must now exceed cost, j would actually want to expand to take over the entire market. This is because it conjectures that any output expansion on its part will be exactly offset by an output reduction by i under Bertrand conjectures, thus leaving the now profitable price unchanged. In fact, as j's optimal response to i's deviation is now non-incremental – under Bertrand conjectures – Makowski shows further that the calculus-based approaches of Breshnahan and of Perry are invalid: j's optimal response to i's deviation from a status quo point is non-differentiable.

In the light of these observations, and others, Makowski draws two broad conclusions. First, the idea of conjectures has not helped in understanding oligopolistic imperfect competition, as its attempt to encapsulate dynamic strategic interactions within static conjecture functions has failed. Thus conjectures about responses require explicit treatment of time, pointing inescapably to game theory as the appropriate tool. Second, as 'consistent' or 'rational' conjectures are built on *ad hoc* foundations involving a *deus ex machina*, restricting the set of admissable conjectural equilibria by imposing arbitrary extra constraints is just as sensible as restricting the set by imposing rationality conditions and a *deus ex machina*. Thus, 'the admittedly "irrational" Cournot conjectures seem at least as rational as [rational conjectural equilibrium] conjectures and a lot simpler than . . . these fancy conjectures.' It seems hard to put the case against 'consistency' any stronger than that.

Daughety (1985) also has produced a critique of consistency which arrives at the conclusion, shared with Boyer and Moreaux, that the Cournot conjecture is consistent. Unlike them, however, he states this conclusion without qualification. He notes, like Ulph and Makowski, that the 'textbook' consistent conjectures equilibrium is not a full equilibrium as there are actions each firm can take which give higher profits. The argument is as follows. With symmetric firms, linear demand and constant marginal costs, the quantity-setting consistent conjectures equilibrium involves outputs at which price equals marginal cost, i.e. the perfect competition outcome with zero profits. But rational firms should know that this will be the outcome if they act in this way, and each could individually choose, rather, to play Cournot. If one chooses to play Cournot while the other plays the consistent CV, a Stackelberg outcome ensues, with positive profits for both. If both jettison the consistent CV conjectures, realising their undesirability, the Cournot equilibrium can ensue. Given that the standard consistent CVs are not 'optimal' in this sense, Daughety attempts to rationalise the concept of a CV in a model where firm i chooses an output level to maximise its own profits subject to a model of its rival, j, which is in turn subject to a model of i, and so on. This yields a static model of infinite regress. He then defines a consistent duopoly equilibrium as one in which the optimal output for each firm i, q_i, equals what firm i believes firm j believes firm i will produce, denoted q_{iji}, which equals what firm i believes firm j believes firm i believes firm j believes firm i will produce, denoted q_{ijiji}, and so on. In this equilibrium, each firm correctly anticipates what the other will do, thus decisions are best responses to correct conjectures. Also, because it is a static model, j cannot actually respond to what i does, but only to what j thinks i will do. When deciding what to do, therefore, i decides on the basis of what it believes j will do, given what it believes j believes about itself. Given this, the CV is actually $\partial x_{ij}/\partial x_{iji}$. Daughety shows that under the assumption that a consistent duopoly equilibrium defined in this way exists, all such duopoly equilibria are Cournot equilibria. Thus, whatever guarantees the existence and uniqueness of one guarantees that of the other. This is also true for the *n*-firm case.

(ii) *A dynamic analysis?*

Given that the principal criticism of the CV notion revolves around the inappropriateness of trying to inject dynamic consider-ations into a static equilibrium concept (or, equivalently, trying to analyse inherently dynamic interactions using static equilibrium tools), it is important to consider efforts to generalise CVs to incorpor-ate some dynamics. Surprisingly, some of the most notable attempts have ended up providing a rationalisation of Cournot behaviour which, as we have seen, everyone began by dismissing as 'naïve'. We will consider briefly one such line of enquiry: the game-theoretic analysis of two-stage models.

Perhaps the best known model of two-stage competition is that of Kreps and Scheinkman (1983). These authors observe that, while prices can be changed rapidly, installing capacity takes time. This means that output decisions at any point in time are likely to be constrained by installed capacity and, in consequence, current capacity decisions will be taken with a view to future output decisions. In a two-stage setting with homogeneous goods, there-fore, they assume that firms will simultaneously install capacity in the first period and then, knowing each other's capacities, compete by setting prices simultaneously in the second period. The solution technique for the game involves working backwards in time. Thus, supposing arbitrary capacities are installed, what is the best that firms can do in period two, given that capacity is installed and its costs are sunk? Consider a duopoly. Kreps and Scheinkman show that, provided capacities are small relative to market demand at zero price (and provided an *efficient rationing rule*[12] is used to handle any excess demand which might arise for a particular firm's output at a given set of prices), then this second stage involves both firms charging the price which equates demand to aggregate capacity. At stage one, the firms (*i* and *j*) know that this will be the outcome in period two. Thus, their profit functions have the so-called *exact Cournot reduced form*, $\bar{q}_i[p(\bar{q}_i + \bar{q}_j) - c]$, where *c* is now the unit cost of installing capacity, capacity being measured in output units and denoted $\bar{q}$. This profit function for each subsumes the outcome of period two's price competition. Kreps and Scheinkman show that the (q_i, q_j) arising in a Cournot equilibrium emerge from this stage of the game. (This is not surprising as, in the first period, the firms are assumed to choose an output pair constituting a Nash equilibrium, given their knowledge of how they will behave in the future, and the Nash equilibrium in outputs coincides with the Cournot equilibrium.) Thus, 'Quantity pre-commitment and Bertrand competition yield Cournot outcomes'!

While the above conclusion is not robust to variations in the rationing scheme or the assumption that 'small' capacities are chosen (see e.g. Davidson and Deneckere 1986 on the former), the important point is that yet again we find a rationalisation, in certain circumstances at least, for proceeding as if Cournot CVs are applicable. There is also a more general point: just as a game in extensive form can be reduced to one in strategic form (though with the loss of some information), so we can consider the CV analysis of static models of oligopoly interactions as representing the reduced form of a more complicated dynamic game.

4.4   THE EVIDENCE

As CVs represent a way of conceptualising actual behaviour in oligopoly, it is important to ask what games businessmen really play. The evidence which we will consider is of two forms: experimental and empirical. Our primary focus in the review of the empirical evidence will be on the results in the papers referred to; methodological issues have been surveyed brilliantly by Breshnahan (1989).

We can deal very swiftly with the main pieces of experimental work in the area, Dolbear *et al.* (1968) and Holt (1985). The former considered behaviour in multiperiod duopoly experiments involving student subjects choosing prices simultaneously at the start of each experimental period. The students were presented with a payoff matrix showing payoffs obtainable from different price choices. A student's price choice determined a row in the matrix; the average of the prices chosen by his competitors determined the column. Payoffs in each cell in the matrix were calculated using a quadratic profit function arising from a differentiated products, linear demand structure. There were *two* symmetric Bertrand–Nash (pricing) equilibria (because of rounding), and a collusive equilibrium involving a higher price. Twelve experiments were run under complete information, each involving students making simultaneous price decisions fifteen times, and the average prices were calculated from rounds 8 to 12. The average price across all experiments (19.5) was found to be slightly above those in the two Bertrand–Nash equilibria (17 and 18). Hence, Dolbear *et al.* concluded that there was some element of tacit collusion present, as the resulting average profits exceeded those obtainable in the Bertrand–Nash cases.[13]

Holt used Dolbear *et al.*'s specification of the profit function and calculated that the price which would be generated by the consistent CVs solution was 19.2. He noted that this was not significantly different from the average price obtained in Dolbear *et al.*'s experiments and concluded that, for this and other reasons, Dolbear *et al's* experiments were not a satisfactory test of the consistent CVs equilibrium concept (or, by implication, of Bertrand–Nash or collusion). Observing that a *homogeneous good, quantity-setting* framework has the implication that the consistent CVs outcome involves zero profits, he regarded this scenario as a more promising setting for oligopoly experiments designed to distinguish between the static Cournot–Nash and consistent CVs behaviour modes.

Accordingly, Holt constructed oligopoly quantity-setting experiments involving, in turn, twenty-four and twelve students, previously uninitiated in economics experiments. There were two types of experiments, one involving random termination (designed to approximate an uncertain, possibly infinite horizon) and the other a single-period experiment which, he argued, gave the Cournot–Nash outcome its best chance. (This was because the single period prevented the use of history-dependent punishment strategies to enforce collusion.) A positive amount was added to all the 'raw' payoffs arising from an unadjusted quadratic profit function so that the consistent CVs outcomes yielded positive profits. (There were many possible consistent CVs solutions for the oligopoly pairs). Moreover, the parameters were structured so that the aggregate outputs yielding Cournot, collusive and consistent CVs, and their associated payoffs to the subjects were relatively far apart. Also, there was no decision by each player which could guarantee a payoff exceeding the consistent CVs outcome. Subjects were given enough information to enable them to compute the profits which would arise for them and their rivals from whatever strategies were pursued.

Against this experimental background, Holt found that the consistent CVs equilibrium did not provide good predictions in his experiments. 'The data was [sic] more consistent with the Cournot equilibrium, although several duopoly pairs managed to achieve perfect collusion tacitly' (Holt, 1985, p. 324). There was also some evidence of rivalry in the sense that some players' behaviour seemed to indicate an interest in maximising the difference of profits. While there was some tendency to collude in the multiperiod, random stopping experiments, there was no such tendency in the single-period experiments, as one would expect.

As Holt notes, experiments using students as subjects can be criticised on the grounds that their behaviour is unlikely to coincide with that of businessmen, given the far greater experience of the latter in actual business contexts. The same charge can be levied against attempts to test for tacit collusion by using game theorists to suggest strategies to be played in repeated prisoner's dilemma games, such as Axelrod's (1981) computerised tournament. However, it is worth stressing that experimentalists can allow for experience effects by allowing their student subjects to 'play the game' several times and, either discounting their initial efforts, or comparing the outcomes from the early plays with those after a certain number of repetitions.

In contrast to the relative paucity of experimental research, there is a voluminous empirical literature which either estimates CVs directly or which throws light on them en route to either estimating the relationship between market structure and performance, motivated by the structure–conduct–performance (SCP) paradigm, or testing for the existence of price-taking behaviour.

Let us consider first the attempts which have been made to estimate firms' CVs directly from empirical data. Iwata (1974) was the first prominent example. Suppose we start with the firm-level equation for the Lerner index for firm i ((4.3)). Rearranging this yields an expression for i's CV in the homogeneous goods case given by

$$\lambda_i = \varepsilon L_i s_i^{-1} - 1 \tag{4.28}$$

As in much of the early SCP empirical work, Iwata assumed that the price–cost margins, L_i, can be obtained from accounting data. Given estimates of s_i and ε, λ_i can be calculated. From what we have said already, a value of $\lambda_i = 0$ would indicate Cournot behaviour while $\lambda_i = -1$ indicates price-taking behaviour. A mixture of observed behaviour patterns amongst the firms in an industry might indicate Stackelberg leader–follower behaviour, but it could indicate other behaviour modes; $\lambda_i > 0$, for example, could indicate collusive behaviour.[14]

Iwata actually estimated pairwise CVs for the three firms in the Japanese flat glass industry. These firms (Asahi, Nippon and Central) each mainly produced window glass and plate glass. Their costs and input demands were estimated from half-yearly accounting data over ten years, from 1956 to 1965. Detailed information on wholesale and retail prices, consumption expenditures and the car industry's demand for plate glass, was used to calculate market demand schedules, and hence elasticities. Non-zero (and unequal) CVs were found for Asahi with respect to Nippon and vice-versa, but not for each of these firms with respect to Central. This suggests that Asahi and Nippon, by far the two largest firms, ignored reactions from the relatively tiny Central Glass Co., but not from each other.

Subsequent studies in a similar vein to Iwata include Gollop and Roberts (1979), using cross-section data from 1972 on the US coffee industry and Appelbaum (1979, 1982) using time-series aggregate data from 1947–1971 on the electrical machinery, rubber, textiles and tobacco industries. These studies estimated cost functions to obtain marginal costs for each firm as a function of output. Gollop and Roberts found that firms' CVs varied according to their own size, and to the size of the rivals they regarded as significant. The positive λ_i they obtained seemed to reflect the collusive behaviour or high likelihood of a retaliatory response to be expected in such a highly concentrated industry as coffee. Appelbaum calculated average CVs (actually, 'conjectural elasticities') for each of the four industries mentioned for the fifteen years of his sample period. He found statistically significant, positive λ_i for electrical machinery and tobacco and concluded that these industries were characterised by a significant degree of 'oligopoly power'. On the other hand, the other two industries were characterised by competitive behaviour.

By far the largest body of empirical work in industrial economics and organisation relates to the SCP. A virtual industry developed around this topic, stimulated by Bain's (1959) seminal work (see Cubbin, 1988; Hay and Morris, 1991, ch. 8; Waterson, 1984, ch. 10; and Scherer, 1980, for substantial surveys). This work was not specifically directed at deriving estimates of CVs; nevertheless, it had as its basis informal theorising about the relationship between industry structure, conduct and performance. This culminated in Cowling and Waterson's (1976) formalisation (see, e.g., equations (4.4) and (4.5) above) which emphasised the role of the CVs which were embedded in the data. In this approach, *inter alia*, the CVs (λ_i) would be interpreted as indicating conduct, the Lerner index would be a performance measure while the Herfindahl index and the demand elasticity would be structure measures. Breshnahan's (1989) introductory comments give a very good summary of why much of the work which Bain, and subsequently Cowling and Waterson, stimulated has been found wanting by economists of the game-theory-inspired 'New Empirical Industrial Organisation' school. Earlier critiques stressed the inappropriateness of inferring causality from equilibrium relationships such as (4.4) or (4.5) (see e.g. Phillips, 1976; Waterson, 1984). Nevertheless, despite the SCP approach's vulnerability to the game theorist's and 'New I-O' critique, even Tirole (1989, n. 12) concedes that: 'the conjectural variations approach may have been a useful way of empirically estimating the degree of non-competitiveness in an industry', especially in view of the absence of, and difficulties in testing, 'fully-fledged' dynamic models. Perhaps for this reason, also, Breshnahan (1989) seems much more sympathetic than Tirole to the CV approach.

It must be noted that there have been *some* empirical attempts to examine conjectures in a dynamic setting. For example, Slade (1987) examined the retail petrol market in Vancouver as an example of a repeated game. Using daily time-series data on retail petrol prices, sales and unit costs for individual petrol stations during a price-war period, she found that actual price responses to rivals were much greater than those that were estimated as appropriate for a 'one-shot' game. She concluded that this possibly indicated that 'punishment strategies' were being employed to enforce collusive discipline, a view supported by the Lerner index which she calculated. At 0.1, this was relatively high for an un-differentiated consumer product industry.[15]

As the estimation of Lerner indices, attempts to identify non-competitive behaviour and the like are concerned ultimately with possible deleterious consequences of market power, it is useful to conclude our empirical review of CVs by returning to Daskin's (1991) paper. This not only incorporates a generalised form of CV, but also provides estimates of oligopoly deadweight loss which improve on Dixit and Stern's (1982) numerical calculations and on the work of Masson and Shanaan (1984). Following Dixit and Stern's methodology, but allowing for different firm-specific proportional conjectures, as detailed above, with the resulting firm-specific and industry Lerner indices as in (4.11) and (4.12), Daskin calculates the deadweight loss for oligopoly (DWL) as:

$$DWL = R\sum_i L_i s_i - R\log_e[1/(1 - L^*)] \qquad \text{for } \varepsilon = 1 \qquad (4.29)$$

$$= R\sum_i L_i s_i - [R/(1 - \varepsilon)]\log_e[1 - (1 - L^*)^{1 - \varepsilon}] \qquad \text{for } \varepsilon \neq 1$$

Here, L^* is the price–cost margin or Lerner index achieved by the lowest-cost firm. In both of these expressions, the first term on the right-hand side represent the total profits (or 'producer surplus') being earned by the oligopolists. This can be expressed alternatively as $R[\sum_i \alpha_i s_i + H - \sum_i \alpha_i s_i^2]/\varepsilon = R[H + \sum_i s_i^2 \alpha_i(1 - s_i)/s_i]\varepsilon^{-1}$ where, we recall, H is the Herfindahl–Hirschman index of market concentration and $\lambda_i \equiv \alpha_i(1 - s_i)/s_i$ is the CV for firm i. The second right-hand terms in (4.30) represent the reduction in aggregate consumer surplus arising from oligopoly pricing rather than having competitive supply at a price equal to the marginal cost of the lowest cost firm. Thus, not surprisingly, oligopoly welfare losses are directly related to the conjectures which represents the market participants' view of conduct in the market, as well as to the structure which emerges from their interactions. Using 1977 US Census of Manufacturing data, Daskin shows that a value of DWL in the range 6–10 per cent of shipments for inelastic or unit elastic demand would be reasonable. For $\varepsilon > 1$, the losses could be considerably higher.[16]

4.5 EXTENSIONS AND CONCLUSIONS

This chapter has reviewed some of the implications of the approach to oligopoly equilibrium which is predicated on the assumption that oligopolists act on the basis of conjectures. This was for long the dominant way of organising thinking about oligopoly, although it has now been partly displaced by more sophisticated game-theoretic investigations of strategic interactions. Nevertheless, we have seen that even the foremost advocates of the 'new', game-theoretic I-O concede some usefulness to the CV approach in providing a basis for testable hypotheses in the quest for evidence of market power. Following most of the literature, we have assumed that oligopolists act cooperatively or non-cooperatively to maximise their profits. This is despite substantial evidence to the contrary (see e.g. Hay and Morris, 1991, ch. 9, for a review). Some authors *have* studied CVs under objectives other than profit maximisation (cf. Shaffer, 1991, and references therein), but space constraints preclude our taking a detour down that route. Space constraints also prevent out relaxing the strong assumption of certainty which we have maintained throughout except briefly in the discussion of Cubbin (1983).

Perhaps the best defence of the CV approach lies in the fact that it has proven such a useful pedagogic device. Its shortcuts and apparent shortcomings have received some *ex post* rationalisation in the hands of the theorists who have shown that decisions arising from some seemingly implausible CVs can be interpreted as being those from the reduced forms of more complicated, dynamic models. (Shapiro, 1989) makes it clear that there are as yet few satisfactory truly dynamic models of oligopoly even in the game theory literature.) To that extent, we can always fall back on Friedman's (1953) position that what matters for the success of a theory is not its descriptive reality but, rather, its predictive ability.

It is perhaps ironic that whereas we began by noting that the CV approach was introduced by economists as a possible way of conceptualising oligopolists' thinking about strategic interdependence, we can conclude by noting that management journals now advocate the use of conjectures by businessmen as one way of improving the business planning process and their competitive position (see e.g. Amit, Domowitz and Fershtman, 1988[17]). Thus, even if businessmen in oligopolies have not hitherto acted on the basis of CVs, if they act on the recommendation of the management literature, at least, there is a reasonable chance that they will come to do so in due course.

5 Oligopoly and Welfare

JOHN CABLE, ALAN CARRUTH AND
AVINASH DIXIT

5.1 INTRODUCTION

Welfare losses due to monopoly have received much attention in the literature since the pioneering work of Harberger (1954). Over the past decade the discussion has *inter alia* been extended to take explicit account of oligopolistic interaction (see, in particular, Dixit and Stern, 1982; Masson and Shaanan, 1984; Daskin, 1991). However the ultimate aim has mostly remained to work towards theoretically well-grounded empirical estimates of actual losses in different industries, sectors or economies. As Daskin observes, the range of estimated losses, though significantly larger than Harberger's original 0.1 per cent of GNP, with one or two notable exceptions rarely exceeds 1–3 per cent of the value of output based on monopoly models[1]; though, using a theoretical extension and empirical implementation of Dixit and Stern, Daskin himself goes on to report an estimate of 6–10 per cent of the value of shipments (for the US manufacturing sector) if industry demand is elastic, and 'considerably higher' with inelastic demand.

Whilst well-based empirical estimates must properly remain the ultimate goal of enquiry, important additional insight can be gained by spelling out the implications for welfare of the various classical oligopoly models at our disposal, as reviewed in Chapter 4. This the present chapter seeks to do. Our method is to postulate a specific welfare function for a simple economy, and then solve directly for the level of welfare (net surplus) under various combinations of market conduct and structure. Our welfare function is consistent with the consumer preferences that generate demand in our model. By 'conduct' we mean alternative conjectural variations determining the way the oligopoly game is played, as discussed in Chapter 4. 'Structure' embraces both the number of firms (which for convenience of exposition is fixed at two throughout the analysis) and also consumer preferences and production technology, as summarised in the relevant demand and cost functions. We then employ numerical simulations to examine the welfare losses both for given modes of conduct across alternative plausible structures, and given structure under different patterns of conduct, all relative to a social optimum characterised by zero profit and marginal cost pricing.

Section 5.2 draws on earlier work by Bramness (1979), Dixit (1978) and Ulph (1983) *inter alia* to provide a unifying framework within which alternative conjectural variations (CV) equilibria may be compared with each other, as well as with the polar cases of monopoly and the 'social optimum' as defined above. When selecting alternative equilibria for inclusion in the analysis, our primary concern is not with the relative merits of the alternative models as oligopoly solution concepts: the 'arbitrariness' or 'correctness' of firms' conjectures and so forth. This has been considered at length in Chapter 4. Here, we focus on the social value of the outcomes produced by alternative behavioural postulates which have at some time been deemed sufficiently compelling to find their way into the existing literature; for our purposes, the pre-existence of a particular solution in the literature is sufficient justification.

Section 5.3 reports the results of the numerical analysis, showing indices of social welfare for different types of oligopolistic interaction under variation in the degree of product homogeneity, and cost and demand asymmetries. The implications of our analysis for antitrust policy are spelled out along with our conclusions in section 5.4.

5.2 ALTERNATIVE CONJECTURAL VARIATIONS EQUILIBRIA

We consider quantity-setting duopoly and assume constant marginal costs c_1, c_2. The utility function is assumed quadratic:

$$U = x_0 + \alpha_1 x_1 + \alpha_2 x_2 - \frac{1}{2}(\beta_1 x_1^2 + 2\gamma x_1 x_2 + \beta_2 x_2^2) \quad (5.1)$$

with α_i, β_i, $\gamma > 0$ and β_1, $\beta_2 \geq \gamma^2$. x_1, x_2 are the duopolists' outputs and x_0 is the composite output of the rest of the economy, assumed competitive.

Inverse demands for the two outputs are obtained by differentiating partially with respect to x_i, $i = 1, 2$, and noting $p_i = MU_i = \dfrac{\partial U}{\partial x_i}$. The quadratic utility function implies that these are linear:

$$\left. \begin{array}{l} p_1 = \alpha_1 - \beta_1 x_1 - \gamma x_2 \\ p_2 = \alpha_2 - \beta_2 x_2 - \gamma x_1 \end{array} \right\} \quad (5.2)$$

γ captures cross-price effects between the competing firms and may be interpreted as a measure of product differentiation. By definition we require that x_1, x_2, are substitutes in an oligopoly, hence $\gamma > 0$. The products are perfect substitutes when both $\alpha_1 = \alpha_2$ and $\beta_1 = \beta_2 = \gamma$ (product homogeneity). Absolute demand advantages for either firm may be captured in a higher value of α_i. With constant marginal costs, c_1, c_2, the duopolists' profit functions are simply $p_i x_i - c_i$, or

$$\left. \begin{array}{ll} & \pi_1 = \theta_1 x_1 - \beta_1 x_1^2 - \gamma x_1 x_2 \\ \text{and} & \pi_2 = \theta_2 x_2 - \beta_2 x_2^2 - \gamma x_1 x_2 \end{array} \right\} \quad (5.3)$$

where $\alpha_i - c_i = \theta_i$.

Equilibrium conditions for the social optimum, pure monopoly and various oligopoly solutions are set out in equations (5.4) – (5.10) in Table 5.1. The derivations of these results are given in the Appendix on pp. 101–4. The social optimum maximises net surplus: $U - (c_1 x_1 + c_2 x_2)$. Equilibrium is characterised by zero profits and marginal cost pricing by both firms, and is the benchmark for subsequent welfare comparisons. The Cournot, Bertrand, and Stackelberg solutions are dealt with in Chapter 4, and require no further comment.

Market share maximisation, or the maintenance of a given market share, is a behavioural strategy that deserves special attention because it allows us to model tacit collusion even in a static setting.

TABLE 5.1 Alternative equilibria

Model	Maximand/ Conjectural variations	Equilibrium conditions ('reaction functions')	
Social optimum (SO)	$\max\{U - (c_1x_1 + c_2x_2)\}$	$\theta_1 = \beta_1x_1 + \gamma x_2$ $\theta_2 = \beta_2x_2 + \gamma x_1$	(5.4)
Cournot (C)	$dx_j/dx_i = 0$ ($i \neq j; i, j = 1, 2$)	$\theta_1 = 2\beta_1x_1 + \gamma x_2$ $\theta_2 = 2\beta_2x_2 + \gamma x_1$	(5.5)
Bertrand (B)	$dx_j/dx_i = -\gamma/\beta_j$ (i.e. firm i chooses x_i assuming x_j changes such that p_j is constant)	$\theta_1 = \left(2 - \dfrac{\gamma^2}{\beta_1\beta_2}\right)\beta_1x_1 + \gamma x_2$ $\theta_2 = \left(2 - \dfrac{\gamma^2}{\beta_1\beta_2}\right)\beta_2x_2 + \gamma x_1$	(5.6)
Market share (MS) Collusion	$dx_j/dx_i = x_j/x_i$ (i.e. firm i chooses x_i assuming x_j changes proportionately) $\max\{\pi_1 + \pi_2\}$	$\theta_1 = 2\beta_1x_1 + 2\gamma x_2$ $\theta_2 = 2\beta_2x_2 + 2\gamma x_1$	(5.7)
Rational conjectures (RCE)		$dx_2/dx_1 = -\beta_1(1 - \delta)/\gamma$ $dx_1/dx_2 = -\beta_2(1 - \delta)/\gamma$ $\theta_1 = \beta_1(1 + \delta)x_1 + \gamma x_2$ $\theta_2 = \beta_2(1 + \delta)x_2 + \gamma x_1$ with $\delta = \sqrt{1 - \gamma^2/\beta_1\beta_2}$	(5.8)
Stackelberg[1] (S_1, S_2)	$\max \pi_i$ s.t. $dx_j/dx_i = -\gamma/2\beta_j$ (i.e. Cournot reaction)	$\theta_1 = (2 - \gamma^2/2\beta_1\beta_2)\beta_1x_1 + \gamma x_2$ $\theta_2 = 2\beta_2x_2 + \gamma x_1$	(5.9)
Dominant firm[1] (D_1, D_2)	$\max \pi_i$ s.t. $dx_j/dx_i = -\gamma/\beta_j$ (i.e. 'fringe' supply priced at marginal cost)	$\theta_1 = (2 - \gamma^2/\beta_1\beta_2)\beta_1x_1 + \gamma x_2$ $\theta_2 = \beta_2x_2 + \gamma x_1$	(5.10)
Monopoly[1,2] (M_1, M_2)	$\max \pi_i$ s.t. $x_j = 0$		

Notes: 1 Equilibrium condition assumes firm 1 'leads'. Similarly for firm 2.
2 Strictly, applies only where products are homogenous ($\alpha_1 = \alpha_2$, $\beta_1 = \beta_2 = \gamma$).

Equilibrium is sometimes, but erroneously, characterised as where firm i maximises profit while j maintains a fixed share of total sales (e.g. Henderson and Quandt, 1980, p. 210). But this is contingent upon Stackelberg-type leader–follower behaviour and a true equilibrium must ensure that compatible market shares are chosen; i.e. must simultaneously satisfy *both* the reaction functions, as in (5.7). As Spence (1978) has shown, it turns out that market share equilibrium coincides with collusive behaviour leading to joint profit maximisation, although this result apparently remains less than well known. That it does can readily be seen in Table 5.1, where (5.7) are also first-order conditions for a maximum of industry profits:

$$\pi_1 + \pi_2 = \theta_1 x_1 + \theta_2 x_2 - \beta_1 x_1^2 - \beta_2 x_2^2 - 2\gamma x_1 x_2$$

With a quadratic welfare function the market share/collusion equilibrium will always generate exactly half the output rate and three-quarters the net surplus obtaining at the social optimum, irrespective of demand and cost parameter values. To see this first note that the social-optimum outputs x_2^0, x_1^0 from (5.4) are:

$$x_2^0 = \frac{\gamma\theta_1 - \beta_1\theta_2}{\gamma^2 - \beta_1\beta_2} \quad \text{and} \quad x_1^0 = \frac{\theta_1 - \gamma x_2^0}{\beta_1} \tag{5.11}$$

The market share reaction functions (5.7) (see Table 5.1 for equations (5.4) – (5.10)), on the other hand, imply:

$$x_2^{ms} = \frac{\gamma\theta_1 - \beta_1\theta_2}{2\gamma^2 - 2\beta_1\beta_2} = \frac{1}{2}\left[\frac{\gamma\theta_1 - \beta_1\theta_2}{\gamma^2 - \beta_1\beta_2}\right] = \frac{1}{2}x_2^0 \tag{5.12}$$

and

$$x_1^{ms} = \frac{\theta_1 - 2\gamma x_2^{ms}}{2\beta_1} = \frac{\theta_1 - 2\gamma(x_2^0/2)}{2\beta_1}$$

$$\tag{5.13}$$

$$= \frac{1}{2}\left[\frac{\theta_1 - \gamma x_2^0}{\beta_1}\right] = \frac{1}{2}x_1^0$$

At the social optimum

$$U^0 = \theta_1 x_1^0 + \theta_2 x_2^0 - \frac{1}{2}(\beta_1(x_1^0)^2 + 2\gamma x_1^0 x_2^0 + \beta_2(x_2^0)^2)$$

Recognising that $\pi_1^0 = \pi_2^0 = 0$ in equilibrium and substituting

$$\theta_1 x_1^0 = \beta_1 (x_1^0)^2 + \gamma x_1^0 x_2^0, \; \theta_2 x_2^0 = \beta_2 (x_2^0)^2 + \gamma x_1^0 x_2^0 \text{ from (5.3)}$$

yields

$$U^0 = \theta_1 x_1^0 + \theta_2 x_2^0 - \frac{1}{2}(\theta_1 x_1^0 + \theta_2 x_2^0) \tag{5.14}$$

Obviously

$$U^0 = \frac{1}{2}(\theta_1 x_1^0 + \theta_2 x_2^0)$$

whereas, substituting for x_1^{ms}, x_2^{ms} from (5.12) and (5.13),

$$U^{ms} = \theta_1 \frac{x_1^0}{2} + \theta_2 \frac{x_2^0}{2} - \frac{1}{2}\left(\theta_1 \frac{x_1^0}{2} + \theta_2 \frac{x_2^0}{2}\right)$$

$$= \left(1 - \frac{1}{4}\right)U^0 \tag{5.15}$$

which completes the demonstration.

The essential requirement for rational conjectures equilibria (RCE) as discussed by Ulph (1983) is that, for a 'self-fulfilling equilibrium', each firm's initial conjectures concerning the rival's reactions are correct. That is, each firm has effectively predicted the slope of its rival's reaction function in the neighbourhood of equilibrium. Thus, for example, Cournot, Bertrand and market share equilibria can be RCE but Stackelberg outcomes cannot be, since only the leader has a correct conjecture whereas the follower does not.

To capture RCE completely we first obtain general reaction functions by setting the partials of (5.3) to zero:

$$\left.\begin{array}{l} \partial \pi_1/\partial x_1 = \theta_1 - 2\beta_1 x_1 - \gamma x_2 - \gamma x_1 (dx_2/dx_1) = 0 \\ \partial \pi_2/\partial x_2 = \theta_2 - 2\beta_2 x_2 - \gamma x_1 - \gamma x_2 (dx_1/dx_2) = 0 \end{array}\right\} \tag{5.16}$$

The self-fulfilling equilibrium so defined need not be unique. Suppose firm 2 changes output from its equilibrium value by an infinitesimal amount dx_2. dx_1 is then found from (5.16):

$$dx_1 = -\gamma/(2\beta_1 + \gamma \, dx_2/dx_1)dx_2$$

Therefore, if firm 2's conjecture is to be correct, we require

$$dx_1/dx_2 = -\gamma/(2\beta_1 + \gamma \, dx_2/dx_1) \qquad (5.17)$$

Similarly, firm 1's conjecture must be

$$dx_2/dx_1 = -\gamma/(2\beta_2 + \gamma \, dx_1/dx_2) \qquad (5.18)$$

Equations (5.16) – (5.18) are four equations in four unknowns, so that it is possible to solve for the equilibrium conjectures and output. Ulph considers both interior and boundary optima; the equilibrium conditions (5.8) in Table 5.1 are for an interior solution with positive profit.[2]

Our dominant-firm solution may be thought of as an extension of Stackelberg's follower–leader solution concept. Follower j is thought of as the aggregate of a competitive fringe of sellers. Leader i maximises π_i over residual demand (market demand minus fringe supply) and costs. Fringe supply is governed by marginal cost pricing hence π_i is maximised subject to $dx_j/dx_i = -\gamma/\beta_j$. The dominant firm is distinguished by a Bertrand reaction function, the fringe by a social optimum. The outcome may be regarded as a *quasi*-RCE, in that the dominant firm's conjecture is correct while the individual fringe suppliers are price-takers.[3]

Inspection of Table 5.1 shows that the extent of product differentiation, captured in the parameter γ, bears importantly on the equilibrium outcomes. Thus with homogeneous products ($\gamma = \beta_1 = \beta_2 = 1$) the Bertrand, RCE and dominant-firm equilibria all converge on the social optimum, since $(2 - \gamma^2/\beta_1\beta_2) = 1$ (Bertrand, dominant-firm), and $\delta = 0$ (RCE) respectively. Conversely, as γ goes to zero ($\delta \to 1$) and there are no cross-price effects (i.e. complete product differentiation) the Cournot, Bertrand, RCE and Stackelberg outcomes converge on the market share/collusion position; in all cases the reaction functions reduce to

$$\theta_1 = 2\beta_1 x_1$$

and

$$\theta_2 = 2\beta_2 x_2$$

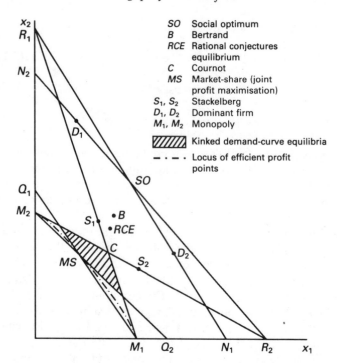

FIGURE 5.1 'Competitive', monopoly and oligopoly equilibria

In effect we are no longer dealing with a duopoly; interaction vanishes as the firms are now monopolists serving disjoint demands. Notice, however, that x_1 and x_2 are both positive and the outcome differs from the pure monopoly case in Table 5.1. This refers to the homogeneous products case where only one firm exists. Hence π_i is maximised subject to $x_j = 0$. Clearly, constraining x_j to zero under complete product differentiation would involve more than merely that firm i has a monopoly.

Each of the foregoing equilibria is depicted in figure 5.1. R_1M_1, R_2M_2, are the familiar Cournot reaction functions. Along each firm's equilibrium locus marginal cost equals perceived marginal revenue and a stable equilibrium exists at C. R_1N_1, R_2N_2 are the social-optimum 'reaction functions', where respectively firm 1's, 2's marginal cost equals price. Market share reaction functions are the loci M_1Q_1, M_2Q_2. The market share equilibrium MS at their intersection necessarily belongs to the *set of efficient profit points*: the curve M_1M_2, which is the locus of points of tangency of the duopolists' iso-profit curves. As we have seen, MS is also the joint profit-maximising equilibrium. The Stackelberg outcomes S_1, S_2 occur at points of tangency between i's iso-profit curve and j's (Cournot) reaction function. Likewise, the dominant-firm equilibria may be found as points of tangency between the dominant-firm's iso-profit curve and the fringe's socially-optimal reaction function, D_1 (D_2). In the homogeneous products case we could legitimately identify the end-points M_1, M_2 of the Cournot reaction functions as the pure monopoly outcomes for firms 1 and 2, respectively; marginal revenue equals marginal cost with x_2, x_1, respectively equal to zero.[4]

Bramness (1979) has delimited the area where *kinked demand-curve equilibria* can arise within the framework we are using. Firm i believes that if x_i is increased x_j will increase equiproportionately, but that if x_i is decreased, x_j will stay unchanged. Then its 'equilibrium locus' is the whole zone between its Cournot and market share reaction functions. The intersection of these zones for firms 1 and 2 covers the whole area where kinked demand-curve equilibria can arise and is the shaded area in Figure 5.1.

5.3 WELFARE COMPARISONS

Our aim now is to use the foregoing framework to examine the extent of welfare losses in duopolistic markets, and how these vary according to:

(i) alternative modes of interaction (conduct), and
(ii) alternative competitive states (structure) as captured in the underlying cost and demand parameters.

In respect to (ii), and with ultimate antitrust policy implications in mind, we focus in particular on the way welfare losses behave as the degree of product differentiation increases (γ falls), and as one firm enjoys progressively larger cost or demand advantages (e.g. c_i/c_j falls or α_i/α_j increases). As any of these happen, competition is reduced in some sense, and we would expect an increase in the shortfall in welfare from the socially-optimal level. The interesting

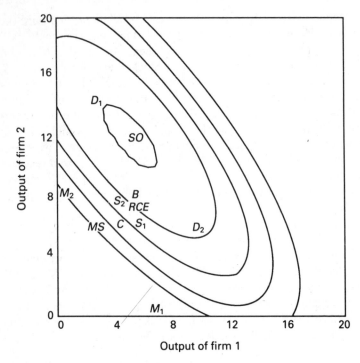

FIGURE 5.2   Duopoly graphics

questions concern the gradient of this relationship between welfare and competition; in whether this relationship dominates or is dwarfed by the impact of alternative modes of conduct on welfare, for a given competitive state; and in whether variations in competitiveness bear on different behaviour patterns uniformly or differentially, i.e. whether the welfare ranking of alternative behavioural outcomes is preserved as the degree of competitiveness varies.

These questions are tackled with the aid of numerical simulations. For specified parameter values we solve for equilibrium prices, outputs, profit, implied elasticities, net surplus (absolute and relative to the social optimum) and level of concentration (as measured by the Herfindahl index).[5] This output can be presented in graphic form and Figure 5.2 is an example. The contours of our social welfare function are ellipses centred on *SO*, with zero slope as they intersect the social optimum reaction functions. The example given features symmetric demands and costs, with $\gamma = 0.75$.[6] Since products are not homogenous M_1, M_2 cannot be considered pure monopoly outcomes. Otherwise, as we would expect, market share (joint profit maximisation) generates least net surplus. Dominant-firm equilibria cause least reduction in welfare from the social optimum, other outcomes tending to cluster in between.

With eight solution concepts and seven parameters to consider the number of possible permutations is large. However, not all make economic sense. Thus product homogeneity is implausible where there are cost or demand asymmetries and vice-versa. For this would necessarily imply non-optimising behaviour by at least one firm or by consumers; if costs are asymmetric one or both firms must be inefficient, and if demands differ consumer preferences are irrational. On the other hand it is only under product homogeneity that, as we have seen, comparison with the pure monopoly outcome is meaningful. Where there is product differentiation, costs and demand may be either symmetric or asymmetric. For differentiation can arise either from *both* firms incurring extra costs to secure customer allegiance, or from *one* firm doing so. Finally, it could be argued that leader–follower behaviour, as under Stackelberg and dominant-firm equilibrium, is plausible only where one firm has a cost or demand advantage. Otherwise the assumption of leader–follower roles is arbitrary. In addition, we may discount Stackelberg and dominant-firm equilibria under which the leader is at a cost or demand *disadvantage* on the grounds of total implausibility.

In presenting our results we first consider the special case of homogeneous products. We then examine separately the impact on the welfare rankings of variations in the degree of differentiation (γ) cost asymmetry (c_1/c_2) and demand asymmetry (α_1/α_2). Although as we have said, not all of the implied combinations make sense, it is helpful to get some feel for the partials of welfare with respect to the parameters in this way. Next we consider *joint* variations in the parameters, focusing our attention on what we consider to be the most plausible or interesting combinations. In particular, we consider cases of low, medium and high product differentiation in conjunction with correspondingly low, medium and high degrees of cost *disadvantage* for one firm (firm 2) accompanied by a concomitant demand advantage. This may be

TABLE 5.2 Price, output and welfare: homogeneous products[1]

Model	X_1	X_2	P_1	P_2	η_1	η_2	Welfare index $(S = 100)$	HERF
Social optimum (*SO*)	7.0		6.0		0.9		100.0	0.50
Cournot (*C*)	4.7		10.7		2.3		88.9	0.50
Bertrand (*B*)	7.0		6.0		0.9		100.0	0.50
Market share (*MS*)	3.5		13.0		3.7		75.0	0.50
RCE	7.0		6.0		0.9		100.0	0.50
S_1	7.0	3.5	9.5		1.4	2.7	93.8	0.56
S_2	3.5	7.0	9.5		2.7	1.4	93.8	0.56
M_1	7.0	–	13.0	–	1.9	–	75.0	1.00
M_2	–	7.0	–	13.0	–	1.9	75.0	1.00

Note: 1 Assumes $\alpha_1, \alpha_2 = 20.0$; $\beta_1, \beta_2 = 1.0$; $c_1, c_2 = 6.0$.
  2 S1, S2, M1, M2 as in Table 5.1.

interpreted as tantamount to extending our analysis to incorporate product quality and selling effort as decision variables to the firm, albeit for the special case where an x per cent cost differential secures the same percentage absolute demand advantage.

Homogeneous products

Table 5.2 confirms the earlier analytical result that with homogeneous products socially-optimal behaviour arises not only from explicit marginal cost pricing, but also under Bertrand interaction and RCE.[7] At the other extreme market share behaviour coincides with pure monopoly, as we expect from the theory, generating only half the socially optimal output at more than twice the competitive price. Monopoly welfare loss in this case is 25 per cent. This is a high value compared with any of the partial equilibrium empirical estimates mentioned in the Introduction, but in the present context is relevant more as a benchmark than for its level. Cournot interaction cuts the monopoly loss to only 11.1 per cent and Stackelberg behaviour to 6.2 per cent.

Note the perverse relationship between 'market structure' and welfare loss. Thus the Herfindahl index fails to distinguish the social optimum, Bertrand and RCE, on the one hand, and the market share equilibrium on the other, whereas these lie at extreme ends of the range of variation in welfare! Furthermore the intermediate Cournot and Stackleberg cases are ranked perversely, the latter generating little over half the welfare loss of the former, despite a more concentrated market structure. Similarly non-discriminating or perverse results occurred throughout our analysis, and this suggests that, in direct contradiction to policy development in the USA in the mid-1980s (US Department of Justice, 1984), the antitrust forum should not place too great a reliance on arguments motivated by Herfindahl information.[8] Evidently the 'new industrial organisation' is correct to emphasise that, contrary to the once strong tradition in industrial organisation, conduct matters.

Product differentiation

Table 5.3 confirms the convergence of the Cournot, Bertrand, RCE and Stackelberg equilibria on the market share/collusion outcome. Notice that the convergence proceeds quite rapidly as

TABLE 5.3 Welfare indices and the degree of product differentiation (γ)[1]

Model	$\gamma \to 1$	$\gamma = 0.75$	$\gamma = 0.5$	$\gamma = 0.25$	$\gamma \to 0$
Social optimum (SO)	100.0	100.0	100.0	100.0	100.0
Cournot (C)	88.9	86.8	84.0	80.2	75.0
Bertrand (B)	100.0	96.0	88.9	81.6	75.0
Market share (MS)	75.0	75.0	75.0	75.0	75.0
RCE	100.0	92.5	86.6	81.0	75.0
$\left.\begin{array}{c} S_1 \\ S_2 \end{array}\right\}$	93.8	89.3	85.2	80.6	75.0
$\left.\begin{array}{c} D_1 \\ D_2 \end{array}\right\}$	(100.0)	96.9	93.7	90.6	87.5
$\left.\begin{array}{c} M_1 \\ M_2 \end{array}\right\}$	75.0	(–)	(–)	(–)	(–)

Note: 1 S1, S2, D1, D2, M1, M2 as in Table 5.1.

the degree of product differentiation increases and γ falls from unity. Thus, despite their differing starting levels, the Cournot, Bertrand, RCE and Stackelberg welfare losses all lie between 18 and 20 per cent of the social optimum when γ = 0.25. At this point the average increase in welfare loss for these solutions compared with the homogenous product case is 15.5 per cent. We conclude that the gradient of the competitiveness–welfare relationship in this plane is quite steep. However, the welfare *ranking* of the alternative equilibria is preserved. Meanwhile the dominant-firm welfare loss also increases as γ falls, to 12.5 per cent – one-half that of other solutions. This simply registers the fact that half the total output produced is subject to pure monopoly pricing and half is priced competitively. However this result is little more than a curiosum, in the absence of the cost asymmetry needed to render the dominant-firm solution concept plausible.

Cost asymmetry

As expected, where rivalry is reduced due to one firm having lower costs (firm 2 in our examples), relative welfare losses increase with the degree of cost advantage (Table 5.4). At high levels of product differentiation (low γ) the effect is barely perceptible (Table 5.4(b)). It remains small even where products are relatively homogeneous; where γ = 0.75 (Table 5.4(a)) the average percentage welfare loss for five meaningful cases (i.e. omitting the social optimum, M, S_1 and D_1) is 10.6 per cent with a 50 per cent cost differential, compared with 7.7 per cent where there is none. Over this range the welfare ranking is substantially unaffected, only Bertrand and dominant-firm interchanging places, these being very close in the original, symmetric cost case. In practice we would expect differential costs and diverse products to go together; if both firms have access to the same technology and are cost minimisers, inter-firm cost differences are most likely to be product-related. Hence, where cost asymmetries are most likely to be found, their impact on welfare, though adverse, is very slight.

Demand asymmetry

A similar conclusion applies in the case of demand asymmetry. Thus, where products are relatively homogeneous there is a sharp

TABLE 5.4   Welfare indices under cost asymmetry

$c_1 = 6.0$;	$c_2 =$	6.0	5.0	4.0	3.0
	Model				
(a)	$\gamma = 0.75$				
	Social optimum (SO)	100.0	100.0	100.0	100.0
	Cournot (C)	86.8	86.4	85.2	83.6
	Bertrand (B)	96.0	95.7	94.9	93.8
	Market share (MS)	75.0	75.0	75.0	75.0
	RCE	92.5	92.1	91.1	89.7
	S_2	89.4	89.6	89.1	88.0
	D_2	96.9	95.2	93.5	91.7
(b)	$\gamma = 0.25$				
	Social optimum (SO)	100.0	100.0	100.0	100.0
	Cournot (C)	80.2	80.2	80.2	80.0
	Bertrand (B)	81.6	81.6	81.5	81.4
	Market share (MS)	75.0	75.0	75.0	75.0
	RCE	81.0	80.9	80.6	80.8
	S_2	80.6	80.6	80.6	80.5
	D_2	90.6	89.5	88.5	87.6

Note: Demand symmetric: α_1, $\alpha_2 = 20$; β_1, $\beta_2 = 1$; $c_1 = 6.0$.

increase in relative welfare loss in all cases (except, of course, market share) as firm 2's demand advantage is increased (Table 5.5(a)). But this is an unlikely state of affairs. More plausible is that a marked demand advantage will be associated with highly differential products. In this case the impact of demand asymmetry on the indices of welfare loss for different types of equilibrium is, with one exception, minimal (Table 5.5(b)). The exception is dominant-firm equilibrium, where relative welfare loss almost doubles from 9.9 per cent where there is no asymmetry to 17.4 per cent where the dominant firm has a 50 per cent absolute demand advantage. Thus the welfare-enhancing effect of a competitive fringe, it appears, is much reduced where it supplies an inferior product.

Joint variation

Table 5.6 shows what happens when the degree of product differentiation varies in the presence of simultaneous, offsetting

TABLE 5.5 Welfare indices under demand asymmetry
$(\alpha_1 \neq \alpha_2; \beta_1 = \beta_2)$

$\alpha_1 = 20;$	$\alpha_2 =$	20	22	24	26	28	30
	Model						
(a)	$\gamma = 0.75$						
	Social optimum (*SO*)	100.0	100.0	100.0	100.0	100.0	100.0
	Cournot (*C*)	86.8	85.3	81.8	77.7	73.7	70.2
	Bertrand (*B*)	96.0	94.9	92.4	89.5	86.6	84.1
	Market share (*MS*)	75.0	75.0	75.0	75.0	75.0	75.0
	RCE	92.5	91.1	88.0	84.4	80.9	77.7
	S_2	89.4	89.1	86.6	83.3	79.8	76.6
	D_2	96.9	93.5	90.1	87.2	84.8	83.0
(b)	$\gamma = 0.25$						
	Social optimum (*SO*)	100.0	100.0	100.0	100.0	100.0	100.0
	Cournot (*C*)	80.3	80.2	79.9	79.6	79.3	78.9
	Bertrand (*B*)	81.6	81.5	81.3	81.0	80.7	80.3
	Market share (*MS*)	75.0	75.0	75.0	75.0	75.0	75.0
	RCE	81.0	80.9	80.6	80.3	80.0	79.6
	S_2	80.6	80.6	80.4	80.1	79.8	79.5
	D_2	90.6	88.5	86.7	85.1	83.7	82.6

asymmetries in both cost and demand. We focus only on plausible combinations: e.g. 'mild' product heterogeneity accompanied by 'modest' additional costs and demand advantage, etc. The results in general confirm previous conclusions. Thus, scanning any column, we see that the type of interactive behaviour in force makes a substantial difference to welfare. Average percentage losses over the nine reported cases are Cournot 16.8; Bertrand 11.5; market share 25.0; RCE 13.7; Stackelberg 15.4; and dominant-firm 6.4. Similarly, welfare losses are much affected by the degree of product differentiation. Average percentage losses across all types of equilibria in Table 5.6(a), 5.6(b) and 5.6(c) are 10.0, 15.8, and 17.7 respectively. However cost and demand asymmetries, in this case across a range of variation appropriate to the degree of product heterogeneity, make very little difference, again with the exception of the dominant firm case.

TABLE 5.6 Joint variation

	(a) Mild differentiation (γ = 0.75)		(b) Medium differentiation (γ = 0.5)		(c) High differentiation (γ = 0.25)				
	a(i)	a(ii)	b(i)	b(ii)	c(i)	c(ii)	c(iii)	c(iv)	c(v)
Social optimum (SO)	100.0	100.0	100.0	100.0	100.0	100.0	100.0	100.0	100.0
Cournot (C)	86.6	86.0	83.8	83.3	80.2	80.1	79.9	79.7	79.4
Bertrand (B)	95.9	95.4	88.7	88.3	81.6	81.5	81.3	81.1	80.9
Market share (MS)	75.0	75.0	75.0	75.0	75.0	75.0	75.0	75.0	75.0
RCE	92.3	91.8	86.4	86.0	80.9	80.8	80.6	80.4	80.2
S_1	88.7	87.7	84.8	84.1	80.5	80.3	80.1	79.9	79.6
S_2	89.6	89.5	85.3	85.1	80.6	80.5	80.4	80.2	80.0
D_1	97.9	98.6	95.4	96.8	92.1	93.3	94.4	95.3	96.1
D_2	95.7	94.5	91.9	90.1	89.1	87.7	86.5	85.4	84.4
Parameter values:									
α_1	20	20	20	20	20	20	20	20	20
α_2	21	22	22	24	22	24	26	28	30
β_1	1	1	1	1	1	1	1	1	1
β_2	1	1	1	1	1	1	1	1	1
c_1	6.0	6.0	6.0	6.0	6.0	6.0	6.0	6.0	6.0
c_2	6.3	6.6	6.6	7.2	6.6	7.2	7.8	8.4	9.0

5.4   CONCLUSIONS

Postulating a specific welfare function for a simple economy, and solving for the level of welfare under various combinations of 'conduct' (as captured in alternative oligopoly models) and 'structure' (in particular, as summarised in underlying demand and cost parameters), yields important additional insights to our understanding of oligopoly welfare loss. The analysis enables us to see directly how sensitive the loss levels are both to variations in conduct across given structures, and to variations in demand and cost conditions for a given conduct pattern. Four main conclusions from our analysis warrant emphasis, as follows.

(i) *Under duopolistic rivalry the particular form of oligopolistic interaction exerts a major influence on the level of welfare*
Conduct matters. Averaging over all cases reported in Tables (5.3) – (5.6) yields the following ranking in Table 5.7:

TABLE 5.7   Average loss of net-surplus

Model	Average loss of net surplus (%)
Market share/Collusion (MS)	25.0
Cournot (C)	17.8
Stackelberg (S_1, S_2)	15.9
RCE	14.5
Bertrand (B)	12.2
Dominant firm (D_1, D_2)	8.3

It follows that the design and execution of antitrust policies should not focus wholly or primarily on structural conditions. Two cases merit special attention.

First, we have seen that market share behaviour coincides with joint profit maximisation and produces the largest welfare loss: 25 per cent in the case of a quadratic social welfare function. Under competition law in most countries where such policy exists, overt collusion is proscribed. However non-competitive, adaptive behaviour generally does not infringe the law unless an agreement can be inferred. Our analysis shows that, where non-cooperative interaction takes the form of mutual market share maximisation, precisely the same outcome will be reached. It thus calls into question the existence of a distinction in law between the two cases. In countries like the UK, where competition policy provides for the application of a test of the public interest on a case-by-case basis, our analysis suggests that evidence of market share interaction should invariably lead to a negative finding, whether or not an implicit agreement can be inferred.

Secondly, our analysis draws attention to the welfare-enhancing effect of competition from a competitive fringe. This almost invariably produces less welfare loss than any other form of rivalry, and in many cases the losses amount to only a few percentage points. However, the constraining influence of competition from the fringe is much weakened where products are heterogeneous. From the standpoint of our static analysis it follows that when evaluating dominant-firm cases antitrust agencies should therefore pay close attention to the cross-elasticities of demand between the fringe and dominant firm's products. However this recommendation may need to be balanced by dynamic considerations, insofar as it may be argued that new and different products are the lifeblood of dynamic market economies.

(ii) *The power of inter-firm rivalry to further social welfare is highly sensitive to the degree of product differentiation in the market*
Where products are homogeneous three types of interactive behaviour generate welfare levels equal to the social optimum, whereas all but the dominant-firm case lead to maximum, market share/collusion losses if there is complete differentiation of products. Furthermore, welfare losses increase rapidly as product heterogeneity enters. Antitrust policy and agencies should therefore pay close attention to the cross-elasticities of demand between rival's products in all cases.

(iii) *Over broad ranges, asymmetric cost and demand conditions as between rivals generally have little effect on the size of welfare losses*
The one (dominant-firm) exception has already been discussed.

(iv) *Measures of market structure are an unreliable guide to the level of welfare in duopolised markets*
This is a corollary of (i). Because conduct matters it cannot be assumed that there is a unique relationship between particular

structural conditions and performance. In particular, measures of seller concentration such as the Herfindahl index may either fail to distinguish different social outcomes, or even rank them perversely. Our results thus lend support to the new directions in industrial organisation, in which conduct moves to centre stage, and structure (in particular, seller concentration) is found jointly with prices, profits, output and welfare, as part of an equilibrium determined by preferences, behaviour and technology.[9]

Appendix: Derivation of the Equilibrium Conditions

Social optimum (*SO*)

Net surplus (utility minus cost) in our model is

$$Z = \alpha_1 x_1 + \alpha_2 x_2 - \frac{1}{2}\left(\beta_1 x_1^2 + 2\gamma x_1 x_2 + \beta_2 x_2^2\right) - (c_1 x_1 + c_2 x_2).$$

The first-order conditions (FOC) for a maximum require

$$\frac{\partial Z}{\partial x_i} = \alpha_i - c_i - \beta_i x_i - \gamma x_j = 0, \quad \text{for } i, j = 1, 2$$

or

$$\theta_i = \beta_i x_i + \gamma x_j \tag{5A.1}$$

where $\theta_i = \alpha_i - c_i$. The 'reaction functions' (equations for optimum x_i in terms of x_j) given as (5.4) in Table 5.1 follow clearly.

Cournot (*C*), Bertrand (*B*) and market share (*MS*)

These three equilibria result from differing specifications of the CVs term dx_j/dx_i in the general FOC for maximum profit for firm i (the partial of the profit function (5.3) with respect to own output):

$$\frac{\partial \pi_i}{\partial x_i} = \theta_i - 2\beta_i x_i - \gamma x_j - \gamma x_i \, dx_j/dx_i = 0 \tag{5A.2}$$

On Cournot assumptions firm i chooses x_i assuming x_j will not change: $dx_j/dx_i = 0$. Hence,

$$\theta_i = 2\beta_i x_i - \gamma x_j = 0 \tag{5A.3}$$

gives firm i's best output for any x_j, and letting $i, j = 1, 2$ we obtain the reaction functions (5.5) in Table 5.1.

In our quantity-setting framework, Bertrand (strictly a price-setting model) requires that firm i chooses x_i assuming x_j will change in such a way that p_j is constant.

Consider increments to firm j's inverse demand:

$$dp_j = -\beta j\, dx_j - \gamma dx_i$$

The Bertrand conjecture requires $dp_j = 0$, so

$$-\beta_j\, dx_j - \gamma dx_i = 0$$

i.e.

$$dx_j/dx_i = -\gamma/\beta_j$$

Substituting (5A.2) gives

$$\theta_i - 2\,\beta_i x_i - \gamma x_j - \gamma x_i\,(-\gamma/\beta_j) = 0,$$

or

$$\theta_i = (2 - \gamma^2/\beta_i\beta_j)\beta_i x_i + \gamma x_j \tag{5A.4}$$

as the reaction functions in this case (equations (5.6) in Table 5.1). Note that $1 < (2 - \gamma^2/\beta_i\beta_j) < 2$, so the Bertrand equilibrium lies between Cournot and the social optimum.

In the market share model firm i chooses x_i assuming x_j changes equiproportionately, i.e. $dx_j/dx_i = x_j/x_i$. Substitution into (5A.2) in this case yields

$$\theta_i - 2\beta_i x_i - \gamma x_j - \gamma x_i\,(x_j/x_i) = 0$$

or

$$\theta_i = 2\beta_i x_i + 2\gamma x_j \tag{5A.5}$$

(cf. equation (5.7) in Table 5.1).

Collusion or joint profit maximisation

$$\pi_1 + \pi_2 = \theta_1 x_1 + \theta_2 x_2 - \beta_1 x_1^2 - \beta_2 x_2^2 - 2\gamma x_1 x_2$$

The FOC require

$$\frac{\partial(\pi_1 + \pi_2)}{\partial x_i} = \theta_i - 2\beta_i x_i - 2\gamma x_j = 0, \quad \text{for } i, j = 1, 2$$

which on rearrangement also yields (5A.5): market share equilibrium maximises joint profit.

Rational conjectures (RCE)

Given equations (5.16) – (5.18) from the text, the procedure is first to solve (5.17) and (5.18) for the rational conjectures dx_2/dx_1 and dx_1/dx_2, and then substitute these solutions in (5.16) to obtain the required reaction functions.

For simplicity let $f_1 \equiv dx_2/dx_1$ and $f_2 \equiv dx_1/dx_2$. Then (5.18) and (5.17) give, respectively:

$$f_1 = \frac{-\gamma}{2\beta_2 + \gamma f_2} \tag{5A.6}$$

and

$$f_2 = \frac{-\gamma}{2\beta_1 + \gamma f_1} \tag{5A.7}$$

Since $-\gamma$ is common in the numerator on the right-hand side of both (5A.6) and (5A.7) we may write

$$f_1(2\beta_2 + \gamma f_2) = f_2(2\beta_1 + \gamma f_1)$$

so that

$$f_1\beta_2 = f_2\beta_1 \tag{5A.8}$$

Substituting for f_2 in (5A.6) and multiplying out gives

$$\gamma\beta_2 f_1^2 + 2\beta_1\beta_2 f_1 + \gamma\beta_1 = 0$$

Taking the quadratic in f_1:

$$\begin{aligned}
f_1 &= \frac{-2\beta_1\beta_2 \pm \sqrt{4\beta_1^2\beta_2^2 - 4\gamma^2\beta_1\beta_2}}{2\gamma\beta_2} \\[2mm]
&= \frac{-\beta_1 \pm \beta_1\sqrt{1 - \gamma^2/\beta_1\beta_2}}{\gamma} \\[2mm]
&= \frac{-\beta_1(1 \pm \delta)}{\gamma} \text{with } \delta = \sqrt{1 - \gamma^2/\beta_1\beta_2}
\end{aligned}$$

As δ is real and $0 < \delta < 1$ the positive root ensures correct relative slopes in (5A.8), so

$$\left.\begin{array}{l} f_1 = dx_2/dx_1 = \dfrac{-\beta_1(1 - \delta)}{\gamma} \\[3mm] \text{and} \qquad f_2 = dx_1/dx_2 = \dfrac{-\beta_2(1 - \delta)}{\gamma} \end{array}\right\} \tag{5A.9}$$

(5A.9) gives the first two conditions of (5.8) in Table 5.1. The remaining (reaction function) conditions are easily obtained by substituting for dx_2/dx_1 and dx_1/dx_2 in (5.16).

Stackelberg (S_1, S_2)

If firm 1 is leader then x_1 is chosen to maximise π_1, subject to firm 2's Cournot reaction function:

$$\theta_2 = 2\,\beta_2 x_2 + \gamma x_1$$

whence

$$x_2 = (\theta_2 - \gamma x_1)/2\beta_2; \; dx_2/dx_1 = -\gamma/2\beta_2$$

Substituting once more for dx_2/dx_1 in (5A.2) gives

$$\theta_1 - 2\,\beta_1 x_1 - \gamma x_2 - \gamma x_1(-\gamma/2\,\beta_2) = 0$$

or

$$\left.\begin{array}{l} \theta_1 = (2 - \gamma^2/2\,\beta_1\beta_2)\,\beta_1 x_1 + \gamma x_2 \\[3mm] \text{which together with} \\[3mm] \theta_2 = 2\beta_2 x_2 + \gamma x_1 \end{array}\right\} \tag{5A.10}$$

are the equilibrium conditions for S_1, given as (5.10) in Table 5.1. Similarly for S_2 when firm 2 is leader.

Dominant firm (D_1, D_2)

In this case the equilibrium conditions are a combination of the Bertrand reaction function for the firm which is dominant, firm 1, say, and the social-optimum reaction function for the 'fringe' firm (cf. equation (5.10) versus equations (5.6) and (5.4) in Table 5.1). Since the fringe firm 2 is a price-taker, firm 1 holds the Bertrand conjecture $dp_2 = 0$, giving $dx_2/dx_1 = -\gamma/\beta_2$ as before. Firm 2 itself obeys the social optimum condition since it chooses output price equals marginal cost.

6 Models of Product Differentiation*

MICHAEL WATERSON

6.1 INTRODUCTION

Product differentiation is one of the pervasive features of modern economies.[1] On entering a department store, say, a customer may choose between a variety of detergents, of dinner plates and of dishwashers. In each case, there is a set of products which may be considered to supply broadly the same needs, for example laundering clothes, but which are different in detail. Since customers differ in their tastes and incomes, they are most likely to exhibit preferences as between the varieties. Modelling product differentiation involves specifying supply and demand sides to the relationship. The aim is to obtain insights into behaviour and performance which cannot be gleaned from homogeneous product models.

The literature which is of potential relevance to a survey of this field is too extensive to permit full coverage. Hence we will largely step aside from what may be considered as less central areas. These include purely monopolistic competition models, most of the technical issues regarding existence, any connections with research and development (R&D) or technical progress, and the relevance of uncertainty, and therefore a role for information. This last exclusion in turn implies that advertising, though in practice intimately linked with some aspects of product differentiation, cannot really be treated. Generally, it implies that our focus is on the supply rather than the demand side (see Caves and

Williamson, 1985). In particular, it may suggest that the models are more likely to be applicable to goods than to services, since most people would be themselves better able to imagine the utility resulting from the purchase of a particular microwave oven, than from employing a particular builder to rectify a defective damp-course. Moreover, since we are reporting on a literature which assumes that firms are unable to ascertain the tastes of *individual* consumers and, more importantly, which confines itself almost exclusively to the (unrealistic) assumption of single-product firms, we shall neglect possibilities for price discrimination.[2] To put it more positively, we focus largely on product differentiation itself, rather than that in association with other things which can exist in the absence of product differentiation. As the title of the chapter suggests, we restrict ourselves to theory.

At the outset, it is important to bear in mind some crucial distinctions between types of product differentiation. Most central (particularly from the point of view of results) is the horizontal–vertical distinction. If we consider a class of goods as being typified by a set of (desirable) characteristics, then two varieties are vertically differentiated when the first contains more of some or all characteristics than the second, so that all rational consumers given a free choice would opt for the first. They are horizontally differentiated when one contains more of some but fewer of other characteristics, so that two consumers exhibiting different tastes offered a free choice would not unambiguously plump for the same one. For example, given the choice between two computers alike in all respects save that one has twice the memory of the other, everyone's choice would be clear, whereas faced with two possible packages, one with a relatively poor printer but a colour screen, the other with a good printer but a monochrome screen, then some people would go for one and some for the other.

A seemingly more technical but nevertheless important distinction may be made between 'address' and 'non-address' goods (to use Archibald, Eaton and Lipsey's 1984, terminology). One way to conceive of the set of all possible goods is by reference to characteristics space (analogous to a geographical space) in which a good may be located using its coordinates (or 'address'), for example its position on the real line from abysmally low to astonishingly high quality, or from sour to sweet. Each good then also has specific neighbours. An alternative, the 'non-address' approach, is to define the set of goods completely, whereupon their number is finite (or countably infinite) as there is no continuum of possible goods. This set may then be viewed as being purchased by the 'representative individual'. The former approach is associated with a tradition originating from Hotelling (1929), the latter with Chamberlin (1933) and followers. More is made of this distinction where we come to Chamberlinian models in section 6.2 (p. 120)

Notice that in raising the issue of horizontal product differentiation, in the address branch we follow Hotelling (1929) and Lancaster (1979) in assuming that consumers make an either/or choice between products, rather than engaging in the (quasi-production) activity of combining them. This need not always be a sensible assumption to make. For example, if none of the varieties of muesli on offer is precisely what one wants, there remains the possibility of buying several different types and combining them in the desired proportions. Then, if price differences exist, one can imagine economising on relatively expensive inputs. Hence, as one price rises relative to others, each consumer buying that variety will gradually shift purchases away from it, though there may be sudden jumps as different goods become 'neighbours'. This alternative approach was explored by Lancaster (1966, 1971). Given heterogeneity between consumers, the outcome will commonly not be very different, in both cases leading to a monotonic non-increasing demand curve for a particular variety (see e.g. Waterson, 1984, section 6.2). However Lancaster's earlier model does seem more likely to produce Giffin-good behaviour, and other peculiarities (see Lipsey and Rosenbluth, 1971). Henceforth we shall concentrate on the either/or case, which is discussed at greater length in the literature.

The other feature of address models which will sometimes be relevant concerns the number of 'neighbours' a product has. In vertical product differentiation models, there are typically two – the immediately superior and the immediately inferior qualities. With horizontal product differentiation, the matter is less clear cut. Suppose you go to the supermarket and find your favourite brand of toothpaste has suddenly increased a great deal in price, relative to the others. Do you choose any other more or less at random, or do you have a list of close substitutes from which you select an alternative? The former behaviour is akin to that represented by Chamberlin's monopolistic competition model where each product is a generalised substitute for all others. The latter behaviour is in line with Lancastrian and Hotelling-type approaches in which the number of relevant product dimensions is 'small'. Hotelling-type frameworks lead typically to two neighbours when there is one dimension and six when there are two. When there are several relevant product dimensions, each product may have many neighbours, for example if there are four or more, each product may have a large number of effective competitors (see Archibald and Rosenbluth, 1975).

Before looking at any models in detail though, we must have very firmly in mind our aims in this survey. Essentially, they are to capture insights into reality which would not be available from homogeneous product models, and in addition to examine the social-welfare implications which arise. For example, when product variety is an important intrinsic feature of a class of goods (e.g. motor cars), we might sensibly ask how much would be optimal, and whether the market left to itself is likely to do a reasonable job of providing that variety.

The plan of the survey is as follows. Section 6.2 covers horizontal product differentiation, starting with Hotelling, and Hotelling-like models, proceeding to social-welfare considerations, some multiproduct insights, then on to Chamberlin-type formulations. Section 6.3 covers vertical product differentiation, first in general, then the specific case of natural oligopoly models and some extensions and comparisons. Section 6.4 attempts to draw some conclusions and make suggestions for further work.

6.2 HORIZONTAL PRODUCT DIFFERENTIATION

Hotelling's model

The logical place to start the analysis is with Hotelling's (1929) own spatial location model which may be developed into a product differentiation model. His assumptions, explicit and implicit, may be stated as follows:

(i) Consumers are uniformly distributed along a line of finite length representing a linear market such as a 'strip' shopping centre or a long narrow beach. We assume there are D consumers

per unit of distance along the line. (Hotelling had D equal to 1.)
(ii) Demand for the product is completely inelastic at one unit per consumer (per time period). If consumers have reservation prices (above which they will not buy) these turn out not to be a binding constraint. Consumers buy from the producer whose delivered price is the lowest, since the products are homogeneous apart from their locations.
(iii) Marginal costs of production are constant and, in the original model, were assumed to be zero (without loss of generality). Firms might face fixed costs of being in production, but it is assumed that they may costlessly change their locations. To pursue the 'beach' analogy, if the product is ice-creams then the seller(s) may easily move around in search of custom.
(iv) There is a fixed number of sellers, constrained often to two. Each has a single location.
(v) A constant cost of transporting one unit of the commodity one unit of distance is incurred. Either buyers pay this transport cost directly, and reckon this in their delivered price calculations, or sellers pass on the direct costs of transport, without discrimination.

To summarise, we have for each consumer:

$$p_d = p_i + x_i t \tag{6.1}$$

where p_d is delivered price, p_i is point-of-sale price of the nearest supplier, and t is the transport cost per unit, x_i, of distance from the supplier. The total market is of length L, say, and the demand, q_i on each firm is proportional to distance sold to left and right:

$$q_i = D \cdot (x_i^L + x_i^R) \tag{6.2}$$

Each firm has a cost function:

$$C(q_i) = F + cq_i \tag{6.3}$$

where F is fixed cost and c is the unit variable cost of production.
Armed with these assumptions, Hotelling proceeds to solve the model in what turns out to be a remarkably modern (though, in terms of his specific framework in which locational decisions are costlessly reversible, rather mistaken) way. Suppose firms take the decisions in sequence, location being decided first, then price. In

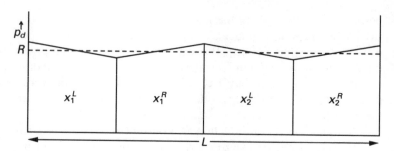

FIGURE 6.1   Optimum location in the Hotelling model

order to choose location though, the firms will have to know what prices are then to be expected. The model thus needs to be solved in reverse; for price in terms of location, then for location itself. Hence it uses a version of Selten's (1975) sequential or perfect equilibrium solution concept.

The framework is illustrated in Figure 6.1, for two firms 1 and 2 (ignore the dashed line for the present). For firm 1, from (6.2), by equating delivered prices to consumers to determine market shares, we obtain

$$q_1 = \frac{1}{2}D[L + (x_1^L - x_2^R) + (p_2 - p_1)/t] \tag{6.4}$$

Profits are:

$$\pi_i = (p_i - c)q_i - F$$

so that firm 1's optimal price is given from the first-order condition, $\partial\pi_1/\partial p_1$, by:

$$p_1^* = c + t[L + (x_1^L - x_2^R)/3] \tag{6.5}$$

and similarly for firm 2. Notice that $\partial q_1/\partial x_1^L > 0$, and also $\partial p_1^*/\partial x_1^L > 0$. Obviously therefore, $\partial\pi_1/\partial x_1^L > 0$. Similarly, $\partial\pi_2/\partial x_2^R > 0$. Thus the firms both wish to move towards the centre as much as possible.

Hotelling therefore concluded that there was a tendency for firms to cluster: 'Buyers are confronted everywhere with an excessive sameness' (1929, p. 54). Moreover, he is clear that distance is a direct analogy for product differentiation, of a particular sort, for example he quotes the case of different types of cider, some sweeter than others.[3]

The formal analogy with product differentiation is in fact remarkably straightforward; the demonstration below follows Salop (1979). A typical consumer whose desired product specification is $\hat{l}$, decides on that product i for which

$$\max_i [U(l_i, \hat{l}) - p_i] \geq \bar{s} \tag{6.6}$$

l_i being the specification of the product and $\bar{s}$ the surplus from consuming a homogeneous good, which is purchased instead if it yields greater utility. Now assume that preferences are given by:

$$U(l_i, \hat{l}) = \vartheta - t[l_i - \hat{l}]$$

i.e. related to the 'distance' between product specifications. Substituting into (6.6), writing product specification distances as x_i and rearranging, we have:

$$\max_i [R - (p_i + tx_i)] \geq 0 \tag{6.7}$$

with $R = \vartheta - \bar{s}$ being the effective reservation price. Thus it appears precisely similar to the problem for a consumer with reservation price R facing a delivered price for the nearest product of $p_i + tx_i$. The dashed line in Figure 6.1 illustrates an example of a reservation price which means some consumers are not served.

Having developed the analogy, we should point out some differences between the location and product differentiation frameworks. First, there is reason to think that price discrimination (which we have ignored) is rather less likely in the product differentiation framework, on the grounds that tastes are less easily observable than consumers' addresses. Secondly, whilst it is sensible to assume linear transport costs in the locational case, we can be rather more eclectic when considering product specification. In particular, it has been argued that the assumption of quadratic distance costs, implying a rather rapid tailing off of utility away from one's most desired products, may be more appropriate to product differentiation, and it will shortly be seen that this modifies the results. Thirdly however, whilst for most purposes in the locational context, one or two dimensions are sufficient, in the product variety context there could be several dimensions along which consumers perceive differences between products.[4] This last point would lead to increases in the number of 'neighbours', as has been outlined in section 6.1, but it has not perhaps received the modelling attention it deserves in the literature.

Modifications to the Hotelling framework

In common with almost every pathbreaking piece of analysis, later authors have been critical of Hotelling's work on the basis of its predictions, its assumptions, and its logical consistency. To take up the last point first, it has been shown that a price equilibrium does not exist in the standard Hotelling framework (see d'Aspremont, Jaskold Gabszewicz and Thisse, 1979). This is because the prices (6.5) are such that neither firm can gain by unilateral departure from them, *assuming the other remains in business*. But, by undercutting, one firm has the potential to drive the other out of business so as to gain the whole market, thus generating instability. Furthermore, since in Hotelling's model the location decision is just as easy to change as the price decision is, it is not clear that his sequential solution approach is appropriate.

The most straightforward way around the first problem is to adopt Eaton's (1972) 'no-mill-price-undercutting' or 'modified zero conjectural variations' assumption. The argument for adopting this assumption is that it would be absurd for a firm to believe it could drive a neighbour (the other firm) out of business, when the neighbour has the option of selling a positive quantity at a price above marginal costs.[5] For it to be worthwhile for firm 1 to drive firm 2 out, firm 1 would want to set:

$$p_2 > p_1 + x_1 t \geq c$$

But firm 2 would find it more profitable to stay in business, so long as $p_2 > c$, which has the potential to force p_1 below c. If this argument be accepted, Hotelling's model stands up as a price-setting equilibrium.[6]

However, there are still several difficulties connected with Hotelling's basic framework, and the predictions one may glean from it. Obviously, one might ask how the prediction of minimum differentiation between products would be influenced by mild perturbations of the assumptions. Early on, Smithies (1940) analysed what happened when the demand curves were less than completely inelastic. He found, as might be expected, that it caused a lessening of the centripetal tendency so noticeable in Hotelling's model. Yet firms still did not choose locations far enough apart to be socially optimal (that is $L/4$ and $3L/4$, the transport cost minimising points). In contrast, one other obvious extension, increasing the number of firms from two to three in Hotelling's model, completely messes it up. This is because of the extremely easy relocation implicit in Hotelling's model which, when coupled with finite markets, leads to leapfrogging behaviour.

Partly for this reason, a lot has been done with other variants of the location framework. One important variant (Samuelson, 1967; Salop, 1979a, etc.) has assumed that preferences can be represented as being distributed around a circle. Hence, there is no captive 'hinterland' for any firm, so that effects arising due to the 'ends' of the line do not (as they did in Hotelling with three firms) arise. If one assumes free entry alongside free relocation, then the equilibrium should involve zero profits (apart from the integer problem), and moreover it is natural to assume it will be symmetric.

Thus Salop demonstrates that (a range of) symmetric zero profit equilibria exist, in which each firm has an equal market area. The equilibrium may be 'competitive', that is like Hotelling in that every customer is served, or 'monopoly' where each firm has its own disjoint market area and some consumers relatively far from any pair of products buy the outside good. Alternatively it may be a 'kinked' equilibrium on the boundary between these two, where the entire market is just served. Adopting the no-mill-price-undercutting assumption rules out 'supercompetitive' possibilities where one firm prices so low as to eclipse its immediate neighbours.

As far as production varieties are concerned, of course, this precise representation is barely relevant. The only real examples are different aircraft, train or coach departure times, where the circle represents a 24-hour clock. Nevertheless, with the help of a minor modification we may analyse more relevant cases. From our point of view, the circle is essentially the same as a line of infinite length, along which consumers are presumed to lie. Products, by analogy, will be equally spaced along this line. The relevant questions then concerns the *density* of products.

From (6.7) (dropping the i subscript given symmetry) we may derive the maximum distance at which products sell as $\bar{x} = (R - p)/t$ and thus obtain consumer demands under 'monopoly' and under 'competition':

$$q_m = 2D\hat{x} = 2D(R - p)/t \qquad (6.8)$$

and

$$q_c = 2D\hat{x} = 2D(\bar{p} - p + tA)/t \qquad (6.9)$$

respectively, where $\bar{p}$ is the price (both) rivals set and brands are a distance A apart. In both cases, we may solve for a symmetric zero profit equilibrium (*szpe*) by setting each firm's marginal revenue equal to marginal cost (profit maximisation) and average revenue equal to average cost (zero profit), to obtain:

$$p_m = c + tA_m/2; \; A_m = \sqrt{2F/tD} \qquad (6.10)$$

and

$$p_c = c + tA_c; \; A_c = \sqrt{F/tD} \qquad (6.11)$$

assuming no 'gaps' in the market.

Under 'monopoly', the firms each serve a broader spectrum of tastes, but with lower mill prices.[7] These results are illustrated in Figure 6.2, solid lines representing 'monopoly', and dashed ones 'competition', for particular parameter values ($F = 2, t = D = c = 1$; $R = 3$ for monopoly, $R = 3.2$ for competition)

One key assumption underlying the Salop-type models above is free relocation of products. For many purposes, this assumption is unrealistic.[8] Indeed, a far more relevant formulation would be to consider product positioning as a long-term policy decision involving substantial sunk costs, with the choice of price as a subsequent and relatively short-term decision. An obvious example would be motor cars, where price for a particular new model is finalised at the last minute.

This reformulation requires us to model a sequence of two (or more) decisions, using the tools, for example, of a subgame-perfect equilibrium. That is, the optimal choice of product position

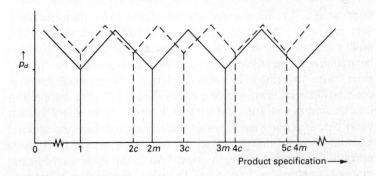

FIGURE 6.2 Spatial distribution of products under 'monopoly' and competition

depends upon the prices anticipated in the second stage, since the strategies are chosen to be Nash equilibria in each subgame. This legitimises Hotelling's approach of solving for prices, given location, then solving for location. It also means that the assumption of zero profits as a necessary condition for free-entry equilibrium must come under examination. When product choice becomes a decision of some consequence, one might expect firms to exercise some foresight in making this decision, and to behave strategically in making a choice which allows them to earn profits above the norm. We now turn to look at these issues.

First, if we turn to a Hotelling-type finite line, retain the assumption that there are only two firms, but impose quadratic distance costs (which may be perfectly appropriate to the product differentiation formulation), then a result in complete opposition to the essential message of Hotelling's paper emerges. The two firms locate at the ends of the market, thus maximising their differentiation, in order to reduce price competition (see e.g. Neven, 1985).

Moving on to the multifirm, free-entry, infinite line framework, several authors (e.g. Hay, 1976; Rothschild, 1976; Schmalensee, 1978; Eaton and Lipsey, 1978) have explored sequential deterrence equilibria in which firms enter in sequence, each a follower with respect to those who have already arrived, but realising that others will subsequently enter. We examine this intuitively by extending the symmetric zero-profit model developed above.

Suppose one firm has located, then the next to locate to its right, say, can with advantage choose a product specification which makes it not quite worthwhile for any firm to choose a position between them, meaning it must not be able to break even. Thus *if* price were to remain constant and the *szpe* involved firms at positions like $1m$, $2m$,. . ., $5m$,. . . in Figure 6.2, then once a firm had located at $1m$, the next firm to the right could guard against entry by positioning itself just to the left of $3m$, since the optimal internal position, marginally to the left of $2m$, would then prove uprofitable. Subsequently, the next firm to the right would locate marginally left of $5m$, and so on. Therefore if each firm in the *szpe* served an area A^*, under our present assumptions of free entry but invariant prices, each firm would be able to serve an area marginally less than $2A^*$ without inviting entry. Substantially above-normal profits could be earned, despite free entry, as a result of the fixed relocation assumption.

Against this, it may be objected we have artificially held price constant, and that price competition may be expected to reduce profits to normal levels. However it is straightforward to design models where price is independent of location; Schmalensee's and Eaton and Lipsey's (1978, section 6) models have this property. Moreover, in models like Hay's where price is a positive function of distance, profits may actually be *more* than twice normal without entry being attracted, since the nature of the model means that the internal entrant would anticipate price falling on entry.[9]

Before closing this subsection, it is worth noting the very different work of de Palma *et al.*, (1985). If we relax the assumption that a consumer at a point Y patronises firm 1, but a consumer at $Y + \varepsilon$ (ε an arbitrarily small number) patronises firm 2, or indeed that the consumer at Y patronises firm 1 at prices (p_1, p_2), but goes to firm 2 at prices $(p_1 + \varepsilon, p_2 - \varepsilon)$, then sudden movements in behaviour which have the tendency to produce non-existence results may be avoided. The de Palma paper manages this in a very logical way by assuming some element of randomness in consumer behaviour, which allows overlapping market areas. It also, incidentally, greatly increases the centripetal tendency.

Social-welfare considerations

In retrospect, it seems that Hotelling's result of there being grossly insufficient variety is overspecific, to say the least. It is not difficult

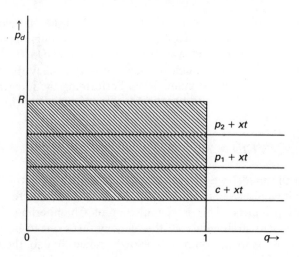

FIGURE 6.3 **Social welfare under alternative delivered prices**

to see why. In his model, not only does a firm's output rise as its captive hinterland is increased (equation (6.4)), but also optimal price rises directly with increases in its hinterland (equation (6.5)). The former result is obviously assisted by the inelastic demand assumption, but it is the latter result which seems unduly specific, in that one might well expect price competition to increase with increased product proximity, as Neven (1985) found, for example.

The degree of variety remains an important question in more general models though. In the case of multifirm frameworks like the Salop variant we have reported on, 'distance' between firms is essentially the only factor which affects social welfare, if measured as the sum of producer and consumer surplus. The point is illustrated in Figure 6.3, for an individual consumer facing two alternative delivered prices, $p_1 + xt$ and $p_2 + xt$. Consumer plus producer surplus is the shaded area in both cases.

In the Salopian framework, social welfare per unit distance when the firms are A units apart (so the furthest consumer buys a product $A/2$ distant) may be written as:

$$W = \frac{1}{A} \left[2 \int_0^{A/2} (R - c - tx) \cdot D \cdot dx - F \right] \qquad (6.12)$$

This function illustrates clearly the nature of the tradeoff involved. Consumers lose utility which firms do *not* gain through having to purchase a product some way from their ideal.[10] On the other hand, society suffers through having to pay too many fixed cost elements if there are too many firms. Performing the integration, then maximising W with respect to A yields an immediate comparison with (6.10) and (6.11):

$$A_w = 2\sqrt{F/tD} > A_m > A_c$$

Thus in the model we have been considering, there is too much variety; it would be better were firms to produce a more restricted range of products. This is reminiscent of Chamberlin's (1933) excess capacity argument (but the analogy turns out to be rather treacherous, as we see on p. 123 below). In fact though, the result is not specific to models with a Salop-type demand function, and there seems to be some general tendency for address models to yield the superabundant variety result. One consequence is that deterrence equilibria which yield pure profits to the producers involved may be socially preferred to zero profit equilibria which involve more firms – see Waterson (1985) for an example.

Of course, social welfare must in general be concerned both with price and with variety. A particular firm considering establishing at a specific location does not take into account either of two sources of divergence between private and social welfare. First, the marginal firm cannot capture all the consumer surplus which arises from a product's introduction, so on those grounds one might expect too little variety, plus socially inefficient pricing when relevant. Secondly, however, there is the 'business' stealing' effect, to use Mankiw and Whinston's (1986) phrase, a force making for too much variety: firms do not take into account adverse effects upon other firms of introducing a new product.

Multiproduct firms

So far, we have artificially restricted discussion to single-product firms. This is substantially at variance with reality, where it would be typical, just to take a random example, for a particular wine distributor to aim to supply a range including a sweet white, a dry white, a rosé and a red, in each price category. There has been relatively little consideration paid to these issues, but it seems clear that relaxing the assumption of single-product firms is likely to have real effects.

Suppose, for example, that a set of firms is located in a growing market. As the density of consumers increases, new opportunities will become available. One possibility is that an entrant firm will seize the advantage. Alternatively, the established firms might seek to prevent entry by setting artificially low prices. This is scarcely credible, however, since once successful entry had taken place, it would be optimal to raise prices again (see e.g. Schmalensee, 1978). More plausibly then, assuming the established firms recognised the gap, one among them who was more alert could set up a new product with the characteristics the entrant would have chosen. It can hardly be more expensive for the established firm than the entrant to do this, and it might be less (e.g. if there are economies of scope involved).

The argument is capable of extension (see Eaton and Lipsey, 1979; but also Hay, 1976, for further relevant considerations). If one firm is occupying a central position in a (finite length) market, and the market is currently capable of supporting only one firm, but is growing, then entry may be predicted to occur in the future on both sides of the central position. A new firm entering, to the left say, would choose a location taking advantage of the (currently) captive hinterland to its left. By contrast, if instead the existing firm were to provide the entering product, it could engage in a more globally optimal locational calculation.[11] This provides an additional reason (besides that of cost) why the established firm can profitably introduce a new product earlier than a *de novo* entrant. If so, it can afford to pre-empt the new entrant in timing its product's introduction. In fact, looked at in this way, the modelling problem regarding multiproduct firms is to explain why new firms never enter[12] (see Prescott and Visscher, 1977, section 3).

However Judd (1985) points out an important implicit assumption in the modelling, namely that the costs of leaving a market are high. Entry costs deter entry if the entrant thinks returns are at best normal after entry. But if the entrant believes the incumbent can be driven into exiting a market, then sinking the costs of entry may be worthwhile because it will lead to a return above costs in the future. The incumbent will in turn be driven into exit if the costs of leaving are low and the low prices which may result from competition following entry will hurt not only products for which there is close competition but also those further away in the spectrum. Judd uses the example of an apple monopolist considering whether to preempt entry to orange production by operating also in that area. Entry by another firm into oranges will lead to duopoly price competition which hurts apple profitability since the products are partial substitutes. Clearly the magnitude of exit costs is an important consideration.

If one restricts articially the numbers of products and firms, then further insights are available. Brander and Eaton (1984) focus on a case where there are two firms, each producing two products. All four products are different, so the major issues of interest concern whether segmenting or interlacing occurs – if we position the four products on a line in places 1 to 4, then interlacing is where firm A, say, produces products 1 and 3, firm B products 2 and 4, whereas under segmenting, A produces 1 and 2, B products 3 and 4. The equilibrium which results then depends, for example, on whether the firms choose their product lines sequentially or simultaneously. Sequential choices strengthen the case for segmentation as an equilibrium, but interlacing may be a better defence against further entry. Really though, such models of multiproduct competition are at a rather early stage of development.

Non-address models

We started the survey with Hotelling. Yet it might have been equally logical to begin with Chamberlin (1933). Would this have led to a different emphasis and results? To examine this question we run through some of the developments in this branch of the theory.

At first sight, the frameworks are rather similar. Suppose there is a range of toothbrushes on sale, in all colours of the rainbow. In the Hotelling construction, an individual consumer might have a specific preference for a green toothbrush, be less keen on yellow and blue, and so on. Under Chamberlinian assumptions, one individual consumer might have a specific preference for orange and be indifferent between the others. However another consumer might favour green over others. Hence it makes sense to analyse Chamberlin's problem in terms of a *typical* consumer who has a preference for variety itself. Thus a better prototype might be a box of chocolates where the typical consumer likes all the centres (even the butterscotch) but values the variety.

In making comparison between the models, then, we should note the distinction between the ways in which variety is developed. In Hotelling-type frameworks, there is an infinity of possible products and tastes. Under Chamberlin, there is a specific set of products entering into the utility function of our typical individual – the colour chart (or whatever) incorporates the complete range. Thus Chamberlinian models describe products while Hotelling describes demands.

The other factor which is of some importance is that, in Chamberlin, neighbour effects are necessarily absent. Most of the recent work on Hotelling models has focused on low-dimension models in which neighbour effects are important. The supernormal profit results rely upon localised crowding which would be much attenuated when each product has a number of neighbours. Hence in Chamberlinian models, those sorts of issues are not raised, and entry reduces profit to zero.

To illustrate Chamberlinian models, we adopt a simple version of a formulation which has been employed by several authors (e.g., Spence, 1980; Dixit and Stiglitz, 1977), then develop the implications. The typical consumer's utility is represented by:

$$U = q_o + Z^\theta; Z = \sum_i z_i; z_i = q_i^{1/\phi}; i = 1, 2, \ldots, n \qquad (6.13)$$

where q_0 is the amount of some numerative commodity, q_i is the amount of variety i of the differentiated product consumed, $\phi > 1$, $0 < \theta <$, and n is the number of varieties produced by the market mechanism. Therefore equating price and marginal utility

$$q_i p_i = q_i \partial U/\partial q_i = (\theta/\phi)Z^{\theta-1}z_i$$

which suggests defining the pseudo-inverse demand curve in terms of Z as:

$$\hat{p}(Z) = (\theta/\phi)Z^{\theta-1} \qquad (6.14)$$

Assuming costs are given by (6.3), a typical (single-product) firm's profit may be written as:

$$\pi_i = p_i q_i - C(q_i) = \hat{p}(Z) \cdot z_i - cz_i^\phi - F \qquad (6.15)$$

Notice that the original differentiated product model has been converted into what amounts to a homogeneous good model in z_i, though distinguished from, say, a standard Cournot oligopoly model by its unusual cost conditions; average cost is 'U' shaped.

Finally, we define $\eta = dlnZ/dlnz_i$ as the conjectural elasticity between i's output and total output, assumed constant across firms. Where $\eta = 0$, each firm expects that it can expand its output without causing price to fall – this is the competitive pricing case where other firms reduce output. A very similar situation obtains if each firm has Cournot beliefs and the number of firms is very large, since here $\eta = 1/n$. By contrast, under collusion, $\eta = 1$. Most of our attention will be devoted to the first special case.

Firm i is assumed to maximise profits by setting $\partial \pi_i/\partial z_i = 0$, given that z_i and q_i are monotonically related (and that the second-order condition holds). Differentiating (6.15) and re-arranging slightly yields, in the general case:

$$(\theta/\phi)[1 - \eta(1 - \theta)]Z^{\theta-1} = c\phi z_i^{\phi-1} \tag{6.16}$$

Since all firms are identical, we may expect a symmetric equilibrium, so $Z = nz_i$. In addition, with the Chamberlinian assumption of free entry, we can assume that price will fall to the level of average cost, thereby determining the numbers of products at equilibrium.[13] Thus, if $\eta = 0$, comparing (6.14) and (6.16) reveals that

$$\hat{p}(Z) = AC(z) = MC(z) \tag{6.17}$$

Therefore under these assumptions (and others slightly more general, see Yarrow, 1985) each firm produces the output Z_m, say, which equates price and marginal cost.

Output Z_m is optimal in the sense that it would also be the output which a social planner maximising welfare subject to a breakeven constraint would require from each firm. Thus, contrary to widespread belief, this Chamberlinian equilibrium does not involve excess capacity. However, it does not reproduce the first-best optimum. To see this, write social welfare from (6.13) and (6.3) as:

$$W = q_0 + Z^{\theta} - n[F + cz_i^{\phi}]$$

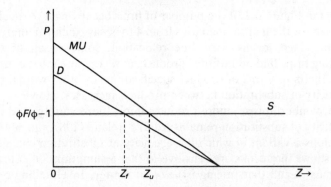

FIGURE 6.4 Firm and industry output in the Chamberlinian model

This can be thought of as a function of n and z, given symmetry. Obtaining the first-order conditions $\partial W/\partial n$ and $\partial W/\partial z$, then rearranging yields:

$$\phi \hat{p}(Z) = AC(z) = MC(z) \tag{6.18}$$

which may be compared with equation (6.17).

The comparison is investigated in Figure 6.4. Condition (6.17) implies that each firm is producing at the minimum point of its $AC(z)$ curve. Given free entry, the supply curve is horizontal at the level $\phi F/(\phi - 1)$. Setting supply equal to demand $\hat{p}(Z)$ yields a total output of Z_f. In maximising social welfare, each firm again has to produce at the minimum average cost point, but in contrast, marginal utility $\phi \hat{p}(Z)$ is set equal to supply, yielding a total output of Z_u. Therefore, despite each firm producing the optimal amount, the market mechanism leads to an industry output which is suboptimal.

To put this conclusion another way, the market system gives rise in this example to insufficient variety, in the sense that too few firms are in production. This result is in complete opposition to the one obtained earlier from the Salopian model, where there were too many firms. Why is this so? Ireland (1987) suggests it arises because of the fundamentally different way in which additional firms enter in the two models. Referring back to the Hotelling model in Figure 6.2, if the number of firms occupying a particular segment of the market increases from 4 to 5, say, then whether we assume fixed locations or free relocation, some or all of the existing firms find other firms' products now compete more closely with theirs in terms of product specification. In other words, the elasticity of substitution between products increases. However, in the Chamberlin case, more products imply more variety, and the elasticity of substitution remains fixed.[14] Ireland (1987, pp. 144–5) develops a variant in which the elasticity of substitution changes, and shows the results are sensitive to that assumption. Of course, we must recall that pricing issues also matter. In Hotelling-type models, firms may only increase output at a location by reducing price, whereas we have been assuming that a firm's output increases have no influence on price in the Chamberlinian case. However if $\eta > 0$ in (6.16), each firm produces on the downward-sloping portion of its average cost curve so that more firms enter and variety increases. Here though, there is true excess capacity.

6.3   VERTICAL PRODUCT DIFFERENTIATION MODELS

A general framework

We now turn to vertical product differentiation. In very general terms, we are concerned with products of different qualities, where the demand for higher quality products is greater, *ceteris paribus*. Thus we might write:

$$q = q(p, u), \quad q_u > 0 \tag{6.19}$$

or alternatively, in terms of the inverse demand function:

$$p = p(q, u), \quad p_u > 0 \tag{6.20}$$

where u is some quality index. Since consumers prefer high- to low-quality products, we might think of (6.19) or (6.20) as arising from some consumer utility function. On the cost side, a fairly general formulation would be:

$$C = c(q, u) + F(u) \tag{6.21}$$

which is more general than (6.3) not only in the way variable costs arise but also because of the dependence of fixed costs upon product quality.

The natural questions which arise in this context include issues regarding the number of products, and range of products over quality space, which are produced, also possibilities for supernormal profits, and the question of qualities relative to the socially-optimal quality. By no means all questions can be addressed easily within the general framework implied by (6.19) or (6.20) and (6.21) above,[15] and we shall concentrate very largely upon two particular models which address specific questions. The first, outlined briefly below, is a special case more appropriate to low-price semi-durable goods while the second is better suited to large consumer durable items.

Before going on to the special cases, we provide a general demonstration of the point that quality is an important issue by following Spence (1975) in his examination of a profit-maximising firm (for simplicity, a monopolist) setting output and quality levels. Profit may be written from (6.2) and (6.21) as:

$$\pi = q \cdot p(q, u) - c(q, u) - F(u)$$

Assuming that social welfare may be measured as the sum of profits and consumer surplus (the area above price and under demand), we have:

$$W = CS + \pi = \int_0^q p(v, u) \cdot dv - q \cdot p(q, u) + \pi$$

It is well know that the first-order condition for maximising social welfare with respect to output, $\partial E / \partial q = 0$, implies $p = c_q$. We focus on the optimality condition with respect to quality:

$$\frac{\partial W}{\partial u} = \int_0^q p_u(v, u) \cdot dv - q p_u(q, u) + \frac{\partial \pi(p, u)}{\partial u} = 0 \quad (6.22)$$

Now at the profit-maximising quality choice, $\partial \pi / \partial u = 0$. Hence unless the first two terms sum to zero at this point, the quality embedded in each unit by the profit-maximising firm will be non-optimal. Notice that this is independent of the quantity supplied being suboptimal; even if quantity were pushed out to the socially-optimal level, this would not ensure that the quality in each unit would be ideal.

Condition (6.22) above may be interpreted, dividing through by q, as that consumer's average valuation of quality,

$$(1/q) \int_0^q p_u(v, u) \cdot dv$$

should equal the marginal consumer's valuation, $p_u(q, u)$. In practice, either one may be the larger. Of course, these are valuations based upon the current output level. The relationship between optimal and actual quality is thus in general determined by a combination of the overall relationship between average and marginal valuations, plus the extent to which output is restricted.[16] This general principle is obviously capable of extension to oligopolistic situations.

One special case of some interest arises where quality takes the form of durability. Prototypical examples are the length of time a lightbulb or a razor blade lasts. In these situations, it is natural to assume that the consumer's concern is essentially about the amount of the service. With what Levhari and Peles (1977) call a 'linear service terminology' we have a special case of (6.20):

$$p(q, u) = p(q \cdot u) = u \cdot r(q \cdot u) \tag{6.23}$$

where $r(\cdot)$ is the inverse demand for the service. Then if on the cost side we assume some sort of separability, it turns out that neither of the quality problems noted above for the general case applies here.[17] The firm, be it competitive, oligopolistic or a monopoly, supplies the correct level of quality in each unit it produces.

Natural oligopoly models

In many instances, quality has more complex effects upon consumer demand. For example, everyone would agree that a colour TV was superior to a monochrome set (since if, perversely, one dislikes colour, the colour set can be tuned to produce monochrome), though the relationship cannot be expressed in the simple terms of equation (6.23). Therefore if both were on sale at the same price, everyone would plump for colour, and it is naturally to be expected that the colour sets would be on the market at a higher price irrespective of their relative costs of production.

This relationship is what Bain (1956) called a product differentiation advantage, and he considered it might lead to supernormal profits, or rents (if the cost conditions were right), also to a limited range of products on the market, with entry being deterred despite the profitability of current market offerings. Building upon two papers by Jaskold, Gabszewicz and Thisse (1979, 1980), they together with Shaked and Sutton (Shaked and Sutton, 1982, 1983, 1984, 1987; Jaskold, Gabszewicz and Thisse, 1986a, b, etc.) have pursued a rigorous examination of these points, and their ramifications. Indeed, some surprising new insights have been generated by this recent work as a result of certain novel features in the model-building. Thus we start from first principles to build a specific model which incorporates these features.

All consumers are assumed to have the same tastes, but to differ in the amount of income with which they are endowed. The typical (ith) consumer faces an array of products of specific quality levels $u_k(u_k > u_{k-1})$, selling at prices $p_k(p_k > p_{k-1})$. The consumer either chooses to consume one unit of one of these various qualities, or instead to consume none. An example might be domestic freezers of different capacities. Utility from consuming variety k is supposed to be of the specific form

$$U_{ik} = (y_i - p_k) \cdot u_k \tag{6.24}$$

where either y_i is the consumer i's income level and the utility U_{io} obtained from spending money on none is referenced $u_o y_i$ or, as an alternative interpretation, y_i is the consumer's reservation price for this general type of good.

It is crucial to the special results of this class of models that incomes (or reservation prices) all lie between two values a and b, i.e. $0 < a \leq y_i \leq b$. For simplicity, there is a uniform density function of consumers, s, between these values.

Consumer i will choose product k in preference to $k - 1$ if $U_{ik} > U_{i, k-1}$. Similarly, the choice will be k rather than $k + 1$ if $U_{ik} > U_{i, k+1}$. Thus, since u_k, p_k (for all k) are parametric to the individual consumer, all those for whom:

$$D_{k+1}p_{k+1} + (1 - D_{k+1})p_k > y_i > D_kp_k$$
$$+ (1 - D_k)p_{k-1} \tag{6.25}$$

$$D_k = u_k/u_k - u_{k-1} > 1$$

will consume product k. By similar reasoning, those for whom $y_i < p_ku_k/(u_k - u_0)$ buy the outside good.

In sum, the model illustrates an income-splitting property whereby everyone within a specific income band buys a certain quality, and the higher the income band the higher the quality. For example, those who are well off buy a big freezer, while those less well off buy a small one and those towards the bottom of the income distribution have to make do without. However it may also be true that the nature of the income distribution strictly limits the number of products. For example, if all incomes were doubled but other things remained unchanged, no one might remain a small freezer buyer. Yet product prices are not of course completely exogenous since they are set by the producers. We must turn to this side of the model.

If we label the income at which the typical consumer is indifferent between products $k - 1$ and k as y_k, then we may use the income-splitting property to write demands for each quality, starting with the highest, n, as:

$$q_n = (b - y_n)s \tag{6.26}$$

$$q_{n-1} = (y_n - y_{n-1})s \tag{6.27}$$

and so on.[18] Now, using (6.25), critical income above which product k is bought is defined as:

$$y_k = D_kp_k + (1 - D_k)p_{k-1} \tag{6.28}$$

On substituting (6.28) into (6.26) and (6.27), it is apparent that we have a special case of equation (6.19) above – demand depends upon quality and price, but also quality and price of neighbours' products. Here, as in Hotelling, the typical product has two neighbours.

On the cost side, the most straightforward assumption to make is that c is independent of u. This simplification will be re-examined later. For the present, we assume the following special case of (6.21):

$$C_k = c(q_k) + F(u_k) = c \cdot q_k + F(u_k) \qquad (6.29)$$

Without loss of generality we set marginal cost c to zero. In terms of our example, large freezers cost more to develop than small ones (greater condenser design problems, perhaps), but production costs are constant at the same level for both, which may as well be set at zero.

Finally we assume there is a three-stage game with the sequence: enter the industry, or not; choose product quality (which is a function of the number of entrants); choose price (a function of product quality). The solution concept employed is the sub-game-perfect equilibrium framework. Thus we first examine the non-cooperative price equilibrium, since price has to be optimal given qualities, and so on.

From equations (6.26), (6.28) and (6.29) (with $c = 0$), we obtain firm n's profits, π_n. The first-order optimality condition $\partial \pi_n / \partial p_n$ then yields:

$$b - 2y_n + (1 - D_n)p_{n-1} = 0$$

after rearrangement and solution of (6.28). Since $D_n > 1$, this implies $b > 2y_n$ and thus $b > 2a$ (assuming $y_n > a$). But, suppose $2a > b$, which is clearly a possibility since the income distribution is exogenous. It must be that there is a corner solution in which there is no room for $n - 1$'s product even at a price of zero. We have everyone buying a giant freezer. In a similar manner, Shaked and Sutton (1982) establish that if $4a > b > 2a$, exactly two firms will be in the market.

Pursuing for the present our natural monopoly case, assuming $2a > b$, we must rewrite demand, since we now know there will be only one firm. From (6.26) and (6.28), and the income restriction, it is:

$$q_1 = s \cdot \min\{(b - D_1 p_1), (b - a)\} \qquad (6.30)$$

It is possible either that $y_1 \leq a$, or $y_1 > a$. In the former case, the final-stage problem, $\max_{pi} \pi_1$, yields a corner solution, with marginal revenue remaining above marginal cost (here zero), and price at a/D_1, the highest price at which all $(b - a)$ units of output can be sold.[19] At the quality-setting stage $\max \pi_1$, we find the firm's optimal quality solves $u_1^2 F'(u_1) = s \cdot a(b \overset{pi}{-} a)u_0$. *Alternatively*, if $y_1 > a$, we obtain $p_1 = b/2D_1$ and $u_1^2 F'(u_1) = sb_2 u_0/4$. These equations may be solved explicitly once $F(u_1)$ is specified. For example[20] if $F(u_1) = u_1^2/2$, then we have $u_1^* = \sqrt[3]{sa(b - a)u_0}$, or $u_1^* = \sqrt[3]{s(b/2)^2 u_0}$ (a higher value) respectively.

Either case implies an equilibrium in which one firm is established, producing a specific quality at a price which, in general, involves supernormal profits, but which attracts no entry. The market is blockaded to entry, in Bain's terms. Notice in particular that increases in market size give rise to increases in optimal quality (in both cases), but *not* to an increase in the number of firms.

Of course, the present example is extremely simplistic and relies on a very narrow income distribution. In fact, both Shaked and Sutton (1982) and Ireland (1987) concentrate their attention on the case where $4a > b > 2a$, which yields a natural duopoly. Here again, some care has to be taken in proceeding from equations (6.26)–(6.28) because of the constraint on total sales. However it is possible to show that a duopoly equilibrium pertains, regardless of market size, in which the firms make distinct products and the higher-quality producer earns more revenue (gross of development costs). Again, larger market sizes lead to higher quality products, but this time price competition between the producers keeps low-quality products from entering the market.

Some extensions and comparisons

One important limitation of these simple natural oligopoly examples is that the whole of the burden of quality improvement falls upon fixed costs. Indeed, this is undoubtedly the reason why market size influences quality, since an increase in size raises the slope of the revenue function in quality space, implying a later intersection of marginal revenue with the marginal cost of increasing quality. To the extent to which this is an accurate reflection of reality, it provides a novel argument for opening up markets to freer international trade: though the broader market remains concentrated, trade spurs on the development of high-quality products, thereby benefiting all consumers (Shaked and Sutton, 1984).

This restrictive cost condition (6.29) also provides a considerable contrast with the earlier models of section 6.3 (p. 124), in which variable costs increased directly with product quality, and in which there were no natural limits to the number of firms. Thus it might be thought necessary to the natural oligopoly results, for variable costs to be uninfluenced by product quality. In fact this is not so, though the result must be carefully qualified.

The persistence of the natural oligopoly result is crucially dependent upon *how much* extra quality costs (among other things). We may think of the above specification as being that if each product sold for its marginal costs (zero) all consumers would have an unambiguous ranking from highest- to lowest-quality product. By extension, if when each product is priced at its marginal production costs (which might differ), consumers have an unambiguous ranking, then the result will go through. (Alternatively, if we could not make such an assumption then, at some price above unit variable cost, *all* product qualities would have some consumers who favoured their product, and hence all firms would achieve some sales. With a large enough market, this would enable all firms to cover fixed costs.)

Jaskold Gabszewicz and Thisse (1986, pp. 32–4) suggest that the assumed properties of these vertical product differentiation models have the effect of producing greater stability in them than in horizontal product differentiation models. In vertical differentiation models, one firm's product is seen by all consumers as strictly preferred to all others, thereby giving that firm a first-mover locational advantage over the others. This aids stability in pricing behaviour. In the horizontal product differentiation models, particularly those with free price *and* location, stability problems are often experienced precisely because *every* firm has available strategies which would attract the whole market to its product.

The type of technology which may be predicted to favour natural oligopoly is one where the quality component is built in at the development stage, and so is largely fixed with respect to output, rather than taking the form of costly additions to a basic model. Indeed, if this characteristic is sufficiently strong, then the finiteness property can be maintained in the face of some horizontal product differentiation. The customer for a word processing package who would rather like some particular special feature may be willing to forego this in favour of a very significant increase in overall quality. Thus, one vertical advance may wipe out otherwise profitable opportunities for horizontal variety. It stands a chance of being able to do so if the burden on *fixed* costs of (perceived or actual) quality improvements is not too heavy, and is bounded from above (Sutton, 1986), so that quality improvements are not too costly to introduce. If consumer responsiveness to such a quality improvement is sufficient, then a firm adopting it can carve out a significant market share, whatever the market size.

6.4　CONCLUDING REMARKS

The literature on product differentiation, after remaining fairly static for some considerable period, moved on considerably in the 1970s and 1980s. Early ideas, such as those of excessive sameness and excess capacity, have been shown to be erroneous, or at least limited.[21] Confusions between horizontal and vertical differentiation, apparent in some early industrial organisation studies (e.g. Comanor and Wilson, 1967) have been ironed out. Certain broad conclusions have been reached, but few general predictions are available.

Among the broad conclusions, it is now clear that variety is valued and needs to be modelled. Moreover, once this is done, some previously inexplicable phenomena become much clearer.[22] Several possible sources of divergence between private and social-benefit maximisation are revealed – not only price but also firm numbers, product qualities and so on may be at socially undesirable values. Supernormal profits need be neither a spur to entry nor a sign of social inefficiency, yet normal profits do not necessarily indicate efficiency. Antitrust policy discussions seem to have taken very few of these issues on board.

At the same time, these new analyses have a more cautionary element. Since product differentiation models can give rise to such a range of predictions, and rather subtle modelling nuances even the form of the demand curve (recall also section 6.2, p. 119) can influence the outcome; it could be said that 'with product differentiation, anything can happen'. This suggests that particular modelling frameworks have to be selected with great care for the particular cases in hand. Many of the models are, after all, developed as building blocks for use in considering the roles of advertising, R&D and so on, that is problems of more practical application. It also endorses the approach of authors such as Sutton (1991), who have shifted away from the proliferation of theoretical nuances towards a search for empirical regularities.

7 Entry and Market Share Mobility*

P. A. GEROSKI

7.1 INTRODUCTION

Competition is an integral part of the way in which markets function. It provides much of the impetus for market growth and development, largely by encouraging the birth and expansion of new innovative firms and the contraction or exit of less dynamic firms. Competition between firms for a place in the market often reflects a competition between different products and processes, and a high rate of turnover amongst firms can reflect bursts of innovative activity and a flowering of new product varieties. Competition can also serve as a source of discipline in markets, encouraging firms to conduct their operations efficiently, and to keep their prices down near to the level of marginal costs. In short, the degree of competitiveness in a market affects how that market responds to change, how progressive it is, and how well it serves consumers' interests.

There are a wide range of factors which help to determine the degree of competition in markets. Permanent (or fixed) features of a market which are exogenous to the short-run price and non-price decisions made by firms are often referred to as elements of 'market structure'. Many economists believe that market structure is a major determinant of market performance, that the vigour of price and non-price competition depends on the fundamentals of cost and demand, the number and type of firms which populate the market, the nature of buyers and the competitiveness of input supply markets. Perhaps the most commonly discussed element of market structure is the number and size distribution of incumbent firms, frequently summarised in the form of a concentration index (like the 5-firm concentration ratio, or the Herfindahl index of concentration). More subtle and, in the view of some economists, far more important, are barriers to entry. Barriers play a central role in determining the number and size distribution of firms and, more important, in affecting the ability of incumbent firms to raise prices above marginal costs. Markets in which there are low barriers to entry will always be surrounded by plenty of potential entrants ready to displace inefficient or technologically stagnant incumbent firms by undercutting prices which have been elevated too far above minimum costs. Markets in which barriers are high, on the other hand, will never be populated by more than a few firms and, lacking a competitive threat from outsiders, they may not perform as efficiently or progressively as they ought.

Our goal in this chapter is to examine the role played by entry and barriers to entry in competitive market processes. We shall proceed in three stages. First, in section 2, we take a close look at the definition of entry barriers, and identify three main sources of such obstacles. In section 3, we examine the relation between entry and market performance, focusing on the effects of actual and potential entry on prices, profits, productivity and innovation. While entry is an important part of the competitive process, it is, however, important not to think of entry as the sole source of dynamics in markets. Thus, in section 4 we shall broaden the discussion somewhat by looking at market share mobility and survival rates throughout the entire size distribution of firms in an industry.

7.2 BARRIERS TO ENTRY

Perfect competition or, more recently, 'perfect contestability' (Baumol *et al.*, 1982) is a benchmark commonly used to evaluate the performance of markets. Roughly speaking, a market is contestable if entry (including subsequent exit) is quick and costless. In such a circumstance, any attempt by incumbents to raise price above costs will be thwarted by 'hit and run' entry and, knowing this, incumbents will desist from raising prices. For entry and exit to be quick and costless, it must be the case that there are no penalties (such as costs of adjustment) to overrapid expansion, there must be no fundamental asymmetries between entrant and incumbent in costs or demand, and entry must not entail the sinking of large, fixed expenditures in highly illiquid assets that would impede exit. In short, there must be no barriers to entry or exit.

Identifying barriers to entry

Barriers to entry are any structural, durable feature of a market or its infrastructure that inhibits the ability of outsiders to enter and compete with established insiders. They are: 'the advantages of established sellers in an industry over potential entrants, these advantages being reflected in the extent to which established sellers can persistently raise their prices above a competitive level without attracting new firms to enter the industry' (Bain, 1956, p. 3; for other definitions of barriers, see Stigler, 1968; von Weisäcker, 1980). The consequence of high barriers is, of course, that incumbents will be able to earn persistently high profits even in the long run, and the size of these profits reflects the height of the barriers which help to sustain them.

Since barriers exist when entrants are attracted to a market (because the pre-entry profits of incumbents are high) but cannot successfully enter (because their expected post-entry profits are negative or lower than could be earned in other activities), they involve a comparison between two equilibria. The problem is that one of these will never be observed (when entry is blocked, the post-entry equilibrium will not be observed). As a consequence, computing the height of barriers to entry is an inherently conjectural exercise. A second complicating feature of any attempt to measure barriers is that they are likely to be 'entrant-specific' to some extent. Some entrants are more capable than others, and some will pursue innovative strategies while others content themselves with imitating the actions of incumbents. Careful attempts to measure the height of entry barriers usually try to compare the most advantaged entrant possible with incumbents (measuring the *immediate condition of entry*; see Bain, 1956, pp. 9–11), and then ask how fast the competitive challenge of entry weakens as one considers less and less able entrants (measuring the *general condition of entry*). Since it is often difficult to anticipate the kinds of innovations that might provide a suitable vehicle for successful entry, most attempts to assess the height of barriers to entry will probably have a systematic bias towards overstatement.

The existence of barriers is reflected in differences between the profit functions of entrants and incumbents. Let us suppose that, pre-entry, the incumbent would choose an output level x^0 and earn profits whose present discounted value is $\pi_1(x^0)$, while post-entry the entrant's best output would be x^* and that it would earn a stream of profits whose expected present discounted value is $\pi_2(x^*)$. A barrier to entry exists if

$$\pi_1(x^0) > 0, \text{ but } \pi_2(x^*) < 0 \tag{7.1}$$

that is, if the entrant wishes to enter but cannot do so profitably. The difference between $\pi_1(x^0)$ and $\pi_2(x^*)$ can be thought of as having two components,

$$\pi_1(x^0) - \pi_2(x^*) = [\pi_1(x^0) - \pi_2(x^0)]$$
$$- [\pi_2(x^0) - \pi_2(x^*)] \tag{7.2}$$

The first element on the right-hand side of (7.2) is a comparison between the profit functions of the entrant and the incumbent evaluated at the same equilibrium levels of output (this is the criterion used by Stigler to identify barriers to entry). It isolates any differences in profits between entrant and incumbent that are independent of the scale of production. The second component of (7.2) is a comparison of the entrant's profit function at two different levels of output, and it measures any disadvantage which the entrant suffers (post-entry) relative to the incumbent (pre-entry) that arises because the entrant operates at a smaller scale of production post-entry than the incumbent did pre-entry.

Since profits are revenues, $R(x)$, less costs, $C(x)$, the first component of (7.2), the difference between π_1 and π_2 evaluated at the pre-entry equilibria, x^0, is a difference that occurs if either

$$R_1(x^0) > R_2(x^0), \text{ or } C_1(x^0) < C_2(x^0) \tag{7.3}$$

These are differences that arise from *product differentiation* or *absolute cost advantages* respectively, and they effectively mean that the incumbent's demand curve lies above that facing the entrant at all levels of output, or that the incumbent's cost curve lies everywhere below that of the entrant. However, the fact that firms must share the market post-entry means that output per firm (for both incumbent and entrant) post-entry is likely to be less than that produced by the incumbent pre-entry; i.e. that $x^0 > x^*$. This is the source of the second type of difference between $\pi_1(x^0)$ and $\pi_2(x^*)$ identified in (7.2), a difference that occurs if

$$R(x)/x \text{ rises in } x, \text{ or } C(x)/x \text{ falls in } x \tag{7.4}$$

This second source of difference between entrant and incumbent springs from *scale-related advantages* that arise in generating revenues or incurring costs of production.

Equations (7.3) and (7.4) make it plain that some entry barriers are not wholly structural in the sense that their effects on entrants are not independent of the output decisions of incumbents. Product differentiation and absolute cost advantages can be measured without knowing the precise details of how incumbents will respond to entry (i.e. without knowing precisely how large x^* is). Scale-related advantages, however, do depend on the nature of post-entry competition. The size of the obstacle that they present to entrants cannot, therefore, be ascertained without further knowledge about market behaviour. Somewhat more generally, the effect that entry barriers have on entrants depends on a range of mediating market conditions. There are numerous factors which might change exogenously, shifting $R_2(x^*)$ and $C_2(x^*)$ in a way which favours or inhibits entry. Most barriers are easier to surmount when markets are growing rapidly, and barriers are often profoundly affected by underlying turbulence in the form of technological advances or changes in tastes. It follows, then, that while barriers to entry are structural and durable features of a market, the effect that they have on entrants may vary over time in a manner determined both by exogenous changes in tastes or technology, and by endogenous changes in the market environment caused by the response of incumbents to entry.

Sources of entry barriers

The preceding analysis identified three main sources of barriers: product differentiation advantages, absolute cost advantages, and scale-related advantages. Let us consider each in turn.

(i) *Product differentiation advantages*

Product differentiation advantages arise from 'buyers' preferences for one of some variety of very similar substitute products . . . and also to the fact that different buyers have different allegiances or preference patterns, so that the preferences in question do not result in some universally agreed upon system of grading or rating of competing products' (Bain, 1956, p. 114). The consequence of such preferences is that entrants will have to charge a lower price to sell the same quantity as incumbents (or, equivalently, will sell less at the same price); i.e. their demand curve will lie everywhere inside that of incumbents. There are lots of reasons why buyers might develop a preference for the products of incumbents, but we shall discuss only three specific examples here to illustrate the general point.

The first example of product differentiation barriers arises from the costs of acquiring information about products. It is often the case that consumers must make a considerable investment in learning about the characteristics of a good in order to use it properly. Such expenditures on information gathering are sunk costs from the point of view of consumers, and learning about one particular brand is likely to weaken a consumer's interest in experimenting with other brands that arrive later on the market (Schmalensee, 1982). This, of course, means that follower brands are likely to sell less than pioneers for the same level of marketing expenditure. Doctors, for example, often digest enormous quantities of technical information before they are willing to prescribe a new drug to their patients. Having made this kind of investment in one drug that works satisfactorily, they are frequently unwilling to do the same for similar drugs that arrive later on the market. As a consequence, 'first movers' often enjoy long-lived advantages over later arriving competitors (see Grabowski and Vernon, 1982; Gorecki, 1986, and others). More generally, Urban *et al.* (1984) examined 129 frequently purchased consumer goods, and discovered that the second arriving brand enjoyed a market share 75 per cent as large as the first mover; to achieve a share as large as the pioneer, the average second mover in their sample would have had to have done nearly 3.5 times as much advertising.

A second example of product differentiation barriers arises either when network externalities exist, or when the consumption of one good needs to be linked to the consumption of a complementary good to provide value for consumers. Network externalities exist whenever the usefulness of a good depends upon how many other people use the good (being the sole person in the world who possesses a telephone is useless). When two different and quite incompatible goods which enjoy network externalities are offered to consumers, the one with the larger network will always be preferred. Hence, an early-moving pioneer who can quickly build up a large customer base will often be proof against entry. In the case of video cassettes, for example, network externalities arise from the fact that a large number of users of a particular type (or standard) of video (VHF, say, or Betamax) living in a given area will support a much larger and more varied library of videos in video rental shops than will the same number of users split between two or more different standards (Grindley and McBryde, 1989). Similarly, it is often necessary to consume collections of goods to get satisfaction (records with record players, gin with tonic, and so on; a car, for example, is really a large collection of complementary goods bought as a single package). Control over the provision of some complementary goods can frequently give a firm considerable advantages in selling its primary good by 'locking in' consumers who have sunk expenditures into particular complementary goods that are not compatible with versions of the primary good offered by rivals (as IBM has demonstrated in the market for mainframe computers – see Brock, 1975, amongst others).

Third and finally, advertising can affect entry through the effect that it has on the choices that consumers make (for discussions of the relationship between advertising and competition, see Schmalensee, 1972; Cowling *et al.*; 1975, Comanor and Wilson, 1974, 1979; Scherer and Ross, 1990, and others). Advertising can be pro-competitive if it enables entrants to make consumers aware of their products, but it can be anti-competitive if it reinforces the market position of incumbents, or if it forces entrants to incur large fixed costs. Rizzo and Zeckhauser (1990), found that less well known physicians advertised more heavily than more established ones (to help establish themselves in the market), but that, nevertheless, the returns to advertising were rather higher for more established physicians (and so that advertising was anti-competitive). Geroski and Murfin (1990) found advertising shares to be highly correlated to market shares in the UK car industry. Entrants able to come into the market and advertise extensively were able to establish a place in the market. However, as more and more entrants appeared in the late 1960s and early 1970s and as incumbents responded to the advertising of entrants by increasing their own advertising, the total volume of industry advertising rose precipitously. This, in turn, made it more and more costly to acquire an advertising share of any given size, and so choked off entry.

Although a wide variety of factors can give rise to product differentiation advantages, they usually create the most problems for imitative entrants who follow 'me-too' strategies. More innovative entrants, by contrast, can often redefine or restructure a market in ways that enable them to secure a place. Entry and expansion by Golden Wonder into the UK crisps market, in the early 1960s, for example, was engineered by the development of new retail outlets. Smiths, the incumbent, had long sold crisps only in pubs, the product being conceived as something men ate while drinking beer. Golden Wonder broadened the appeal of crisps by persuading people that it was a family snack, and then sold it through supermarkets (Bevan, 1974).

(ii) *Absolute cost advantages*

Absolute cost advantages to incumbents arise when their unit cost curves lie everywhere below those of entrants, opening up a gap that enables them to raise prices somewhat above their own costs without attracting entry. 'For a given product, potential entrant firms should be able to secure just as low a minimal average cost of production after entry as established firms had prior to entry. This, in turn, implies (a) that established firms should have no price or other advantages over entrants in purchasing or securing any productive factor (including investible funds); (b) that the entry of an added firm should have no perceptible effect on the going level of any factor price; and (c) that established firms have no preferred access to productive techniques' (Bain, 1956, p. 12).

Much the most common types of absolute cost advantage are created by monopoly control over various scarce inputs (such as natural resources like copper, sulphur, nickel and so on). More generally, control over the infrastructure supporting the production and sales of a particular product can also create advantages for incumbents. Express coach travel in the UK was deregulated in 1980 but, despite numerous attempts by other entrants, National Express, one of the two original public sector companies, has retained its dominant position. This occurred in the main because it controlled coach terminals in many of the larger cities in the UK, and refused access to rivals (Davis, 1984).

Patents are a source of absolute cost advantages because they restrict the access of entrants to up-to-date, state of the art technology. Their effectiveness depends on how difficult imitation is. Mansfield *et al.* (1981) examined a sample of 48 product innovations and discovered that the imitation costs (and the time required to imitate) were roughly two-thirds the costs of the original innovation, and that 60 per cent of patented innovations were imitated within four years (patents in drugs were, however, particularly effective at deterring imitators). More generally, legal restrictions on entry (e.g. licensing taxi cabs) and a whole range of government policies can also create absolute cost advantages (a taxi driver without a licence has, effectively, an infinitely high cost of production). Tariff and non-tariff barriers to trade are a prominent example of such barriers, as are the subsidies doled out to 'national champions' suffering from a surfeit of foreign competition (e.g. see OECD, 1985, and for a survey of barriers which fragment the internal EEC market, see EEC, 1988). Procurement policies by national governments are also often used to support certain firms against their rivals.

Factors like patents which delay the arrival of entrants often give incumbents time to build up other types of cost advantage, usually by learning and accumulating experience in production or sales. For example, Lieberman (1984) uncovered strong learning effects in the chemicals processing industry, with costs of production falling appreciably with increases in cumulative output or investment. Learning, however, brings advantages only to firms who can prevent rivals from benefiting from their experience, and

Lieberman found (in subsequent work) that cost advantages based on cumulative production did not block entry (although it did reduce the survival prospects of entrants somewhat) because incumbents could not completely restrict access to their technology.

As with product differentiation advantages, it is possible to find a wide range of specific factors that give rise to absolute cost advantages. Innovative entrants facing barriers associated with product differentiation advantages can often wriggle their way into a market by refining it in some way, and much the same principle applies to innovative entrants facing absolute cost barriers. In this second case, however, it is often the creative use of old technology or the development of new methods of production that hold the key to successful entry in the face of barriers created by absolute cost advantages.

(iii) *Scale-related advantages*

Economies of scale create problems for entrants in two ways. First, whenever economies of scale make large plants efficient relative to small ones, the need to raise finance to construct such plants may create problems for entrants. Second, and more subtly, economies of scale squeeze entrants. Should entrants attempt to enter at efficient scale and produce as cost effectively as incumbents, they will inevitably depress market price. On the other hand, should they choose to operate at a small and inefficient scale (and so leave price unaffected), they will suffer a cost penalty. Either way, they are unlikely to be able to enjoy the same margin between price and costs post-entry that incumbents enjoyed pre-entry. If economies of scale are large enough, if incumbents respond aggressively to entry and if the market does not expand much, then prices may fall below an entrant's expected post-entry costs and entry will be blocked.

There have now been a wide range of studies of economies of scale (for a thorough survey, see Scherer and Ross, 1990), and they suggest that the advantages of scale economies in production are in general fairly modest. Probably more substantive are scale effects arising whenever entrants need to sink substantial fixed costs to enter. Many of these are associated with marketing expenditures, and advertising in particular. Brown (1978), for example, calculated that a new entrant into the US cigarette industry would need to devote nearly 50 per cent more of its sales revenue to advertising than an established incumbent in order to compete on a par. Biggadike (1976) studied a small sample of advantaged entrants (subsidiaries of large firms well established in other markets) in a number of US industries, and discovered that they might need as much as eight years to break even, and 10–12 years to earn returns comparable to those enjoyed by incumbents. The primary cause of this was the extremely high levels of marketing and R&D expenditures needed to effect entry (being 41 per cent and 51 per cent of revenue on average in his sample).

Scale effects can often have a big impact on entry in markets where competition is 'localised' due to product differentiation barriers (Eaton and Lipsey, 1978). The localisation of competition restricts the market open to an entrant who chooses to produce a particular product in a particular location in geographic or product characteristics space, and scale effects mean that the entrant must capture a large share of the local market if it is to be viable. However, in markets where consumers' tastes are diverse and change rapidly, entrants can overcome the disadvantages of scale by adopting flexible production techniques, trading off the ability to produce one product very efficiently at one specific (and often very large) output level against the ability to produce a range of products at a range of different (and generally rather smaller) output levels (Carlsson, 1989). Scale economies give rise to cost advantages for firms that choose to produce a standardised good in large volume. If, however, consumers have a taste for product variety or if different consumers have different tastes, then entrants who choose to target one or more specific product niches may sometimes compete effectively against a large, mainline producer.

The strategic exploitation of barriers

As we have seen, entry barriers arise from differences between the cost and demand functions of entrants and incumbents, and from differences in their scale of operations pre- and post-entry. In both cases, the problems faced by entrants can be exacerbated by the strategic actions of incumbents. Of necessity, these take on the character of investment decisions, with costs incurred pre-entry and benefits realised (if entry is blocked) over the future life of the market. Needless to say, strategic entry deterrence is more likely to be undertaken by far-sighted incumbents in markets which seem to be profitable, stable and predictable. Since blocking entry is a public good enjoyed by all members of the industry whether or not they contribute to it, strategic entry deterrence is more likely to be undertaken when the industry is dominated by one or a few giant firms than when it is more competitive in appearance. Finally, investments in strategic entry deterrence will occur when they are relatively costless; that is, when entry is already difficult (because of high barriers) and not much is needed to make it impossible.

In thinking about entry deterrence, it is useful to conceptualise the problem as one in which new entrants will need to produce at least a certain minimum level of output, say x^m, if they are to cover their average costs. For example, suppose that their costs are

$$c(x) = cx + f \tag{7.5}$$

where c is (constant) marginal costs and f is fixed costs. If the price that is expected to prevail post-entry is p, then to just break even, the entrant will need to produce

$$x_m = f/(p - c) \tag{7.6}$$

while to make positive profits, it will need to produce more than x^m. Anything that lowers p, raises c or raises f is likely to make entry more difficult.

One strategy that an incumbent might follow is to try to lower p, the price that the entrant expects to prevail post-entry. What is needed is some credible pre-entry signal which will persuade the entrant that the incumbent plans to produce a large output post-entry, thus insuring that its own arrival and attempt to produce x^m will depress prices below average costs, $c(x^m)/x^m$. Some economists believe that a low pre-entry price (a so-called 'limit price') will do the trick (Modgliani, 1958 and, for a more recent version of this argument, Milgrom and Roberts, 1982), but most now accept that something much more substantial and irreversible is needed (see the discussion in Geroski *et al.*, 1990; Gilbert, 1989; Tirole, 1988, and others). Irreversibility matters because threats made pre-entry (such as the threat that post-entry prices will be driven below entrant's unit costs) which can be undone post-entry lack the credibility needed to deter entrants. In fact, what the incumbent would like to do is to produce at monopoly levels pre-entry while threatening to produce more post-entry should the entrant begin its assault on the market. One obvious way to implement this strategy is to instal sufficient capacity pre-entry to wipe the entrant out post-entry, but then to leave it idle (or under utilised) until entry actually occurs (Spence, 1977; Dixit, 1980, and others). A strategic stockpiling of inventories can have very much the same kinds of effects (Ware, 1985).

Problems can also arise if incumbents can limit the demand facing an entrant by restricting its potential market (effectively shifting in the demand curve facing the entrant, reducing the quantity that it can sell at any given price). The smaller the potential market open to it, the less likely it will be that the entrant can sell x^m. Many markets are naturally segmented, either because consumers live in different geographical areas and must incur substantial transportation costs to visit other areas, or because consumers have well defined and strongly held differences in tastes for different product attributes. Either way, an entrant will want to locate in an area that is large enough to enable it to earn positive post-entry profits, and the obvious strategy for incumbents to follow is to fill the available product and geographical space with their own products, leaving no room for the entrant. The higher are fixed costs, the larger the market that the entrant will need to reach in order to break even and, therefore, the less densely packed the available product and geographical space needs to be to deter entry. This kind of strategy can be pursued pre-entry by excessive product proliferation (for an example, see the discussion of the ready-to-eat breakfast cereal market in Schmalensee, 1978), or post-entry by the use of 'fighting brands' (new products introduced by incumbents that exactly match those introduced by entrants) which distract attention away from entrant's products and so limit their market.

Finally, incumbents can pursue strategies that raise entrant's costs (either marginal costs c or fixed costs f), effectively forcing entrants to sell a larger output x^m in order to break even. Such strategies often raise incumbents' costs as well, but as long as they raise rivals' costs more than they raise incumbents' costs, they will be attractive to incumbents (Salop and Scheffman, 1983). For example, computer reservation systems are now the major method by which travel agents book airline flights. These are owned by a few airlines, and are often offered to travel agents at or below costs. Rival airlines' costs are raised by this tactic because the system can be used to shift bookings toward the proprietor airline, forcing rival airlines to incur substantially increased marketing expenditures in an effort to attract new customers and retain the loyalty of older ones. The problem for rivals arises because travel agents have a tendency to select the first flights for a particular route that appear on the screen, and it is a simple matter for proprietors of these systems to list their own flights first and put rival airlines at a disadvantage (Fisher, 1987).

7.3 ENTRY AND MARKET PERFORMANCE

Economists are fond of using 'natural selection' as a kind of metaphor to describe the workings of competition in markets. Selection between different species occurs in the wild because resources are scarce, and those species that are well adapted to their environment will survive and prosper at the expense of other, less well adapted species (i.e. the relative size of their population will increase). Using this analogy to analyse market processes leads one to think of entry as a source of discipline in markets, as a force which insures that all surviving firms in a market are as well adapted to the market environment as possible (i.e. that they efficiently produce the products that consumers wish to have). Of course, since human beings can anticipate selection pressures, they can begin to adapt to environmental changes before they occur, and they can actively try to change the environment in ways that suit them. In the context of market competition, this means that incumbents may choose to respond to the competitive pressure created by entry before entry actually occurs. Still, the basic principle is the same: entry – actual or potential – is a source of competitive discipline in markets and ought, therefore, to play a major role in driving profits down to competitive levels.

There is, however, more to natural selection than competitive discipline. Environmental changes call for new types of species, new characteristics in the individuals of existing species and new patterns in behaviour. In the wild, the search process is initiated by mutations, random 'errors' that occur during the reproductive process and lead to an individual with one or more new characteristics.

These 'errors' are like innovations, and the process of natural selection is a way of choosing between different innovations as Nature's 'invisible hand' struggles to use the resources available in the new environment as efficiently as possible. Although the process of innovation in markets is far more complicated than genetic mutation, it is, nevertheless, important to see entry as being potentially a creative force in markets. Entry is often the vehicle that is used to bring a new innovation to the market, and the threat of entry often encourages incumbent firms to innovate much more promptly than they otherwise might have.

To analyse the effect of entry on market performance, we shall focus first on those effects that spring from the competitive discipline that entry brings to markets, and then move on to consider entry as a creative and innovative force in markets.

The effects of entry on prices and profit margins

Entry can have one of two effects on pricing behaviour. First, a stream of new entrants may arrive in the market whenever prices exceed competitive levels. The consequence of this is likely to be some sort of price war as entrants attempt to undercut incumbents in order to penetrate into the market, and as incumbents respond in an effort to defend their market positions. Second, entry can effect prices even if it does not actually occur if the anticipation of potential entry by incumbents leads them to cut prices in advance of entry (in order to deter entrants). This outcome is particularly likely to occur when fixed costs are not sunk (so that exit is costless), and when product differentiation and absolute cost advantages do not exist (so that entry is easy). Markets in which the threat of potential entry is so severe that incumbents make no supernormal profits are often referred to as 'perfectly contestable' (Baumol *et al.*, 1982).

While no one disputes that entry is, in principle, likely to lead to a bidding down of prices and a narrowing of profit margins, the interesting questions are how fast and how completely the process works. Answering these questions is a good deal more difficult than it looks at first sight, mainly because potential entry is difficult to observe. If potential entry is a perfect substitute for actual entry from the point of view of imposing competitive discipline on incumbents (as would be the case if markets were 'perfectly contestable'), then any assessment of the effects of entry that is based only on observed entry flows will be hopelessly biased. More fundamentally, it is important to explore whether potential entry is, in fact, a perfect substitute for actual entry, and to do this one needs to develop a strategy for dealing with this unobservable.

To fix ideas, it is worth developing a simple model of entry and market dynamics. Let $\pi(t)$ denote profits at time t, which we assume depend on market structure, $S(t)$, and potential entry, $P(t)$, and other things (which for convenience we suppress),

$$\pi(t) = \beta_0 S(t) + \beta_1 P(t) \tag{7.7}$$

Thinking of market structure as the level of industry concentration, one then expects that $\beta_0 > 0$ (high concentration creates market power, enabling incumbents to raise prices above marginal costs) but that $\beta_1 < 0$ (potential entry acts as a source of competitive discipline). Changes in market structure, $\Delta S(t)$ are caused by actual entry flows, $E(t)$, and other things (which for simplicity we neglect),

$$\Delta S(t) = \rho E(t) \tag{7.8}$$

where $\Delta S(t) \equiv S(t) - S(t - 1)$, and $\rho < 0$ because actual entry diminishes the control that leading firms have on the market. Both actual and potential entry depend on expected post-entry profits and, for simplicity, we suppose that entrants assume that pre-entry profits, $\pi(t - 1)$, will prevail post-entry. Hence,

$$P(t) = \gamma_0\{\pi(t - 1) - \pi^*\} \tag{7.9}$$

and

$$E(t) = \gamma_1\{\pi(t - 1) - \pi^*\} \tag{7.10}$$

where γ_0 and $\gamma_1 > 0$ (this is a model of entry first used by Orr, 1974; for more sophisticated models, see Masson and Shaanan, 1982; Kessides, 1986; Breshnahan and Reiss, 1988, and others). π^* is often called the level of 'limit profits'; i.e. that level of profits which is sustainable forever in the face of entry (if $\pi(t - 1) = \pi^*$, then $P(t) = E(t) = \Delta S(t) = 0$ and, as a consequence, $\pi(t) =$

$\pi(t + 1) = \ldots = \pi^*$). π^* is, of course, a natural measure of the height of entry barriers, since it reflects the ability of incumbents persistently to raise prices above costs without attracting entry.

The system in (7.7)–(7.10) describes a simple error correction or feedback system. Whenever profits rise above π^*, then both potential and actual entry occur in proportions determined by the relative sizes of γ_0 and γ_1. Potential entry has a direct effect in reducing profits (measured by β_1), while actual entry affects market structure (via ρ) which, in turn, affects profits (via β_0). The process continues until profits reach the level of π^*, at which point equilibrium is re-established.

The major problem with estimating the system in (7.7)–(7.10) is that $P(t)$ is unobservable (we assume that π^* can be written as a linear function of observables which proxy various types of entry barriers), and three solutions suggest themselves: first, one might find some observable to proxy $P(t)$; second, one might estimate a 'full reduced-form model'; and third, one might estimate a 'partial reduced form'. The second and third options arise because one can observe the causes and consequences of $P(t)$, and then use this information to substitute out for the unobserved $P(t)$. The partial reduced form uses equation (7.9) to substitute out for the term $P(t)$ in (7.7), yielding

$$\pi(t) = \beta_0 S(t) + \alpha_0 \pi(t - 1) + \alpha_1 \pi^* \tag{7.11}$$

where $\alpha_0 = \beta_1 \gamma_0$ and $\alpha_1 = -\alpha_0$. The full reduced form uses both (7.9) and (7.10) to substitute out for both $P(t)$ and, indirectly via (7.8), for $E(t)$ in (7.7), yielding

$$\pi(t) = \alpha_2 \pi(t - 1) + \alpha_3 \pi^* \tag{7.12}$$

where $\alpha_2 = (\beta_1 \gamma_0 + \beta_0 \rho \gamma_1)$, $\alpha_3 = -\alpha_2$ and where we have neglected terms in $\pi(t - 2)$, $\pi(t - 3)$ and so on whose coefficients are likely to be of second order in magnitude. Equations (7.11), (7.8) and (7.10) are an estimable three-equation system in $\pi(t)$, $S(t)$ and $E(t)$ (which, in fact, can be reduced to a two-equation system in $\pi(t)$ and $E(t)$), while (7.12) can be estimated on its own, using only information on $\pi(t)$. The three-equation system enables one to get an estimate of all the individual structural parameters of the system (7.7)–(7.10) except for β_1 and γ_0. However, it is possible to get an estimate of the product of these last two parameters and use them to assess the relative size of the joint effects of actual and potential entry on profits (which are $\beta_0 \rho \gamma_1$ and $\beta_1 \gamma_0$ respectively). The single-equation system (12) scrambles all the parameters of (7.7)–(7.10) together, and one gets an overall estimate only of the effect of total entry – actual plus potential – on margins (i.e. an estimate of $\beta_1 \gamma_0 + \beta_0 \rho \gamma_1$, and not of its two components).

There have been a number of estimates of (7.12) reported in the literature (see Mueller, 1986, 1990), and they generally suggest that profits converge to π^* fairly quickly, but that long-run profits are not equalised across firms, much less driven to zero. Firms with large market shares, and firms in industries where particularly heavy advertising occurs, often show noticeably higher long-run profits than others. Rather few estimates of the fuller system (7.8), (7.11) and (7.10) have been reported, but Geroski (1989a) found that profits converged fairly rapidly towards π^* for a sample of UK industries in the late 1970s, but that, on average $\pi^* = 15$–20 per cent. Actual and potential entry each seemed to have a (fairly) weak effect on the dynamics of margins, and the effects attributable to each seemed to be roughly of the same order of magnitude. Industries that were highly concentrated and in which advertising was particularly heavy showed both slower adjustment to and higher levels of long-run profits.

On the face of it, these results indicate that entry has rather weak effects on profits. In effect, they suggest that entry barriers are generally rather high and that most entrants are simply not innovative enough to make a major impact on the sectors that they choose to operate in. However it is important to recognise at least three caveats which may be lodged against this conclusion. First, virtually all of the studies of this type use accounting measures of profitability, and these have a number of drawbacks. This problem may not, however, be too severe. Although accounting and economic rates of return can diverge spectacularly, persistently high accounting rates of return imply persistently high economic rates of return, and this is what we observe in the data. Second, the effects of entry may be particularly slow to come, but very powerful when they finally arrive. Most of the studies that we have examined effectively search for rather short-run effects (say, one or two years) of entry on profits, and it may be that this kind of methodology exaggerates the height of barriers to entry. Third and finally, entry may have a big impact on prices but very little impact on margins if it causes incumbents to reduce costs in line with prices. There is some evidence to suggest that one of the principal responses of incumbents to major waves of entry is savage cost cutting to maintain margins, and this almost certainly means that entry has a bigger effect on prices than it has on margins.

The effects of entry on productivity and innovation

Although firms that enjoy positions of market power can raise prices above competitive levels and above their actual costs to generate supernormal profits, some may opt for the quiet life and tolerate a degree of inefficiency. It follows that their first reaction to competitive shocks may be to reduce slack. This type of effect has been particularly evident in a number of the newly deregulated industries (Bailey, 1976). In the US airline industry, for example, the carriers who have faced increases in competition have put pressures on labour suppliers, freight transporters, telecommunications suppliers and so on to renegotiate supply contracts, and unit cost savings have been substantial. The same sort of effect is also often observed when collusive agreements break down (Erickson, 1976). The elimination of price conspiracies in the US gymnasium seating industry, for example, led to a 23 per cent reduction in costs, and substantial cuts in the salaries of senior management. Somewhat more broadly, there is also some evidence to suggest that entry has an effect on the productivity performance of a sector. Geroski (1989b) studied a sample of 79 UK industries over the period 1976–9, and found that entry accounted for roughly 30 per cent of the total factor productivity growth over the period. Much the same effects are regularly observed in industries faced with substantial competition from imports.

It is also widely believed that entry is likely to stimulate either the generation or diffusion of innovations in markets. Although large and powerful incumbent firms may have the means to conduct large-scale R&D projects, they often lack the incentive to introduce new products that displace the stream of profits currently earned on their existing operations (Arrow, 1962). Rapid entry into the UK dry cleaning industry in the late 1950s, for example, was based on the adoption of new technology by entrants that incumbents had known about since the 1930s. Since the new technology facilitated the introduction of on-the-premises dry cleaning operations which totally displaced the elaborate factory cleaning systems run by incumbents (and would, therefore, have mandated a total change in the internal operating structures of these firms), they held back from adopting the new innovations as long as possible (Shaw, 1973).

Somewhat more speculatively, there is evidence to suggest that entry plays a major role in stimulating innovation early in the life cycle of new products. Gort and Klepper (1982) have observed that new products typically evolve through a number of stages defined in terms of net entry (i.e. entry minus exit). Following the initial introduction of a generically new product, net entry is positive as the number of new firms operating in the market rises, often at a phenomenal rate. Sooner or later, however, the rate of increase of new firms levels out, and is soon followed by a period of consolidation in which the less efficient producers are weeded out. Net entry is negative at this point, with the number of producers often falling by some 40–50 per cent before a new equilibrium is established at which net entry is again zero. Defining industry life cycles in terms of these variations in net entry, Gort and Klepper discovered that the number of major innovations introduced into the market peaked during the expansion phase, while the number of minor innovations peaked just before the contraction phase began. What is more, during the early phases of market evolution, most innovations were introduced by outsiders (that is, entry was used as a vehicle for introducing new innovations). However, as the market continued to develop and mature, the relative contribution of outsiders to total innovation activity fell.

It is not too difficult to account for this pattern of activity. When new products are first introduced, the market that they serve is often rather poorly defined. Consumers have only rather vague ideas about the potential uses of the new product, and most producers have yet to explore the full range of product characteristics that it is possible to produce. This uncertainty in the market makes it very difficult for any substantive barriers to entry to build up, and innovative entry is often rather easy. Competition at this stage of industry evolution is a selection process fuelled by the wide variety of slightly different products that are brought to, and tested in, the market. At some point, however, the product begins to standardise, the range of product variants shrinks considerably, and the basis of competition shifts from determining what the product is to determining how efficiently it can be produced. Exploiting economies of scale, learning and other cost advantages become important elements of competitive strategy, and industry rationalisation begins to occur. Entry falls as entry barriers rise, and both entry and innovation rates diminish. Particularly interesting examples of this evolutionary process can be observed, *inter alia*, in the US semiconductor industry and in computer aided designs (see Tilton, 1971 and Kaplinsky, 1983, respectively).

At the risk of oversimplifying, one might sum up the discussion in this section up by distinguishing 'imitative' from 'innovative' entry. Imitative entrants are those new firms who more or less exactly replicate the activities of incumbents, generally competing on the basis of lower prices or some rather minor modification in the ancillary services they provide with the product that they sell. Such firms can provide a competitive discipline on incumbents whenever barriers to entry are not too high, and their activities can play an important role in the competitive process in markets where products are well defined, consumer tastes are stable and technology is both well understood and mature. Imitative entrants are likely to have an effect on prices both directly (because they undercut incumbents and generally force the latter to respond) and indirectly (because the stimulate incumbents to operate more efficiently, and this may, in turn, exert a downward pressure on prices), but they will not have more profound effects on the structure or evolution of the market. Innovative entrants, on the other hand, compete on the basis of product characteristics, playing the role that mutations play in natural selection processes by throwing up new and different variants of the generic product. Such entrants are likely to thrive when markets are young and product characteristics matter far more than product price and, because they introduce variety and change into the competitive area, they can have a substantive effect on the direction and speed of market development.

7.4 MARKET SHARE MOBILITY

The competitive process is one of turbulence and change in which some firms grow, and others stagnate or contract. Entry feeds this process by introducing new firms into the market, and it is, in turn, fed by the process as the contraction and failure of old firms makes room for new ones. The turbulence and change that we observe in markets is, of course, no more than the visible manifestation of a selection process which weeds out those firms whose products are poorly conceived or inefficiently produced, and rewards those whose products are well designed and whose operations are well run. Although it is difficult to say anything general about the processs of selection as it occurs in most markets on the basis of our existing knowledge, it is possible to piece together some parts of the story from various fragments of data.

It is natural to start with entry. The first and perhaps most surprising observation to be made about flows of entry is that most markets are flooded with entry. In the UK over the period 1973–9, an average of 50 new firms entered each of 87 three-digit manufacturing industries per year (with a maximum of 877 reached in one industry in 1977). Expressed as a percentage of the stock of existing firms, entry rates often run in the 5–10 per cent range per annum, particularly during cyclical upswings (see Geroski, 1990, 1991 for some international comparisons). Over the five-year period 1978–82, entry rates into US industry averaged some 40 per cent (Dunne *et al.*, 1988). However, although the number of entrants into most markets is large, most of these firms are rather small. On average, they are 25–30 per cent of the size of the average incumbent (itself a rather small firm) and, as a consequence, the market penetration of new entrants is rather modest. In the UK during the 1970s, for example, the collective market share (in three-digit industries) of all entrants averaged 2.9 per cent.

The notion that entry and exit are part of a broader process of selection that occurs in markets suggests that one will observe both entry and exit occurring simultaneously, and this is what we do observe. Entry and exit are generally positively correlated across industries in any given year, and over time in any given industry. In terms of the number of firms involved, entry and exit rates in the UK were correlated year by year across industries with coefficients on the order of 0.30–0.40; for entry and exit expressed in terms of market shares, the correlations were more like 0.6 (similar numbers were obtained for the USA). The 50 or so new entrants to the typical three-digit UK industry each year were matched by an outflow of about 38, leaving a net addition to the stock of firms of 12, or a net entry rate of just over 1 per cent. In fact, over the period 1972–9, exiting firms accounted for more sales than entrants, so that net entry penetration averaged −0.5 per cent. In the USA, net entry rates at the end of the 1970s averaged 3.1 per cent, and the net market share penetration of all entrants averaged 0.5 per cent.

In fact, the high correlation that we observe between entry and exit arises in no small part because entrants in one year often exit in the following year. A special tabulation made for the UK which tracked four cohorts of entrants (those entering in 1975, 1976, 1977 and 1978) over the first five years of their life showed that at least 30 per cent had failed before their fifth birthday. What is more, it also turned out to be the case that survivors contracted somewhat over the first five years of their life. Together, failure and contraction meant that the total employment accounted for by each cohort of entrants declined by some 40–50 per cent over the first five years of the life of that cohort. Similarly, the market share of each cohort of US entrants was highest in its initial year – the 1967 cohort, for example, saw a collective market share of 13.9 per cent fall to 8.3 per cent in 1972, 6.7 per cent in 1977 and 5.3 per cent in 1982. As with the UK, the main reason for this loss of collective market share was exit.

In short, entry seems to be rather easy in the sense that gross entry rates are fairly high in most markets. However, entry often causes exit (if not immediately, then subsequently), and most entrants are, in any case, rather small. Further, their post-entry growth in the host market is often quite modest, and their expected life is quite limited. Entry in this sense, then, is rather difficult. Put another way, the data suggest that entry barriers are not so much obstacles that prevent the arrival of new firms to a market as they are obstacles that make it difficult for these firms to find a secure foothold in that market.

Life at the other end of the size distribution of firms is quite different. Davies *et ai.*, 1991, identified the leading five firms in each of 54 three-digit industries in the UK, calculating their market shares and tracing their growth over the period 1979–86. Only 54 of the 270 market leaders they examined left the top five by 1986, and only 10 of these disappeared through liquidation. More interesting, the probability of exit declined rather sharply with rank. Only two of the 54 firms ranked first in 1979 were not present somewhere in the top five in 1986 (31 were still ranked first), while four of the second-ranked firms, 10 of the third-ranked firms, 18 of the fourth-ranked firms and 20 of the fifth-ranked firms exited.

Put together, the data on entry and on market leaders suggest that selection pressures are fairly strong at the bottom of the size distribution of firms in most industries. Turnover rates are high, and the post-entry performance of new firms is often rather unimpressive. At the top of the size distribution, however, selection pressures seem to be somewhat weaker and, what is more, even within the leading five, selection pressures appear to fall off markedly as one approaches the top. One might describe this pattern stylistically as one in which an entrant that first comes into a market and then gradually expands over time faces fewer and few substantial hurdles. With each one that it successfully surmounts, it becomes stronger and better prepared to meet the next challenge.

There are several reasons why one might expect this kind of pattern to emerge from the data, but the most interesting of these centres on the notion of 'mobility barriers' (Caves and Porter, 1977). Entry barriers are, as we have seen, obstacles that protect 'insiders' (i.e. incumbents) from 'outsiders' (new firms, potential and actual). However, most markets have a rich internal structure, and some insiders occupy particularly favourable positions that are protected from the incursions of other insiders who occupy less favourable positions within the market. These obstacles to mobility within markets are often called 'mobility barriers', and they have the same basic features and arise from the same kinds of sources as entry barriers do. In the car market, for example, large mass volume producers like GM and Ford compete side by side with more specialist producers such as Rolls Royce. Both types of producer occupy well defined niches, and both would have some difficulty in moving into the niche occupied by the other. In the case of Rolls Royce, entry would be hampered by the sheer scale of investments in production and distribution that would be needed to make it a mass market producer; for Ford and GM, the principal issue is one of acquiring the kind of reputation for quality and prestige associted with Rolls Royce.

Mobility barriers enrich the notion of entry barriers in an important way, for if mobility barriers exist, then it matters where in the market an entrant chooses to compete and which 'entry path' it chooses to follow. Thinking of an industry as a map with a number of protected niches, the question that entrants face is whether it is better to enter some attractive niche A directly, or to do so indirectly by first entering niche B and then moving on to A. Several considerations suggest that indirect paths may often be optimal. The ability of an entrant to compete in niche A may depend on the accumulation of consumer goodwill or production experience, and it may be more efficient and less risky to accumulate these intangibles by first producing in niche B. Further, when entrants must make substantial commitments before entering highly profitable markets, then a sequential sinking of smaller commitments built up by producing first in less attractive niches may be much less risky than heading straight for the most profitable niche.

The notion that an entrant must accumulate something like 'experience' or consumer 'goodwill' if it is to survive (much less to prosper) takes us some way towards understanding the pattern of intra-industry dynamics that seem to emerge from the data. Small firms who first enter and then try to expand in the market will have to cross a number of thresholds (or mobility barriers) to get to the top. Different challengers are likely to take different routes to the top, depending on their skills, expectations, time horizon and so on. If it is indeed the case that crossing these thresholds requires a firm to accumulate more skills and a growing base of consumer goodwill, then it is not unlikely that those who manage to surmount the first thresholds they encounter will find themselves progressively more and more able to cross subsequent thresholds.

Indeed, it is possible that the structure of mobility barriers which protects market leaders emerges from the characteristics of the core product that they supply, and from the relationship between that core product and more customised variants. Entrants often start life as fringe producers located in local market niches, and their expansion must necessarily take the form of expanding into more and more such niches. To do this, they need to produce a product that is suited to a wider and wider range of buyers, and this means moving away from a strategy of customising their product to one of standardising it. The relatively intense selection pressures that we observe at the bottom of the size distribution of firms may be the consequence of having to expand into a succession of local market niches, each surrounded by mobility barriers of one type of another. At first, this expansion process is bound to cause a tension between serving niche *C* and niche *D* that is exacerbated by the need to satisfy the slightly different consumers in each. However, once the trick of serving *C* and *D* successfully has been mastered, moving on to serve *E*, *F*, *G* and so on may prove to be rather easier.

These are, of course, only speculations. At the moment, we know relatively little about intra-industry market dynamics, or about the nature of the selection process that operates within industries. However, what is clear is that entry is only one part of a much broader picture of mobility and change in markets.

8 Strategic R&D and Innovation

JOHN BEATH, YANNIS KATSOULACOS
AND DAVID ULPH

8.1 INTRODUCTION

Innovation is important to an economy for a variety of reasons. First, it is through innovation and the resulting investment in new and better processes that technical progress comes about and such change is essential for economic growth. In the second place, the new products that result from innovation are crucial in improving living standards. Thirdly, in an international context, there is considerable evidence that a country's trade performance depends significantly on its non-price competitiveness and innovation contributes directly to this (Fagerberg, 1988). Because of the central importance of innovation, it is therefore not surprising that the resurgence of interest in industrial organisation has resulted in a considerable improvement in our analytical understanding of the process and of the relationship between the market equilibrium and the social optimum. The technique that has proved to be most useful is game theory and our aim in this chapter is to give a straightforward and coherent account of what has been learned from its application to the analysis of strategic technological competiton.

Firms invest in R&D not only to pursue new product and process innovation directly but also to develop and maintain their broader capabilities to assimilate and exploit externally available information. This dual role for R&D has been pointed out by

Cohen and Levinthal (1989). However, here we shall concentrate on the first of these. Behind this 'innovative' reason for R&D are two motivating forces: profitable investment and strategic advantage. Consider the former first. Allocating resources to innovative research and development will, if successful, increase a firm's profits. There is thus a 'profit incentive' to innovate. One can usefully think of this as the incentive that would face a firm that was taking a decision in isolation. This is why Katz and Shapiro (1987) refer to it as the 'stand-alone' incentive and it was on this that Arrow (1962) focused in his analysis of the value of a patent under different types of market structure. The second incentive that makes firms engage in R&D is to give themselves a strategic advantage. A better process or a better product can enhance a firm's market share. If a firm knows that its rival is engaging in R&D then its own competitive position is under threat and the fear of losing out to its rival will help to explain the amount of resources that it allocates to R&D itself. For this reason, then, we can refer to this strategic component of the overall incentive to do R&D as the 'competitive threat'. In the literature it is also referred to by another name: the 'replacement effect'. The reason is that the size of this incentive is determined by the difference between the payoff if the firm wins and its payoff if it loses; i.e. it is the loss it suffers from failing to maintain its current market position and being 'replaced' by the victorious rival. This incentive is particularly important in models where R&D is deterministic; in these R&D competition takes the form either of a bidding game or else a game of pure timing.

The game-theoretic literature on R&D contains four paradigms. The first of these is the deterministic auction model. Its origins are in Barzel (1968) and Scherer (1967) but its most recent use has been by Gilbert and Newbery (1982), Katz and Shapiro (1987), Vickers (1986) and Beath, Katsoulacos and Ulph (1987, 1992). A second deterministic model, but one with an investment rather than auction story, is the 'non-tournament' model of Dasgupta and Stiglitz (1980) and Flaherty (1980). Most recently this has been used by Spence (1984), Judd (1985b), Beath and Ulph (1990) and Katsoulacos and Ulph (1990b) to examine market performance and by Brander and Spencer (1983) to discuss strategic technology policy. The third paradigm is the 'tournament model' in which R&D success is stochastic and the contest takes the form of a race.

Early single-firm versions of this are Lucas (1971) and Kamien and Schwartz (1971). More general treatments came with the papers by Loury (1979), Lee and Wilde (1980), Dasgupta and Stiglitz (1980a), Reinganum (1982), Grossman and Shapiro (1987), Harris and Vickers (1987) and Beath, Katsoulacos and Ulph (1989a). A fourth paradigm is the probabilistic contest model used by Futia (1980) and Rogerson (1982). Here, if firm i invests x_i, its probability of being the successful innovator is $p_i = \dfrac{x_i}{\Sigma x_i}$. However, since this model has attracted little attention we shall concentrate in this chapter on the first three.

An important reason for starting our discussion with the auction model is that it places the strategic motive in centre stage. This is because there can only be one successful bidder.[1] The maximum bid that a firm would be prepared to make would be the difference between the profits it could expect were it successful in the auction and those it would get were it not. This is what we called above the competitive threat. However, an unsatisfactory feature of the auction model is that losers never end up committing resources to match the bids they make.

In auction models, the innovation is there and there are no problems associated with its expected date of arrival. The same feature is essentially true in the second class of model we look at: the non-tournament model. This is because there is a deterministic relationship between the amount of R&D effort a firm undertakes and the innovative output that results. In this model there are strategic issues but the contest is not of the winner-takes-all form because of the potentially infinite number of discoveries to be made. Firms obtain patents that protect them from costless imitation, but not from equally costly imitation. We look at these models in section 8.3.

Absent in the models of sections 8.2 and 8.3 is the issue of the timing. However a common view would be that a feature of R&D that a model should seek to capture is that increased effort brings forward the date of successful innovation. If a firm should succeed before one of its rivals, it may enjoy important first-mover advantages (Schmalensee, 1982b) and, in the case where patent protection is perfect, would give it a dominant market position. The issue of timing is a central feature in the tournament model of section 8.4. In this model firms compete for a single innovation and engage in R&D for both investment and strategic reasons. In the version we present there is technological uncertainty and a stochastic relationship between R&D effort and innovative success. It allows us to see both the profit incentive and the competitive threat at work, and to separate them out.

8.2 R&D AS A BIDDING GAME: THE AUCTION MODEL

A Single Innovation

Consider the following model: there are two firms producing an identical product under constant returns to scale technologies. Each firm has some innovative history with the result that their unit costs are c_1 and c_2, $c_2 < c_1$. A new technology is discovered which lowers costs to $c_3 < c_2$, and an infinitely-lived and completely effective patent for this technology is put up for auction. The auction is an English one[2] and so the patent is awarded to the firm which values it most highly. This firm has to bid an amount equal to the value placed on it by the other firm, while the losing firm pays nothing. If the winner is the current low-cost firm (leader) we have persistent dominance, while if the winner is the current high-cost firm (follower) we have action–reaction. The question is which of these two outcomes will occur.

Let $\pi(\alpha, \beta)$ be the (present value of) profits in equilibrium of a firm whose unit costs are α while those of its rival are β. In order for the leader to be indifferent between acquiring the patent or not is just to say that

$$\pi(c_3, c_1) - B^l = \pi(c_2, c_3) \tag{8.1}$$

This condition defines the maximum bid, B^l, that the leader would be prepared to make since, if the leader wins the patent its profits will be $\pi(c_3, c_1)$ while, if the follower wins, the leader's profits will be $\pi(c_2, c_3)$. Similarly the maximum bid that the follower is willing to make, B^f, is

$$B^f = \pi(c_3, c_2) - \pi(c_1, c_3). \tag{8.2}$$

Since these maximum bids reflect the fall in its future profits that each firm would suffer if its rival were to innovate and it were not, they reflect one of the two incentives that we said drove firms to innovate: the competitive threat.

Let $\sigma(\alpha, \beta)$ be the industry profits made in equilibrium when the unit costs of one firm are α and those of the other are β. Then we will have persistent dominance iff

$$\sigma(c_3, c_1) > \sigma(c_3, c_2) \tag{8.3}$$

since if (8.3) holds, $B^l > B^f$. The factor that differentiates the two sides of the inequality (8.3) is the unit cost of the high-cost firm in the *post-auction* market and so, to understand when the inequality is satisfied, we need to know how industry profits vary with the cost of this firm.

Suppose we start from a position where the two firms have identical costs and consider the case where competition in the product market is Cournot.[3] If the costs of one of the firms should now rise, this will have a first-order negative effect on its profits and will increase the market share of its rival. However, this will have only a second-order positive effect on the profits of the rival. Hence it follows that industry profits will fall. However, as the cost gap widens and the market share of the high-cost firm falls while that of the low-cost firm rises, the first effect declines in size and the second increases. Thus we should find that as the cost gap opens, industry profits first fall, reach a minimum, and then rise reaching the monopoly level once the cost gap is wide enough.[4] However, note that once the gap is sufficiently wide that industry profits equal monopoly profits, (8.1) and (8.2) show us that both firms have the same maximum bid. We should therefore need some mechanism to resolve ties. Let us suppose that the leader has some 'incumbent advantage' and so theirs is the bid that is accepted. We then have the result that under Cournot competition, a large innovation or a large initial gap results in persistent dominance while a small initial gap and a small innovation results in action–reaction. However, if the market competition were Bertrand, then industry profits would be increasing in gap. This is because the low-cost firm will always set its price so as to undercut its rival. Hence industry profits are just the profits of the low-cost firm[5] and so are increasing in the cost gap between the firms. Thus we get persistent dominance irrespective of the size of the innovation or the initial gap. This suggests the possibility that the more competitive 'static' behaviour (Bertrand as opposed to Cournot) may give rise to the less competitive 'dynamic' outcome – a point that has also been noted by Vickers (1986).

The auction model is of course a tournament model in the sense that there is only one winner. It is obviously highly stylised and suffers from two particular drawbacks that were mentioned briefly in section 8.1. The first of these is that the innovation date is exogenous and does not depend on the level of R&D spending. This amounts to treating the whole process of technological advance as exogenous. The second is that the unsuccessful bidder commits no real resources to R&D. Katz and Shapiro (1987) have a tournament model that overcomes the first limitation and takes account of timing. However, because there is no uncertainty it suffers from the second drawback: the loser commits no resources to R&D. The reason is as follows. The loser can see that any attempt by him to advance the date of innovation can always be profitably preempted by the winner. The perfect equilibrium of this game is one in which the loser does not participate and the winner invests in R&D the resources needed to enable him to bring the innovation on stream at the date that he would have done in the absence of rivalry.

A key feature of deterministic tournament models is that the only force that matters is the competitive threat. As we shall show in section 8.4, when we introduce uncertainty the profit incentive comes into play as well. This also gets us around the second drawback since typically firms will commit resources to R&D. We shall find that all the essential features of the Katz and Shapiro model appear in this more general framework, so we shall not discuss it further at this stage.

Despite these limitations, the model we have been considering so far captures in a very direct way the competitive threats that will be an essential part of any model of strategic innovation, and shows clearly that the amount of R&D done by the successful firm will be strongly affected by the valuation placed on the innovation by the unsuccessful firm. Moreover it provides an insight into the effects of factors such as the size of the innovation, the initial difference between the firms, and the nature of market competition on the outcome of the innovation process.

Sequences of innovations

Single-innovation models – like that covered in the last section – suffer from three deficiencies. First, in thinking about the resources that they should devote to current R&D, there is no way that firms can take account of the possibility that a lead lost today may be regained in the future. If they were able to do so it could make action–reaction more likely simply because this could now be a correctly anticipated future outcome. The second is that, with only one innovation, the lead gained by the winner is fixed, and so firms cannot contemplate the possibility that current success might breed future success. If this were the case, not only would it give the current leader an even greater incentive to win, but it could also strengthen the desire of the follower to prevent the leader opening up too big a gap. Finally, in a sequential framework firms have to contemplate not just the future profits that flow from gaining particular strategic positions, but the costs of maintaining those positions. If winning the current race makes rival firms even more determined to stop the leader winning future races then, from the leader's point of view, winning may be more expensive than losing. However if winning the current race so discourages rivals that they reduce their effort in the future, then winning will mean a lowering of future bid costs for the leader. These deficiencies therefore suggest that the whole question of persistent dominance versus action–reaction is better posed in the context of sequences of innovations rather than in that of a single innovation.

There is now a literature on such models and examples are Vickers (1986) and Beath, Katsoulacos and Ulph (1987, 1992). Vickers considers the case of two firms who initially have unit cost levels $c_2 < c_1$. There is, however, a sequence of T auctions. These take place at the start of period $\tau(= 1, \ldots, T)$, and are for technologies of successively lower unit costs $c_{\tau+2} < c_{\tau+1}$, $\tau = 1, \ldots, T$. Over the sequence of auctions, each firm will build up a portfolio of patents on various technologies. However, at any date, each will only employ the most cost efficient of the technologies that they own and thus the state of the game can be described by specifying just these two cost levels.

General results are harder to come by in the sequential case than when there is a single innovation, but Vickers proves two results. The first result is

● A sufficient condition for action–reaction is that for all auctions $\tau = 1, \ldots, T$ and for all $k = 1, \ldots, \tau$,

$$\sigma(c_{\tau+2}, c_{\tau+1}) > \sigma(c_{\tau+2}, c_k) \tag{8.4}$$

To understand this result, notice first of all that, for $\tau = 1$, (8.4) is just (8.3) with the inequality reversed. This is a sufficient condition for the high-cost firm to win the first auction. Now consider the second auction ($\tau = 2$). Condition (8.4) says that the following two inequalities need to be satisfied:

$$\sigma(c_4, c_3) > \sigma(c_4, c_1)$$
$$\sigma(c_4, c_3) > \sigma(c_4, c_2)$$

This tells us that, for all cost levels that the high-cost firm may have, industry profits decrease, the lower that cost level. Thus the condition can be (somewhat loosely) restated as requiring that industry profits be strictly decreasing in the costs of the high-cost firm throughout the entire range of costs spanned by the all T auctions. It should be clear that this condition will be sufficient to guarantee action–reaction in the final (Tth) auction. Now consider the second-last auction. Each firm knows that because of action–reaction in the final auction, if it wins this auction it will lose the next and vice versa. What will each firm bid? Consider the firm that is currently the low-cost firm. Its bid will be the difference between the profit flow it would get from winning and that it would get from losing. This is

$$B_{T-2}^l = [\pi(c_{T+1}, c_{T+2-k}) + \delta V^H(T)] - [\pi(c_T, c_{T+1}) + \delta V^L(T)]$$

The δV terms are simply the present values of being the high-cost or low-cost firm in the final period. So the first of the square brackets says that if the low-cost firm wins, it will remain the low-cost firm for one period and then lose in the next auction and become the high-cost firm. Similar reasoning establishes that the bid made by the high-cost firm will be

$$B_{T-2}^f = [\pi(c_{T+1}, c_T) + \delta V^H(T)] - [\pi(c_{T+2-k}, c_{T+1}) + \delta V^L(T)]$$

Thus, in the bids B_{T-2}^l and B_{T-2}^f, those components that are attributable to future profits and future bid costs will be the same for l as for f. Thus all that can matter in determining whether or not $B^f_{T-2} > B^l_{T-2}$ are the components attributable to current profits, and then (8.4) again guarantees that the outcome of the second-last auction will be action–reaction. Hence, by induction, action–reaction occurs in every auction.

This is a completely general argument establishing the result that provided conditions sufficient to establish action–reaction in a single auction hold throughout the range of circumstances spanned by T auctions, we will get action–reaction in every auction. However (8.4) is a much more stringent condition than the corresponding one-period one, for it requires the inequality in industry profits to hold however wide a gap opens up between the firms over the course of the sequence, and this will require much slower rates of technical change than would be involved in the single-innovation case.

Although (8.4) is only sufficient for action–reaction, we can see intuitively how failure to satisfy it could generate dominance. For suppose that (8.4) held in the final period if the cost gaps were small, but not if they were large. Then there would be action–reaction in the final auction if firms entered it close together in terms of cost, but not if they were far apart. But then the outcome of the auction in the previous period could affect the kind of auction that will take place in the final period, in which case the leader (at $T-1$) will enter the auction knowing that a win at $T-1$ guarantees a win at T, while the follower knows a win at $T-1$ guarantees a loss at T. This does not automatically imply that the leader at $T-1$ will necessarily win, because though his guaranteed win at T will bring it more profits, the firm may have to bid more in T to get those.

Vickers' second result is:

• If the high-cost firm's profits are always zero, and industry profits are strictly increasing in the costs of the high-cost firm, then the outcome is always persistent dominance.

These are precisely the conditions that prevail under Bertrand competition, so this again is just an extension of an earlier result for single innovations. The intuition is as follows. Given Bertrand competition, the leader will always win the final auction, and given that the loser's profits are zero, the bid he will have to make to win the patent is $\pi(c_{T+2}, c_{T+1})$, which is independent of which firm wins the second-last auction. But then since the only thing that can matter in the second-last auction are the profit streams of the leader and follower, and these are higher for the leader, the leader will win the second-last auction. Moreover, the high-cost firm in $T-1$ makes no profits in that period, none in the last and has no bid costs, so the value of being the high-cost firm is zero.

Now move back one period to $T-1$. Each firm knows that whoever wins this auction will win the last auction and that the profits net of bid costs that it will make in period T are $[\pi(c_{T+2}, c_T) - \pi(c_{T+2}, c_{T+1})]$. Hence the bids that both make in the $T-1$ auction will incorporate this.

However since this is common to both, the only thing that can determine the outcome of the auction is the one-period profit streams as leader or follower. But the zero-profit condition again ensures that the leader wins this auction. We can continue this form of argument backwards and will find each time that the bid that the leader needs to make to win the patent in any period τ is independent of the outcome of the previous auction.

The zero-profit condition is therefore quite important because it guarantees that anticipated future bid costs do not depend on the outcome of earlier auctions. What both these results therefore show is that it is only some of the strongest conditions for dominance or action–reaction in the single-innovation models that carry over to sequences, and that, in general, conditions that are sufficient for dominance or action–reaction in single-innovation models can produce the opposite outcomes in at least some of the auctions in a sequence.

Product innovation

In much of the innovation literature no great distinction is drawn between process and product innovation – they are both just ways in which firms can increase their profits. In the context of strategic innovation, however, the distinction is vital.

As we noted above, in the Vickers model of process innovation, firms will employ only the most cost efficient of the technologies they own. Matters are much more complicated with product innovation. Consider instead a model with vertically differentiated goods[6] (e.g. Shaked and Sutton, 1982) and in which there is Bertrand competition. If the sequence involves such goods of successively higher quality, then as a firm builds up its portfolio of patents, it will in general want to produce more than one of the goods on which it holds a patent as it will be better able to target different consumer groups the wider its range of products. This makes the analysis more difficult since we now have to keep track of the entire patent portfolio of each firm. In Beath, Katsoulacos and Ulph (1987), the problem is simplified by assuming that there are diseconomies of scope that limit each firm to producing only one good chosen in a profit-maximising manner from its portfolio. This makes the model formally similar to Vickers. However the conclusions are almost precisely reversed. Very slow technical progress is now associated with persistent dominance, while very rapid technical change produces action–reaction.

To see why the results are reversed, we need to examine how industry profits vary with the quality gap between the two firms. It is easiest to see the argument that they are first increasing and then decreasing by considering the case where the quality of the high-quality good is held constant and that of the low-quality good is gradually reduced. With a zero gap, both firms are producing the same product and Bertrand competition will eliminate profits. As the gap appears, at least one firm (the high-quality one) can make positive profits so that industry profits must initially increase with the gap. However, a feature of models of vertical differentiation is that consumers always have the option of not buying the differentiated products. Given the level of the high-quality good, widening the gap involves a lowering of the quality of the low-quality good. If prices did not change, the low-income consumers would increasingly find the no-purchase option attractive and to combat the fall in demand for its product, the low-quality firm will start to cut its price. In order to compete and maintain market share, the high-quality firm has to do the same. Hence industry profits start to fall when the gap gets sufficiently wide. Now recall that the logic of Vickers' argument depended on whether industry profits rose or fell with the gap between the firms. In his Cournot competition case, the graph of industry profits against the cost gap was U-shaped. What the argument above has illustrated is that in the product differentiation case with Bertrand competition, the graph is an inverted U-shape. This explains why the conclusions are reversed.

This analysis of product innovation assumed infinitely-lived patents. In a subsequent analysis, Beath, Katsoulacos and Ulph (1992) drop the previous assumption of infinitely-lived patents and also assume that while there are only two firms engaged in the R&D race, there are many firms capable of producing goods whose patents have lapsed. Because of this free-entry assumption and Bertrand competition, the price of such goods is driven to marginal cost,[7] so only the highest quality of these non-protected goods is ever bought. This keeps the number of goods actually being produced fixed as we move through the sequence: the goods with patent protection and the highest-quality good whose patent has lapsed. However there is a more important implication of having finitely-lived patents. For now if the outcome of the innovation process is persistent dominance, one firm will own all the extant patents and will be able to act as a monopolist restricted only by the presence of the highest-quality non-protected good available at a zero price. If however the outcome of the race is action–reaction firms will end up holding patents on more than one good, but each of these goods will be separated in the quality spectrum from the other goods they own by goods held by the rival firm. The outcome of Bertrand competition between the two firms will then be the same as if all the goods were owned by separate firms – and hence will be competitive.

Beath, Katsoulacos and Ulph show that if patents last for only two periods the outcome is always persistent dominance. The reason is the same as that behind Vickers' action–reaction result in the case of process innovation. Recall that at any auction, all that mattered in determining the bids were industry profits with the new technology; the impact of profits further into the future was the same for both the high- and low-cost firm. In the product innovation case with two-period patents the nature of future patent races is independent of the outcome of the current race. Hence all that can matter in determining this are the current levels of industry profits. But since leaders get monopoly profits if they win which exceed profits in any non-cooperative duopoly, we must have persistent dominance. However if patent life is extended to three periods, the outcome of the race can be action–reaction. The reason is that while leaders get more profits if they win, followers are willing to pay a lot to stop them winning, so a leader's profits net of bid costs can be lower than those of a follower.

This is another example of the possibility that market situations which would be regarded as more competitive on the basis of static theory can produce less competitive outcome under dynamic competition.

Summary

While these auction models are undoubtedly excessively stylised, they do provide the following valuable insights:

- single-period models can give very misleading results;
- there are crucial differences between product and process innovation;
- policies which, on the basis of static arguments, may be thought to produce more competitive outcomes can, in dynamic models, generate less competition.

A major difficulty with the sequential models, however, is that because the outcome depends to some extent on the anticipated future bid costs, then the rather artificial auction construction in which the loser effectively commits no resources to R&D, while the leader could put in a lot, may excessively bias the results towards action–reaction. An important feature of R&D in practice is that resources can often be lost if a rival manages to develop a new idea first. What is therefore needed is a model in which each firm has to commit resources to R&D if it is to be have any chance of innovating. In the next section we examine a model that allows for this.

8.3 NON-TOURNAMENT MODELS OF R&D RIVALRY: MULTIPLE WINNERS

A non-tournament model is one in which there can be multiple discoverers. The model we shall focus on is that of process innovation which was introduced by Dasgupta and Stiglitz (1980). In this, firms are engaged in the production of a homogeneous good and devote an amount z to R&D. This determines their level of unit costs c according to the relationship

$$c = \gamma z^{-\beta} \tag{8.5}$$

where β is the elasticity of cost reduction. Thus a firm's unit costs (assumed independent of output) depend on the level of technology it uses, and this is improved by R&D. This specification also captures several relevant features of R&D: doing it is critical if a firm is to maintain its market position, however it is subject to diminishing returns in the level of R&D activity (though its costs do not depend on firm size).

Demand is given by the constant elasticity function and so we can write the price of the good as

$$p = \alpha X^{-\varepsilon} \tag{8.6}$$

with ε denoting the inverse elasticity and X market demand.

Denoting the social welfare and n-firm oligopoly profit functions by $W(X, z)$ and $\Pi(x, z)$ respectively, where x is firm output, the social optimum and the symmetric n-firm market equilibrium are characterised by

$$W_x = \alpha X^{-\varepsilon} - \gamma z^{-\beta} = 0 \tag{8.7a}$$

$$W_z = \gamma \beta z^{-(1+\beta)} X - 1 = 0 \tag{8.7b}$$

and

$$\Pi_x = \alpha\left(1 - \frac{\varepsilon}{n}\right)X^{-\varepsilon} - \gamma z^{-\beta} = 0 \tag{8.8a}$$

$$\Pi_z = \gamma \beta z^{-(1+\beta)}x - 1 = 0 \tag{8.8b}$$

respectively.

The first point to note about these conditions is that from (8.7b) and (8.8b) we can see that the marginal benefit of R&D (i.e. $x \, dc/dz$) should equal its marginal cost (= 1). However, the *amount* of R&D done per firm (the amount of cost reduction) is *not independent* of market structure because the level of output per firm will be different. The second point is to note from (8.7a) and (8.8a) that Π_x lies inside W_x, but that the condition characterising

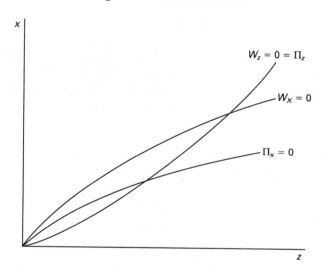

FIGURE 8.1 R & D: market equilibrium versus social optimum

the optimal choice of R&D for the social planner and the firm are the same. However, the amount of R&D done per firm (the amount of cost reduction) is not independent of market structure because the level of output per firm will be lower the larger is n.

These relationships are illustrated in Figure 8.1.

In Figure 8.1, the locus $W_z = 0$ will cut the $W_x = 0$ locus from below. Since the $\Pi_x = 0$ locus lies inside the $W_x = 0$ locus, and increasingly so as n increases, we see that z is a decreasing function of n. Thus a feature of this model is that increased competition reduces the extent to which firms can expect to appropriate the rents from R&D but, in aggregate, there is excessive duplication of research. Thus we have another result:

● In the symmetric market equilibrium of this model, firms engage in too little cost reduction from the social point of view. Furthermore, the greater the number of firms that the market equilibrium can support the less R&D will be done per firm.

For the $W_z = 0$ locus to cut the $W_x = 0$ locus from below, it is necessary that demand is not too elastic relative to the effectiveness of R&D in lowering the costs of production. This condition is also important for a further result:

• In aggregate, there is excessive duplication of research (nz is increasing in n).

A feature of the homogeneous product model above is the assumption that research paths are interchangeable: all firms really face the same problem and all paths potentially lead to its solution. This may not always be the case. It may be that each firm faces its own particular problem and so each requires that an independent research path be completed if it is successfully to reduce its costs (or improve its product). This problem has recently been examined by Katsoulacos and Ulph (1990a, 1990b) in a differentiated products framework. It is again the case that the equilibrium amount of R&D *per firm* is less than optimal but, as the market becomes larger, it approaches the socially-optimal level. In addition, because there is too little entry, a feature of the market equilibrium is that *aggregate* R&D is less than is socially optimal. There is insufficient entry for two reasons. The first is that, given the level of R&D – and hence production costs – the incentive to enter depends on profits net of fixed costs. Since profits are less than consumers' surplus, this will result in too little entry. However, there is a second effect that arises from the fact that, given the number of products produced, there is too little R&D undertaken in the market equilibrium and since a consequence of this is a reduction in the effective size of the market, fewer firms can be supported in the free-entry market equilibrium than in the social optimum.

8.4 TOURNAMENT MODELS: THE TIMING OF INNOVATION

It is true to say that by the amount of resources they commit to R&D, firms can affect not only the size but also the date of successful innovation. In a strategic setting this means that firms engaged in technological competition are likely to be involved in something akin to a race. While it is possible to explore the timing of innovation in a deterministic context (see Scherer, 1967; Gilbert and Newbery, 1982 and, especially, Katz and Shapiro, 1987), it is more natural to look at this in the case where there is technological uncertainty. The strategic element of timing is further emphasised if we model the technological competition as a 'tournament'. This means that the contest has a winner and a loser and carries the implication that the innovation can be effectively protected (by a patent, for example).

The model

The model we shall use is the simple duopoly one of Beath, Katsoulacos and Ulph (1989a). This model differs from Dasgupta and Stiglitz (1980) and Lee and Wilde (1980) by allowing for asymmetry between the contestants in both the value of the winner's prize and in current profits. These values are information that is assumed to be common to all the parties. The relationship between R&D effort and success is stochastic. Specifically, the probability that a firm successfully innovates in a small interval of time, given that the other has not succeeded up till then, is a constant function of its current flow rate of R&D expenditure. This conditional probability is called the 'hazard rate'. There is no accumulation of knowledge and, at any instant as the race for a particular innovation proceeds, the decision problem faced by the firm over its choice of R&D level remains unchanged. The firm therefore chooses a single time-independent flow rate of R&D effort. In fact we can think of the firm as choosing its hazard rate rather than R&D level as this simplifies the notation. We denote this hazard rate x_i, for firm i and let $c(x_i)$, the flow cost of achieving this, be given by x_i^2.

The time-independent nature of the model and the fact that success probabilities are uncorrelated means that we can derive the value function for firm i in a particularly simple way. Consider a firm i that is considering investing some effort x_i in R&D at an instantaneous cost of $c(x_i)$. Denote the value of participating in this instantaneous R&D competition as $V(x_i)$. Let (a/r) (resp. (d/r)) be the present value at the date of discovery of the profits made by firm 1 (resp. 2) if it is the successful innovator and let (b/r) (resp. (e/r)) be the present value of its profits if its rival succeeds. (r is the common rate of discount.) Since (a/r) is the present value from successful innovation by firm 1 and (b/r) the present value to firm 1 if firm 2 should succeed, it follows that $(a/r)>(b/r)$. (Similarly $(d/r)>(e/r)$.)

Without loss of generality we can concentrate on firm 1. If it is successful, it will enjoy a 'capital gain' of $G = [(a/r) - V_1(x_1)]$ with probability x_1. If its rival is successful, it will suffer a 'capital loss' of

$L = [V_1(x_1) - (b/r)]$. The probability of this occurring is x_2.[8] Denote the profits that firm 1 is currently earning by s_1. The equilibrium instantaneous investment decision for the firm must satisfy

$$rV_1(x_1) = x_1G + x_2L + s_1 - x_1^2 \qquad (8.9)$$

Rearranging this gives

$$V_1(x) = \frac{x_1(a/r) + x_2(a/r) + s_1 - x_1^2}{x_1 + x_2 + r} \qquad (8.10)$$

where $x = (x_1, x_2)$.

This model incorporates the two basic incentives that firms have to undertake innovative R&D that were mentioned at the outset. First there is the profit incentive (marginal return to the innovation). This would determine just how much R&D effort a firm that faced no R&D rivalry would put in. If there were no rivalry ($x_2 = 0$), firm 1's R&D effort would depend only on the comparison between $(a - s_1)$ and $c'(x_1)(= 2x_1)$. The effort level corresponding to this pure investment incentive we shall denote by x_1^0.

Secondly there is the incentive reflecting the threat posed by the existence of an active rival: the competitive threat. Its size is determined by the difference between the value of profits if the firm is successful and their value if it were to lose out to a rival: $(a-b)$. Suppose that firm 2 was to increase its effort level to infinity. It is then almost certain that the innovation will occur and the prize be awarded instantaneously. The marginal benefit of an increase in firm 1's effort rate is simply $\left(\frac{a-b}{r}\right)$, and the marginal cost is $c'(x_1)$. Firm 1 should thus equate marginal benefit to marginal cost and we denote the value of x_1 that satisfies this by $\bar{x}_1$.

The R&D effort levels corresponding to the profit incentive and the competitive threat set bounds on the reaction function for the firm. This reaction function shows the optimal effort level for one firm, given the effort undertaken by its rival. Thus, the R&D game between the two duopolists can be illustrated in a simple diagram in which these reaction functions are drawn. This is shown in Figure 8.2.

Figure 8.2 shows that a firm's R&D reaction function starts at the effort corresponding to its profit incentive and is asymptotic to

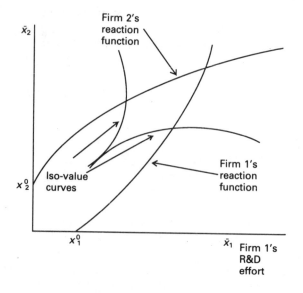

FIGURE 8.2   R & D reaction functions in duopoly

a line defined by its competitive threat. The Nash equilibrium effort level is given by the intersection of the two reaction functions. Clearly, by comparing the position of the equilibrium to a 45-degree line drawn from the origin, we can predict which firm is the more likely to innovate.

Also shown in Figure 8.2 are typical iso-value (of profits) curves for the two firms. The tangency between these shows that both firms could be made better off (in expected present value terms) by moving from the non-cooperative Nash equilibrium to the cooperative solution indicated by the tangency point. This also illustrates the negative externality on firms that is present in the patent race: if a firm wishes to *maintain* its relative probability of success, an increase in the rival's effort level forces it to do the same, but this reduces the expected present value of profits.

Both the profit incentive and the competitive threat will depend on a firm's identity (i.e. its current market position). This is because the post-innovation market structure (number of firms and degree of asymmetry between them) will depend on who wins and who loses and also because the current market position determines the size of the current profit flow. Clearly, the greater the profit incentive or the greater the competitive threat, the greater the overall incentive to innovate. However, there is nothing to rule out asymmetries in these forces such that while one firm may face the greater competitive threat, another has the greater incentive. Thus to identify the likely winner in these patent races, we need to look at all of the elements.

Beath, Katsoulacos and Ulph (1989a)show that the relative size of the profit incentive and competitive threat for any firm depends on whether imitation is easy or difficult. If the former is less than the latter we have the case shown in Figure 8.2 in which reaction functions are positively sloped. However, if the reverse holds and the profit incentive exceeds the competitive threat, reaction functions are negatively sloped. (This case arises when there is easy imitation.) Thus, as Beath, Katsoulacos and Ulph show, the race between the two duopolists could be one of four types depending on the slope of the reaction function for each of the firms. This model also has some fairly straightforward comparative statics results. These are

● If there is an increase in the prize to successful innovation, the competitive threat will increase.
● If one firm faces both a greater competitive threat and a larger profit incentive than the other it will undertake more R&D and hence be more likely to win the race.
● If the threats and incentives that face each party are identical then the outcome cannot be predicted. However, it requires only that one of these forces be satisfied as a strict positive inequality for the likely outcome to become clear.

An important point about the existing literature is that it uses assumptions that ensure that the equilibrium is the one that corresponds to the case where for both firms the competitive threat exceeds the profit incentive. Furthermore, these assumptions are also sufficiently strong to generate *either* 'persistent dominance' (the incumbent wins) (e.g. Gilbert and Newbery, 1982; Harris and Vickers, 1987) *or* 'action–reaction' (the challenger wins) (e.g. Reinganum, 1983). However, as we have seen, any outcome is possible. One that Katz and Shapiro (1987) point to in their analysis is the possibility of the competition taking the form of a 'waiting game' rather than a race. In the model outlined above, this outcome emerges when the profit incentive exceeds the competitive threat for both firms. The best response to observing one's rival increase R&D effort is then to reduce one's own. This saves the firm current R&D costs but has little or no effect on the likely date of success, and hence is profit increasing. This structure of incentives results in a Nash equilibrium in which both firms behave rather like free-riders and invest relatively little effort in R&D. Hence we can describe this as a waiting game.

Competition in the R&D game

So far in this section we have focused on a particular market structure: duopoly. A natural question to ask is 'how does the degree of rivalry and the degree of appropriability affect technological progressiveness in tournaments?' We have already seen that these weaken incentives in a non-tournament setting. The analyses contained in the literature on tournament models have differed in two ways. The first is in the assumption made about behaviour in the R&D game. For example, Dasgupta and Stiglitz (1980) make use of a 'large numbers' assumption to the effect that each firm believes its actions will have no impact on the likely date of discovery. The alternative is to allow firms to take into account the effects of their actions on their rivals. This is the approach used by Loury (1979), Lee and Wilde (1980) and Reinganum (1981, 1982).

The second is the distinction between those models that assume fixed or contractual R&D expenditures (Dasgupta and Stiglitz, 1980, Loury 1979), which take the form of a lump-sum incurred at the outset, and those models where R&D is non-contractual in the sense that it is a flow cost that is incurred until someone successfully innovates. Models falling into this latter category are Lee and Wilde (1980) and Reinganum (1981, 1982). In Lee and Wilde this flow rate is constant. This is an implication of the time-independent nature of the hazard rate. On the other hand, Reinganum has firms choosing a development plan that specifies the optimal R&D expenditure at each instant.

In the discussion here, we will follow the Lee and Wilde approach and indicate, in passing, where different results would be obtained were one to assume contractual costs.[9] The starting point is the function (8.10) which defines the value of participating in R&D competition. Suppose that there are n identical firms, each of them currently earning zero profit and that they are engaged in an R&D competition to win a perfectly protected patent whose capitalised value is P. Those who are unsuccessful get nothing. Thus in this case $a = d = rP$ and $b = e = s = 0$.[10]

In this case (8.10) becomes

$$V_i(x) = \frac{x_i P - x_i^2}{h + x_i + r} - F, \qquad i = 1, \ldots, n \qquad (8.11)$$

where h denotes the aggregate R&D effort of firm i's rivals. The first-order condition for the maximisation of expected value is

$$(h + r)(P - 2x_i) = x_i^2 \qquad (8.12)$$

This defines the optimal R&D effort for firm i given the effort levels of the $(n - 1)$ other competitors.

We can now ask what will be the effect of an increase in rivalry on firm i's R&D effort. To establish this, totally differentiate (8.12) to yield

$$\frac{dx_i^e}{dh} = \frac{P - 2x_i^e}{2(h + x_i^e + r)} \qquad (8.13)$$

By the first-order condition, we know that $[P - 2x_i^e]$ is positive. It therefore follows that $\frac{dx_i^e}{dh} > 0$. Since h can be thought of as generalised rivalry, we see the following result:

- Greater rivalry stimulates greater R&D activity.

This is the feature that makes these tournaments so competitive.

Focus now on the industry equilibrium and ask how changes in the equilibrium number of firms affects equilibrium R&D effort. Since we are dealing with identical firms, we can restrict our attention to symmetric equilibria. This means that $x_i^e = x^e$, $\forall i$ and so $h = (n - 1)x^e$. Now the first-order condition yields x^e as a function of h – call it $\phi(h)$. In equilibrium we therefore have $x^e = \phi[(n - 1)x^e]$ and so

$$\frac{dx^e}{dn} = \frac{\phi_h}{1 - (n - 1)\phi_h} \qquad (8.14)$$

So we have the result:

● Suppose $1 - (n - 1)\phi_h > 0$, then as the number of firms in the industry increases, so does equilibrium R&D per firm.[11]

What this suggests is that when R&D is of this non-contractual nature, it is the competitive threat posed by rivals that is the more important of the determinants of a firm's R&D. However if we had assumed instead that R&D was in the nature of a fixed cost, the condition that determines how much effort is committed in equilibrium is of a more simple marginal benefit/marginal cost sort. Indeed, as Loury shows, in equilibrium each firm's R&D choice must satisfy the following first-order condition

$$\frac{P}{nx^e + r} = c'(x^e) \tag{8.15}$$

This says that, in equilibrium, the firm chooses its effort level so as to equate the expected value of the 'prize' to the marginal cost of effort. Now, increased rivalry reduces expected profit and hence reduces equilibrium R&D effort. Thus the relationship between R&D effort and market structure depends on whether R&D costs are of a contractual or non-contractual nature.

The economic intuition behind these differing results is the following. In the contractual case, firms are really being asked to sink their R&D spending up-front. In this case, it is almost as if the typical firm were putting itself in the shoes of a potential entrant. This is why the equilibrium R&D is determined by the investment-like condition that characterises the profit incentive (8.15). Competition makes investment in this industry look less attractive, and so the typical firm does less of it.

The position with non-contractual costs is different. Here the correct way to view the firm is as someone committed to the industry. Now increases in rivalry heighten the competitive threat for the typical firm and so cause it to increase its R&D effort in response. Thus we see that in these two models the relative importance of the two basic forces we have argued determine R&D – the profit incentive and the competitive threat – differs and so it is not surprising that the results on R&D competition obtained by Loury and by Lee and Wilde are at odds.

Let us now consider social optimality and proceed by comparing the market equilibrium with the choice that would be made by the social planner. The planner's problem is to choose the number of projects and the level of R&D effort so as to maximise the capitalised value of net social surplus.[12]

As we saw in the discussion of equilibrium in the duopoly model above (p. 178) there is a negative externality in patent races that can be usefully internalised by moving to the cooperative solution that the social planner would choose. In the example we are discussing here, it turns out that this negative externality means that the market equilibrium is one that is characterised by socially excessive competition in the search for rents. In order to show this, we need to look at the R&D effort per firm and the number of firms that the social planner would operate.

Let us focus first on R&D per firm and start by supposing that the 'prize', P, that faces the social planner and the typical firm in the market is the same. Given that n firms are to be operated, R&D effort will be chosen to maximise $n^s V$ and this yields the first-order condition defining the socially-optimal level of R&D effort per firm, x^s,:

$$r(P - c'(x^s)) = n(x^s c'(x^s) - c(x^s)) \qquad (8.16)$$

We can now ask if, at the level of effort chosen by the planner, the typical firm in the market would choose more or less. To answer this we evaluate $\partial V_i / \partial x_i$ at $x_i = x^s$. Since we have

$$\frac{\partial V_i}{\partial x_i} = \frac{(h + r)(P - c'(x_i)) - (x_i c'(x_i) - c(x_i))}{(h + x_i + r)^2}$$

we can use (8.16) to eliminate $(P - c'(x_i))$ and so deduce that

$$\frac{\partial V_i}{\partial x_i} = \frac{[(h + r)n - r][x^s c'(x^s) - c(x^s)]}{r(h + x^s + r)^2} > 0 \qquad (8.17)$$

when evaluated at $x_i = x^s$. This follows because the second set of square brackets in the numerator is positive as a result of the convexity of the R&D cost function. Hence we can conclude that $x^s < x^e$.

Now consider the number of firms (or projects), n^s, which the social planner sets. This is determined by the condition $\partial(n^s V)/\partial n^s = 0$, and this yields the result that

$$\frac{xP - c(x)}{nx + r} = \frac{F(nx + r)}{r}$$

This defines n^s and so holds true for $n = n^s$. Now consider V evaluated at $n = n^s$. This is

$$V = \frac{F(n^s x + r)}{r} - F = \frac{n^s x F}{r} > 0$$

However this tells us that at $n = n^s$, a competitive firm would find it profitable to enter and hence $n^s < n^e$. Since $x^s < x^e$, we have the result:

• The social planner will operate fewer projects and run each at a lower effort rate than would be the case for the independent firms in the market equilibrium.

Thus we see that, faced with a common prize, the market suffers from two excesses in equilibrium: there are too many firms engaged in the race and each is investing more effort than is socially desirable. Since the expected date of success is $1/nx$, the market innovates too rapidly from a social point of view. There is a caveat to this result, however, and that is that, in general, the social planner will be seeking to maximise the present value of consumer surplus net of R&D costs rather than the (smaller) present value of monopoly profits so that the 'prizes' are different. Thus the question is whether the smaller prize that the firm faces will result in the market innovating too rapidly or too slowly. Unfortunately there is no clear answer in theory. However an analysis of efficiency losses in a tournament model with an endogenous number of firms has been carried out by Beath, Katsoulacos and Ulph (1991). This suggests that the market equilibrium may be one in which there is either socially 'excessive' or else socially 'insufficient' rent-seeking.

The degree of appropriability

A final point to consider in the case of tournament models is the effect of variations in the degree of appropriability. We therefore drop the assumption that a patent gives a firm complete protection from imitation. Now an increase in n can reduce each firm's equilibrium R&D effort. The intuition is as follows. With patent protection, a firm is anxious not to be left behind its rivals in the race. However, with imitation it is not so critical to be first and the addition of a new firm means that existing firms will want to push on to it some of the costs of innovation and thus reduce their own R&D costs. This has a real current value to them. Indeed, Futia (1980) shows that, with sufficiently rapid and complete imitation, there can be an inverse relationship between *aggregate* R&D and the number of firms in the industry.

A similar phenomenon (noted by Spence, 1984) arises when rival firms experience significant positive spillovers from each other's R&D. This is another example of non-appropriability which, if sufficiently large, gives rise to an inverse relationship between aggregate expenditures and the number of firms.

8.5 SEQUENCES OF TOURNAMENTS

A disadvantage of the sequential auction models of section 8.2 was the absence of uncertainty. It was this that we sought to remedy in section 8.4. There are already a number of sequential models with technological uncertainty in the literature. These include Fudenberg *et al.* (1983), Harris and Vickers (1987), Grossman and Shapiro (1987) and Park (1987). In these models firms have to complete a number of stages before it is possible to obtain the single innovation (patent). Thus at any time up to the date of successful innovation, firms can be either at the same or at different stages. Only when the last breakthrough is made and the patent is awarded is there product market competition. Since there are no intermediate payoffs, the incentive for succeeding before your rival at any stage other than the last one is that this moves you nearer than your rival to the ultimate goal.

An important issue which we need to consider in this section concerns the nature of the innovative process. Implicit in the discussion of section 8.2 is the assumption that at all times firms are competing for the same innovation. This means that although one firm has a patent on the technology that prevents everyone from using it, nevertheless all the relevant technological information has become common knowledge and, moreover, those who were unsuccessful in the previous race are just as able to exploit this common knowledge as the actual discoverer.

However, in the Grossman and Shapiro, Park, and Harris and Vickers models the assumption is that either because technological information does not become common knowledge, or else because there are extremely strong learning-by-doing effects, each firm essentially has to discover each technological step by itself before it can move on to discover the next. In this case, then, at any one time, the firm that is ahead (the leader) and the firm that is behind (the follower) will be competing for *different* innovations. If the leader succeeds before the follower it will pull ahead of its rival, while if the follower succeeds first it will simply move one stage closer. In this case, the best that the follower can do is to *catch up*. Models in which followers must first move, in a step-by-step fashion, to the leader's position can be called *catch-up models*. These are to be contrasted with *leapfrog models*. The Vickers (1986) and Beath *et al.* (1987, 1992) auction models of section 8.2 are examples of this genre, as is Reinganum (1985). In leapfrog models a follower is allowed at any given time to compete directly with the leader for the new best-practice technology. Such models therefore implicitly assume that once an innovation is patented, all the knowledge that is encapsulated in it becomes a public good – although patent protection ensures that it cannot be currently exploited by rivals in the market.

Fudenberg *et al.* (1983) emphasise the importance of leapfrogging by considering a model where the probability of success depends only on the total time spent in research (they call this 'experience'). If there is a single stage, then timing of entry is crucial and the perfect equilibrium is one in which only one firm enters and does R&D. Introducing a second stage allows a follower the possibility of leapfrogging the leader, and the equilibrium can now involve more than one firm doing R&D.

Grossman and Shapiro, Park and Harris and Vickers not only use a catchup model, they also focus on the case where the competitive threat exceeds the profit incentive. The former two analyse a two-stage race while Harris and Vickers allow for many stages. These analyses obtain the following results:

- If a follower should catch up with the leader, the latter will increase its R&D effort.
- A leader puts in more effort than a follower.
- R&D efforts are at their most intensive when the competitors are neck-and-neck.
- In a head-to-head race, effort increases as the race proceeds.
- If a leader emerges, his efforts increase and those of the follower decrease. The further ahead the leader moves, the more disillusioned becomes the follower and at some point may give up altogether.

These results relate to *multi-stage races*. There are no analytic results from models dealing with *sequences of innovations*. In principle it is just a matter of incorporating the one-period tournament model into a sequential framework. The formal structure for doing this is contained in Beath, Katsoulacos and Ulph (1993).

One real difficulty is that the equilibrium in such models need not be unique. While it is true that in some cases one of these may be the obvious equilibrium, in others it may be quite unclear what equilibrium should be selected. However, even if non-uniqueness were not a problem, it would still be very hard to get analytical results. Because the equilibrium values of R&D expenditures in one race enter into the present values that appear in the previous race, it is necessary to have an explicit link between these equilibrium levels of R&D expenditure and the parameters of the associated R&D race in order to be able to link together what is happening in the various races. This link was extremely simple in the certainty model but it was nevertheless the case that analytical results were fewer than in the single-period model. In the model with uncertainty the link between equilibrium levels of R&D expenditure and the parameters of the model cannot be expressed in a simple closed form, even for a simple form of cost function like the quadratic of section 8.4. This is why analytical results are so hard to come by.

For this reason it is necessary to resort to computer simulation to explore behaviour. While this involves a loss of generality, it has the compensation that we can explore a wide range of cases and so get a good feel for the essential features of such sequential tournaments. We have undertaken such simulation and will end this section by reporting our own findings on sequential innovation.

The results relate to the following model. Two firms are producing a homogeneous product whose inverse demand function is the constant elasticity function

$$p = S^\varepsilon X^{-\varepsilon}$$

where p is the (market) price, X total output, ε, $0 < \varepsilon < 1$, is the inverse elasticity of demand, and S is a scaling parameter which allows us to explore the effects of exogenous changes in market size. There is a sequence of T cost-reducing innovations. Technical progress occurs at the constant rate g, where

$$g = (c_k/c_{k+1}) - 1, k = 1, \ldots, T + 1$$

and c_k is unit cost. The R&D cost function is again quadratic, and there is a positive rate of interest, r. In addition to varying these parameters,[13] we also varied the two main structural features of the model: whether the nature of market competition was Cournot or Bertrand; and whether the structure of moves in the sequence was leapfrog or catch-up. The results are summarised in Table 8.1.

With Bertrand competition and a catch-up move structure, the outcome is one of persistent dominance. At the outset both firms compete vigorously but as the leader pulls away, the challenger gives up. As this happens, the leader's effort is also falling. This is precisely what we would expect from the work of Harris and Vickers.

However, if we move to a leapfrog structure then, while the last races in the sequence are again characterised by persistent dominance, there is action–reaction in the early stages as the firms vie for the eventual persistent dominance. Higher growth and interest rates are associated with dominance over a smaller number of races. However the striking feature is that, as the gap widens between the two firms, R&D spending rises sharply, reflecting the greater threat the leader faces of being leapfrogged by its rival.

With the leapfrog move structure but Cournot competition, the outcome is one of action–reaction in every race. However, probably the most interesting set of outcomes arises with the pairing of

TABLE 8.1 Sequential innovation, simulation results

	Catch-up			*Leap-frog*
Bertrand	Persistent dominance, high initial efforts The follower gives up			Action–reaction in early races Persistent dominance in later races As the gap develops, R&D rises with the leader's competitive threat
	$\dfrac{g}{r}$	*Low*	*High*	
Cournot	*Low*	Action–reaction	Persistent dominance, catch-up, then action–reaction	Action–reaction
	High	Persistent dominance, then catch-up	Persistent dominance Follower gives up	

catch-up and Cournot. When the rate of technical progress is high and the rate of interest low, the incumbent wins at first and opens up a considerable gap. The challenger then completely closes this and thereafter, whenever one firm pulls ahead, the other immediately puts in more R&D effort and closes the gap again. However, when the rate of technical change and rate of interest are low, the challenger always closes any gap that opens up, and in this sense we have action–reaction all the time. When the rate of interest is high, the leader pulls away to the finish line. Provided the rate of technical progress is not too high, the follower then comes home in his own time. However, with a sequence of large innovations, the follower gives up before reaching the finishing line.

Thus it still remains true that Bertrand competition produces 'more' dominance than does Cournot. However, unlike the case of certainty where, with a leapfrog move-structure, Bertrand competition always produced dominance, with the introduction of uncertainty this result is no longer true, and it can produce action–reaction, at least over some of the races in a sequence. Similarly, while in the work of Harris and Vickers where the sequence of races were stages in a single race, it was shown that the catch-up move structure always produced dominance, in the case of a sequence of races this is no longer the case, and we can get action–reaction when there is Cournot competition and low rates of technical change. However, drawing on the whole range of simulations, we can say that the combination of leapfrog moves and Cournot competition almost always produces action–reaction, while the combination of catch-up moves and Bertrand competition almost always produces persistent dominance.

8.6   CONCLUSION

As we said at the outset, there is strong evidence of the importance of technological competitiveness as a determinant of a country's relative trade performance. This is not just a matter of technological leadership; it is also a matter of technological capability. However, the literature that we have explored here has been on the whole concerned with the former. We have dealt with the latter only in our discussion of sequential races where we drew a distinction between catching-up and leapfrogging. What we hope we have shown is that while the forces that drive R&D effort are few and basic, the ways in which they come together results in a surprisingly varied tapestry of potential outcomes.

Thus we saw that, even when only the competitive threat was present, as in the auction models of section 8.2, some markets would be characterised by persistent dominance and others by action–reaction. Which outcome arose depended on the particular features of the market (Bertrand or Cournot competition), the nature of the innovation (process or product) and its size, the rate of innovation and patent life. When both profit incentive and competitive threat are present, the analysis of the single tournament revealed that we could might have a patent race or a waiting game. When these tournaments were brought together in a sequence, the array of possibilities was extremely rich as the simulation results summarised in Table 8.1 revealed.

An omission from our story has been the links between R&D and other input markets: in particular the markets for labour and capital. For example, we have implicitly assumed throughout this chapter that there was no asymmetry in information and that firms faced perfect capital markets. However, it is often claimed that one of the factors that is responsible for the UK's lack of technological leadership is the short-term view of R&D taken by the capital markets. The implication is that firms are reluctant to invest in R&D as much as they would wish because of the fear of the depressing effect that this might have on their share price. This of course is a claim and an obvious area for research is to examine its legitimacy and to build models that would allow one to explore the question theoretically. There is little work to report on.

Equally important is the link between R&D and the labour market. Here, fortunately, there is already some valuable work on the relation between firm/union bargaining structure and the likely outcome of technological competition. It is of course still too early to assess these contributions fully but the interested reader is referred to the series of papers on the topic by Ulph and Ulph (1988, 1989, 1990).

9 Recent Developments in the Economics of Public Utility Regulation

THOMAS G. WEYMAN-JONES

9.1 INTRODUCTION

The industries discussed in this chapter comprise firms which are natural monopolies and for which a system of regulation has been devised by Government. This system is referred to as the regulatory contract between the Government's regulator and the industry.

Briefly, natural monopoly arises when the production level corresponding to the lowest unit cost of the firm is sufficient to meet all market demand when price is set at that unit cost. The industries which supply the traditional public services through networks, i.e. telecommunications, electricity, gas, and water services, usually have the characteristics of natural monopolies and are conventionally referred to as public utilities. Particularly in Europe and many developing countries, such industries have been in public ownership, while elsewhere, notably the USA, they have been owned by private shareholders (investor owned utilities), but universally there has been some form of implicit or explicit regulatory contract between local or national government and the utility. Doubts about the efficient performance of US utilities together with the impetus towards privatisation of European public utilities, i.e. the transfer of the industries from public ownership to investor owned utility status, has prompted a fundamental re-examination of the economic principles underlying traditional regulatory contracts. This has coincided with the incorporation of game theory and incentive issues into industrial economics in a way that has revolutionised traditional ideas about regulation.

The chapter is organised as follows. It begins with a review of two traditional regulatory ideas: cost of service and Ramsey pricing, together with a discussion of the meaning of efficiency in regulatory economics. The topic of governance structures for natural monopolies and the alternative costs and benefits of incentive regulation is then introduced. The critical issue of the differences in the information available to regulators and utilities then requires an examination of the principal–agent game between regulator and utility, and yields two broad categories of regulatory contract: Bayesian and non-Bayesian regulation. The second of these leads naturally to discussion of the leading practical innovation in incentive regulation: price caps.

9.2 COST OF SERVICE OR RATE OF RETURN REGULATION

The form of regulatory contract used for investor owned utilities in the USA is known as cost of service regulation. In essence a public utilities commission, appointed by the state government, adjudicates on the prices set by a firm which has a monopoly franchise to provide one or more utility services. The conventional criterion is that the monopoly cannot earn more than a *fair and reasonable* rate of return on its capital, so that its prices reflect the cost of service provided to its customers. There are several different ways that this cost of service or rate of return model can be written, and what follows is only one (though the most frequent), stylised version. It is based on the work of Averch and Johnson (1962) and Cowing (1978).

The utility has a regulated price, p, for its output y, which is provided from the use of two inputs, capital and labour: $y = f(L, K)$. It faces fixed input prices: w per unit of labour services, and r per unit of capital services, so that its costs are $C = wL + rK$. Its operating profits relative to its capital base are limited to a fair and reasonable rate of return, s, per year. The utility's problem is to maximise profit, π, under this regime:

$$\max \pi = pf(L, K) - wL - rK \text{ subject to: } [pf(L, K) - wL]/K \leq s$$

The constraint limits operating profits before interest to a fixed proportion, s, of the capital base. Since p is fixed when s is fixed, we can arbitrarily set $p = 1$ for simplicity. The Lagrangean (with multiplier θ) for the problem is:

$$L = f(L, K) - wL - rK + \theta[sK - f(L, K) + wL] \qquad (9.1)$$

and the first-order conditions are:

$$[\partial f/\partial L - w][1 - \theta] = 0 \qquad (9.2)$$

$$\partial f/\partial K - r + \theta s - \theta \partial f/\partial K = 0 \qquad (9.3)$$

$$sK - f(L, K) + wL = 0 \qquad (9.4)$$

By the envelope theorem, $\theta K = \partial\pi/\partial s$, so that $\theta = [1/K]\partial\pi/\partial s > 0$, since raising s relaxes the constraint allowing π to increase.

From (9.3), $\theta = [r - \partial f/\partial K]/[s - \partial f/\partial K] < 1$ if we make the usual assumption that: $r < s < \partial f/\partial K$; i.e. the allowed rate of return is above the cost of capital but below the profit-maximising marginal revenue product of capital; hence: $0 < \theta < 1$.

From (9.2) and (9.3), the fundamental results (9.5) and (9.6) are derived:

$$[\partial f/\partial K]/[\partial f/\partial L] = \{[r - \theta s]/[1 - \theta]\}/w = r^*/w \qquad (9.5)$$

$$[r^* - r] = [r - \theta s - (1 - \theta)r]/(1 - \theta)$$
$$= [\theta/(1 - \theta)](r - s) < 0 \qquad (9.6)$$

and therefore $[r^*/w] < [r/w]$, so that the regulated firm faces a distorted factor price ratio that causes it to overinvest in the capital stock – so called 'gold plating of the rate base'. In Figure 9.1, the regulated choice of production process to minimise costs, (OR), has a lower labour to capital ratio than the unregulated choice, (OF).

Differentiating (9.2)–(9.4) and applying the second-order conditions for a maximum, gives the result:

$$dK/ds = -[K/(s - \partial f/\partial K)] > 0 \qquad (9.7)$$

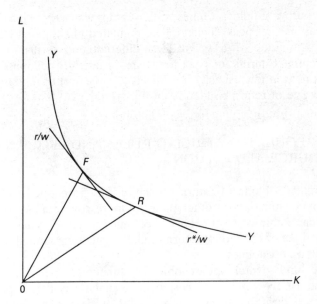

FIGURE 9.1 Rate of return regulation

so that increasing the allowed rate of return allows π to be increased by expanding the capital base. If the regulated price is now set at the level of unit cost, then:

$$p = C/y = \Psi(y, s, w, r) \tag{9.8}$$

and prices are therefore driven by the utility's choice of output, its allowed rate of return and its input prices. In this sense, given a value for *s*, the regulations are a form of *cost plus contract* since the utility simply passes on the costs of its own performance and its input charges. In practice the regulators often express a view on whether or not particular investments are justified for meeting demand, a factor which in conjunction with the vagueness of the phrase 'fair and reasonable rate of return' has led to the US regulatory system becoming notorious for its litigiousness.

This incentive to overinvest and pass on cost increases has been regarded as one of the prime sources of technical inefficiency due to regulation in US utilities. In particular, suppose a utility produces output at different times of the year for which there is a cycle of peak and off-peak demand. The regulated price, p, may then be some index of a set of time-differentiated tariffs. Time-differentiated tariffs for peak loads are designed to minimise the investment in idle capacity, but this is just the sort of investment which rate of return regulation encourages.

9.3 REGULATORY PRICING RULES AND EFFICIENT RESOURCE ALLOCATION

The model of rate of return regulation has no explicit welfare economics foundations other than the loose commitment to fair and reasonable costs of service, but regulatory theory including the critique of the rate of return model is usually grounded firmly in welfare economics.

The fundamental welfare objective function underlying most regulatory economics and cost benefit analysis is that a policy change is desirable from society's point of view if the potential gainers could compensate the potential losers in monetary units i.e. a potential Pareto improvement. If the compensation actually occurs then we have a Pareto improvement. One definition of an efficient allocation of resources is a situation in which potential Pareto improvements have all been exhausted. Adopting this criterion, we write economic welfare as the unweighted sum of consumers' surplus, S, and producers' profits, π, each of which depends on the price structure of the firm:

$$W = S(p) + \pi(p) \tag{9.9}$$

For natural monopolies subject to decreasing unit costs as output expands we may wish to impose the constraint that the producer at least breaks even: $\pi \geq 0$. This is important for public enterprises subject to a public sector budget constraint, or natural monopolies for whom the regulator has to ensure the viability of production. The Lagrangean function for this constrained (or second-best) Pareto problem is:

$$W = S + \pi + \lambda\pi = S + (1 + \lambda)\pi \tag{9.10}$$

where λ is the shadow price on the breakeven constraint ($\lambda \geq 0$). It measures the welfare benefit to society (in £) of relaxing the profit constraint by £1. Note that this affects a regulator's interest in consumers compared with producers. The regulator would accept a distortion of resource allocation at the margin that transferred resources from consumers to producers in order to ensure the producers' financial viability. Vogelsang (1990) gives an interesting alternative interpretation of this $(1 + \lambda)$ term as the opportunity cost of public funds. If a natural monopoly pricing at marginal cost (the pricing rule implied by the unweighted surplus criterion) has a deficit which must be financed by a transfer from the Treasury, this transfer has real opportunity costs: (a) it encourages the firm receiving the subsidy to engage in rent-seeking or lobbying or other inefficient behaviour; (b) the subsidy may require distortionary taxes elsewhere in the economy; (c) there are transaction costs in collecting and transferring the subsidy. The net result is that it costs $£(1 + \lambda)$ to transfer £1 to a loss-making producer.

Alternatively, we could easily imagine a situation in which the regulator favoured consumers at the margin with a welfare criterion:

$$W = S(p) + \mu\pi(p); \quad \mu < 1/2 \tag{9.11}$$

The first-order conditions for the maximisation of the unweighted welfare criterion (9.10) are, where subscripts denote vector differentiation:

$$S_p = -(1 + \lambda)\pi_p \tag{9.12}$$

But $S_p = -q'$, i.e. minus the vector of quantities demanded (e.g. if S is the unweighted sum of the indirect utility functions) and π_p is $(q' + [p - C_q]q_p)$, i.e. the vector of (marginal revenues – marginal costs) with respect to price changes. Written out more explicitly and concentrating on the situation where cross-price effects are negligible, we have the following n conditions, one for each of the utility's products:

$$-(\lambda/1 + \lambda)[q_j] = [p_j - \partial C/\partial q_j][dq_j/dp_j] \quad j = 1, \ldots, n \tag{9.13}$$

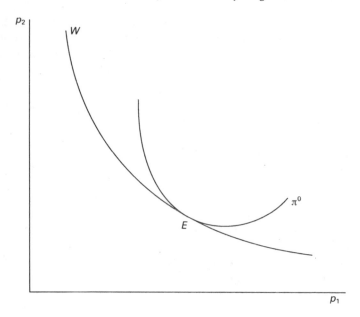

FIGURE 9.2 Ramsey pricing

The n equations in (9.13) state that at a second-best welfare optimum that allows the utility to break even, the price–marginal cost markup weighted by the slope of the product's (compensated) demand schedule should be proportional to the amount of the product consumed. Now recalling that marginal revenue has a simple proportional relationship to price depending on the product's price elasticity of demand, e_j: $MR_j/p_j = [1 + (1/e_j)]$, we can derive from (9.13) two alternative relationships for the cases of a binding and a non-binding breakeven constraint:

For $\lambda > 0$, $[p_j - \partial C/\partial q_j]/p_j = -[\lambda/(1 + \lambda)][1/e_j]$;

(Ramsey pricing)   (9.14)

and for $\lambda = 0$, $p_j = \partial C/\partial q_j$; (Marginal cost pricing)   (9.15)

Figure 9.2 illustrates the basic idea for a producer of two commodities, (e.g. peak and off-peak electricity). The axes are the prices of the two commodities. There are two contours: π^0 represents combinations of the two prices which just cause the firm to break even, and it acts as a constraint. With decreasing costs assumed, welfare is maximised by finding the lowest W contour subject to being on or above the π^0 contour. At the optimal combination of prices, the contours have a common slope at which the marginal rate of substitution of welfare gains (i.e. $[(p_1 - MC_1)/(p_2 - MC_2)]$) equals the marginal rate of substitution of profit gains (i.e. $[(MR_1 - MC_1)/(MR_2 - MC_2)]$). Rearranging this tangency yields equation (9.14) above. In the simplest case of a single-product firm, Ramsey pricing is average cost pricing.

9.4 ECONOMIC EFFICIENCY AND GOVERNANCE STRUCTURES FOR NATURAL MONOPOLY

The concept of economic efficiency used in the pricing analysis above is that of allocative (pricing) efficiency. Economists such as Farrell (1957) and Leibenstein (1966) introduced an additional dimension of efficiency measurement, productive or x-efficiency.

In Figure 9.3, inputs can be combined in several different ways to make a constant level of output along the iso-quant yy. At given input prices represented by the slope of the line CC the cheapest total costs involved in making the output represented by yy arises from using the input combination E. A firm making the same level of output but using input levels at R is clearly inefficient. Farrell's decomposition measures the firm's efficiency by the following ratios which can be at most unity (or 100 per cent) in the case of a firm which is productively efficient.

- OP/OQ = Allocative efficiency – representing a failure to choose the cheapest process or input combination.
- OQ/OR = Technical efficiency – representing a failure to maximise output from the chosen process or input combination.
- OP/OR = Productive (or overall) efficiency – representing the product of allocative and technical efficiency ratios $[OP/OQ][OQ/OR]$.

For our purposes it is convenient, if simplistic, to equate the Farrell and Leibenstein ideas and simply refer to this concept by the shorthand expression x-efficiency.

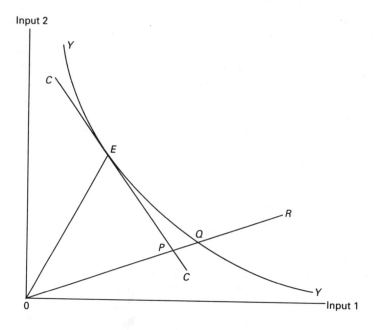

FIGURE 9.3   Types of x-inefficiency

Regulation has therefore to be directed at removing different kinds of inefficiency by incentives to: (a) lower prices, and (b) lower costs. This opens up the topic of what we mean by incentive regulation. We can begin by classifying the institutional types of regulation:

1. *No regulation*: the industry is open to entry and exit with no price rules, profit constraints or prohibition of barriers to entry.
2. *Public enterprise*: the industry is publicly owned and price guidelines are laid down, e.g. Ramsey or marginal cost pricing. Examples are the old UK nationalised industries and many other state owned European utilities such as Electricité de France.
3. *Cost of service, (rate of return)*: e.g. traditional US-style regulation, and UK pharmaceuticals for the NHS. The traditional objection is gold plating the capital base on which the allowed rate of return is calculated.

4. *Franchise bidding*: e.g. broadcasting. Here the franchise contract to be the natural monopolist is auctioned to the highest bidder, or lowest-price-commitment bidder. It emphasises competition for the field in place of competition in the field. Suggested by Demsetz (1968) it was challenged by Williamson (1976) and became the focus of a famous debate on the transactions costs of contract monitoring for quality and performance.

5. *Incentive-based regulation*: this is a widely used term treated in detail in the very influential paper by Joskow and Schmalensee (1986). Their definition is that it comprises any form of regulation in which the utility's price structure is partially or completely decoupled from its own reported cost structure.

The treatment by Joskow and Schmalensee allows us to classify these institutions in terms of their implied regulatory contracts in a very simple way:
Define:

p_t: regulated price in period t
c_t^*: regulator's estimate of the x-efficient unit cost
c_t: utility's reported unit cost
b: proportion of cost overrun risk borne by consumers.

The general regulatory contract is then:

$$p_t = [1 - b]c_t^* + b\,c_t; \quad 0 \le b \le 1 \tag{9.16}$$

$b = 0$: fixed price regulatory contract – incentive-based regulations

$b = 1$: cost plus regulatory contract – public enterprises, and cost of service regulation when there is no regulatory lag.

When $b = 0$, the utility's prices are capped by the regulator's guess at the x-efficient unit cost. The utility is allowed to retain any profits it makes from keeping its unit costs below the price cap. Hence it has every incentive to be x-efficient. This type of contract is also called a residual claimant contract, since the utility is the residual claimant to the profits from beating the cap. However, the regulator may have set too lenient a cap, and the utility may be able to make profits which are very large in absolute terms. The regulator may then be tempted to set $b > 0$. As long as $b < 1$, the utility's prices are partly decoupled from its reported unit costs, and a cost-reducing incentive is available.

When $b = 1$, the utility's abnormal profits are confiscated, but it can pass through to consumers any changes in its costs which it reports to the regulator. Traditional public enterprise, where the utility is instructed to relate prices to the marginal cost base which it reports to the regulator falls into this category, as does cost of service regulation. However, if the regulator in a cost of service contract is slow to update the regulated price in terms of current reported costs, there is an incentive for the utility to reduce its costs below the previously allowed level. This regulatory lag can reintroduce an element of incentive regulation to cost of service contracts whenever costs are rising.

In general, there emerges for the regulator a fundamental dilemma between profits confiscation (cost plus) contracts which may be allocatively efficient but give no incentive to lower costs before pass through, and residual claimant (fixed price) contracts which may be x-efficient, but leave the utility with what the regulator might regard as inequitably large profits.

Economists have tried to weigh the attractions of different institutional types, or natural monopoly governance structures, and two such analyses are compared here. The first is that of Littlechild (1983) designed to evaluate the different possibilities for regulating the privatised UK telecommunications industry. Littlechild's options were: no regulation; two profits-confiscation regimes (rate of return, and profits ceiling); and two incentive schemes (a profits tax that diminished proportionally with output increases, or output-related profits levy, and a price cap based on the rate of inflation or local tariff reduction). These regulatory options were compared against a set of desirable criteria in five categories. The first two were protection against monopoly and efficiency and innovation, traditional concerns of welfare economists. Littlechild's next two categories were the burden of regulation and promotion of competition. One of his objectives was to implement 'regulation with a light hand' so as to avoid the regulatory distortions and costs characteristic of US regulatory experience. By competition Littlechild seems to have had in mind the idea of rivalry, since he simultaneously scored the unregulated regime as best on competition but worst on protection against monopoly. His last category was the likely proceeds of the share flotation for

TABLE 9.1 Littlechild (1983): final ranking of schemes for regulating BT's profitability (1 = best, 5 = worst)

	No constraints	Max. rate of return	Output-related profit levy	Profit ceiling	Local tariff reduction
Protection against monopoly	5	3	2	4	1
Efficiency and innovation	1 =	4 =	4 =	3	1 =
Burden of regulation	1	5	4	3	2
Promotion of competition	1	5	4	2 =	2 =
Proceeds and prospects	1 =	4	5	3	1 =

Reproduced with the permission of the Controller, HMSO.

the Government. Note that the confusion between a method of funding the Government's budget deficit, i.e. asset sales, and a reduction in the deficit itself has been characteristic of deregulation in many parts of the world. Table 9.1 sets out Littlechild's cost benefit analysis.

On all categories except protection against monopoly, Little-child felt that a regime of no constraints scored best, but his overall winner was the incentive regulation mechanism based on a price cap which he referred to as local tariff reduction. A similar tabulation was suggested by Crew and Kleindorfer (1986) and a summary version of this is illustrated in Table 9.2. In their matrix Crew and Kleindorfer divided the attributes of alternative governance structures into three major categories: efficiency, equity and transactions costs. The efficiency attributes were subdivided into the familiar categories of price efficiency, x-efficiency, dynamic efficiency and scale effects, while equity attributes included the control of prices and 'fairness' by which Crew and Kleindorfer meant equal audience in the regulatory process for all parties, utility, consumers, and government. Their third category reflected the transactions costs of the regulatory process and accounted for both the burden of regulatory expenditures and the incentive to incur the sunk costs of investing in the types of capital asset specific

TABLE 9.2   Crew and Kleindorfer (1986): properties of alternative regulatory governance structures (1 = good, 0 = bad)

	Regulation structure	Regulated rate of return	Incentive regulation	Public enterprise	Franchise auctions	No regulation
Efficiency attributes	Price	0	1	0	0	0
	x-efficiency	0	1	0	1	1
	Dynamic	0	1	0	0	1
	Scale	1	1	1	1	0
Equity attributes						
	Price control	1	1	1	1	0
	Fairness	1	0	0	1	0
Transaction cost attributes						
	Burden	1	1	1	0	1
	Asset-Specific	1	1	1	0	0

to the industry. These subdivisions gave eight attributes in all. Crew and Kleindorfer compared five governance structures: regulated rate of return (i.e. cost of service regulation), incentive regulation in the sense of decoupling prices from reported costs described earlier, nationalised public enterprises, auctioning the natural monopoly franchise and, finally, no regulation. Crew and Kleindorfer's subjective scoring (1 = good, 0 = bad) set out in Table 9.2 indicates their belief that incentive regulation scores well on the widest range of criteria. They argue that franchise auctions and no regulation fail to provide an incentive to incur sunk cost investments in specific assets (a reflection of the fact that contestable markets theory is not applicable to the network-specific public utilities). Public enterprise and rate of return regulation, on the other hand, offer little incentive to cost reduction or the provision of efficient price structures such as those reflecting peak loads.

Nevertheless, practical problems of implementation not addressed in Tables 9.1 and 9.2 do arise with incentive regulation.

For example in the context of equation (9.16), how is c_t^* to be estimated in practice? One possibility is a full-scale econometric/ accounting audit – but this implies heavy regulatory costs, thereby destroying the argument for regulation with a light hand. A second possibility is to use the average cost reported by other comparable firms – yardstick competition, which allows the regulated utility to keep a share of the difference between its costs and those of the other firms. However this raises problems of *collusion* as the utilities have a counter-incentive to cooperate in misleading the regulator and *comparability* when the utilities differ in important cost-related factors. A more practicable possibility is to use $c_{t-1}[1 + RPI - X]$; where $RPI - X$ is the rate of retail price inflation less some allowance for efficiency improvement. This could be inaccurate unless X is frequently reviewed, but it is an inexpensive form of incentive. The implied question is, how is X to be decided at the regulatory review? This is almost precisely the suggestion made by Littlechild (1983) and it is discussed in more detail in section 9.8 below.

9.5 REGULATION UNDER ASYMMETRIC INFORMATION

A fundamental assumption made throughout the analysis so far is that the regulator and the utility have access to the same information, so that each is engaged in a game of symmetric information. Dropping this assumption means examining regulatory models which make use of principal–agent analysis. The analysis of regulation as a principal–agent game stems from the view that a regulated utility will generally know more about its costs and performance than the regulator. The regulator, however, must persuade the utility to carry out its production and pricing decisions in a way which optimises the regulator's social welfare criterion. The literature on this topic is very large but is superbly summarised in Baron (1989) and Besanko and Sappington (1987).

There are at least four different aspects to the asymmetric information issue. Firstly, the utility may be better informed about the technological possibilities available for meeting its output target at minimum cost. This is the problem of hidden information or *adverse selection*. This term arises in the literature on risk and insurance and reflects the idea that when the typifying character-istics of a consumer cannot be observed by the insurance company, the company is likely to attract the worst risks if it offers a standard contract. The problem of adverse selection is to design a menu of contracts that indicate by their different choices the consumers' individual characteristics. Secondly, the utility knows how much unobservable effort it puts into reducing costs when those costs are also affected by unobservable random shocks. This is the problem of hidden action or *moral hazard*. Again, this is an insurance market term and it refers to the fact that once a contract is settled the insured party may no longer undertake the precautionary but unobservable care and effort to minimise his risk. The problem is to provide an agent with an incentive to use his best efforts. Thirdly, even if the regulator and utility agree on costs, the utility's owners may be risk-averse so that there are efficiency gains to trading some of their risks with the regulator. Fourthly, the vari-ables of particular interest to the regulator e.g. output or quality of supply may not be directly measurable or observable so that there is a monitoring issue.

We begin with a very naïve regulatory model which has never-theless been useful for setting the parameters of the debate on these issues. Loeb and Magat (1979) (hereafter LM) introduced an idea which has led to many developments in the regulatory litera-ture. Its importance is not in its practicality (which is nearly non-existent), but in its ability to illustrate important ideas in a clear light. Here I will adopt the LM contract to illustrate what economists mean by a 'truth-telling mechanism'. It is linked to the ideas of incentive-compatible preference revelation mechanisms in auction theory, and public goods theory.

There are two players; the principal is the regulator, and the agent is the utility. The regulator knows:

(i) the utility's demand curve: $q = D(p)$
(ii) how to calculate marginal cost given the value of an unknown parameter γ: $MC = MC(\gamma)$.

Figure 9.4 sets out the basic analysis.

The utility knows the value of the parameter γ, which measures its technical efficiency or productivity or other exogenous factors affecting costs. However, γ does not measure effort in our example – in the words we met earlier we are looking at an adverse

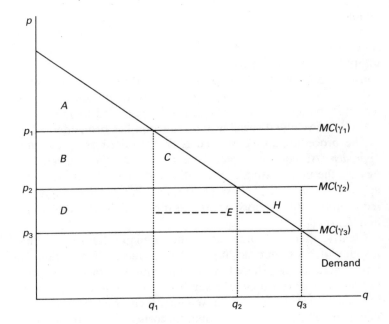

FIGURE 9.4   Loeb–Magat (LM) mechanism

selection model rather than a moral hazard model. LM did not distinguish these. The usual model has γ as a random variable, with the utility able to observe its realisation and act upon it prior to selling its output at the regulated price, while the regulator remains ignorant of γ. Suppose the realisation of the random variable is $γ_2$ in Figure 9.4.

If the regulator simply asks the utility to report γ and then sets price so that $p = MC(γ)$, the utility will report $γ_1$ and obtain a high price. The regulator needs a mechanism to persuade the utility to say γ is $γ_2$ and accept a price of $p = MC(γ_2)$. The LM contract says the utility is to announce γ; the regulator stipulates $p = MC$(announced γ) and observes the market demand at this price. The regulator then pays the utility all the consumer surplus up to the observed price and quantity. If the utility announces $γ_1$, it sells q_1 at p_1 and receives the transfer of consumer surplus (in addition to its profit) of A. But by announcing $γ_2$, it would receive a transfer of $A + B + C$, which it prefers. However, it does not go further and announce γ_3, because while it would receive $A + B + C + D + E$, it would incur costs of $D + E + H$ over and above its actual revenues, leaving it with $A + B + C - H < A + B + C$. Hence the utility tells the truth, price is set at marginal cost, and the sum of consumer and producer surplus is maximised. Note that the preoccupation here is with finding the allocatively efficient outcome. The distribution of the social surplus is regarded as immaterial since an unweighted social-welfare function has been adopted.

The procedure just described is characterised as a *revelation approach*. An equivalent procedure would have the regulator delegating the price-setting to the utility and simply transferring the appropriate amount of consumer surplus when the demand resulting from the utility's price decision is observed. This is the *delegation approach*.

Clearly, there are drawbacks: the regulator transfers a huge amount of consumer surplus to the producer. If we adopt an unweighted social-welfare function this equity problem is ignored, but one way of recouping the surplus is to auction the right to be the monopolist. If we adopt a weighted social-welfare function so that every £1 transferred to producers costs £$(1 + \lambda)$ to raise from consumers or the rest of the economy, then we will want to qualify the LM contract, perhaps by trading off a loss of allocative efficiency for a gain in terms of the regulator's distributive weighting of consumers against the producing utility. These qualifications make up the literature on adverse selection regulatory contracts, to which we now turn.

9.6   REGULATION UNDER ADVERSE SELECTION

Here I take the simplest standard adverse selection problem to illustrate the basic ideas of this literature with a model analysed in Besanko and Sappington (1987).

A regulator knows the utility's demand schedule, $q = D(p)$, and how to calculate marginal cost given a cost parameter, c_i, where $i = H$ or L for high and low costs. The regulator does not know the realisation of the binary random variable c_i but has a set of prior beliefs which amount to a probability distribution for c_i: ϕ_H, ϕ_L. The regulator wishes to maximise a weighted social-welfare function in which the relative weights on consumer and producer surplus (β and $(1 - \beta)$) are different. This is shown in equation (9.17).

$$W = \beta[S(p) + T] + (1 - \beta)[\pi] \qquad (9.17)$$

where S is consumers' surplus, π is utility's profit, and T is a negative lump-sum transfer from the consumers to the utility. The utility has a reservation profit, π^*, e.g. the breakeven level at which it just decides to participate in the business.

The regulator's instruments are contained in the range of contracts offered: $[p_i, T_i]$ i.e. a combination of a price cap and a transfer payment for each possible cost announcement by the utility. The choices correspond to the possible realisations of the cost parameter, high or low. If the regulator knew the realisation of marginal cost, she could implement the first-best solution: $\pi = \pi^*$, $p_i = MC(c_i)$, $q_i = D(p_i)$. However, the regulator can only design a contract to ensure truth-telling in the face of her uncertainty. She maximises the expected value of social welfare subject to the constraints of (i) inducing participation in the business, and (ii) ensuring truth-telling (incentive compatibility). This formulation of the objective which incorporates the regulator's prior beliefs about the probability distribution of the random elements in the model corresponds to the *Bayesian* approach to regulatory mechanism design:

$$\max EW = \sum_i \phi_i \{\beta[S(p(c_i) + T(c_i)] + (1 - \beta)[\pi(c_i)]\};$$
$$\text{where } i = H \text{ or } L \qquad (9.18)$$

subject to:

$$\pi(c_i) \geq \pi^* \qquad [IR] \qquad (9.19)$$

and

$$\pi(p(c_i), T(c_i), c_i) \geq \pi(p(c_j), T(c_j), c_i);$$
$$i, j = H \text{ or } L \qquad [ICC] \qquad (9.20)$$

The first constraint is the participation or individual rationality constraint, IR, while the second is a set of incentive compatibility constraints, ICC. These ensure that when the utility really has cost parameter c_i, it cannot do better than self-select the contract offered for announcing that value, compared with the contract for announcing some other value, c_j.

The optimal solution is characterised by the following behaviour.

If the cost parameter realisation is c_L, then:

the utility selects p_L, T_L, where $p_L = MC(c_L)$,
the first-best output is produced; but
T_L is large enough to ensure strictly $\pi > \pi^*$.

If the cost parameter realisation is c_H, then:

the utility selects p_H, T_H, where $p_H = MC(c_H) + I_H$,
the second-best output, $q_H < q_H^*$ is produced; and
T_H is only large enough to ensure strictly $\pi = \pi^*$.

The term I_H is the incentive correction, and $I_H = [\phi_L/\phi_H][2\beta - 1][MC(c_H) - MC(c_L)]$ with $I_H = 0$, when $\beta = [1/2]$. This means it is the existence of unequal weights in the social-welfare function which gives rise to the divergence of price from marginal cost when the high cost parameter is realised.

Figure 9.5 illustrates the argument behind the solution. Along the horizontal axis is measured the output level permitted to the firm – i.e. the output that results from the permitted price. The first-best (symmetric information) levels are q_H^* if cost is $MC(c_H)$ and q_L^* if cost is $MC(c_L)$. Along the vertical axis are the payments to the firm under the regulatory contract: $R = pq - T$. The permitted price is p, which implies output q, and the lump-sum transfer is T. Apart from c_i, these completely determine the firm's profits. Start at q_H^* and point B on the $\pi(c_H)$ curve. This curve is the iso-profit locus (profit-indifference curve) between output and regulatory payments for a firm with the c_H realisation. The curve rises steeply because large increments in R are needed to induce higher output when cost is high. Higher profits are indicated by curves to the northwest, (upper left). The particular $\pi(c_H)$ curve chosen is the one which intercepts the vertical axis at π^*, the reservation level of profit.

Now for cost announcements which imply output levels below

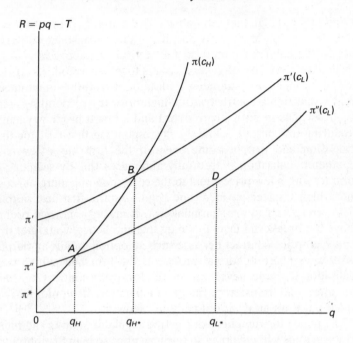

FIGURE 9.5 Regulation with adverse selection

q_H^*, the firm will be regulated as if it is a c_H firm. An example is the second best q_H at A. This contract will however be rejected by a c_L firm. Why? Because the $\pi(c_L)$ iso-profit curves for c_L realisations are always less steeply sloped than the $\pi(c_H)$ curves, since with low costs the firm will always be able to raise profits more readily than a c_H firm by expanding output when it has a given set of regulatory payments. This means that if it was to be treated as a c_H firm and offered compensation along $\pi(c_H)$ in reducing output from B, the c_L firm would actually be moving to a lower iso-profit curve – e.g. $\pi''(c_L)$ instead of $\pi'(c_L)$. It would reject such a contract.

Now start at point A. For cost announcements which imply output levels above the second best q_H at A, the firm is compensated along $\pi''(c_L)$ as if it has a c_L realisation. This leaves the c_L firm indifferent between, say, D and A, so that we shall assume it does produce the first-best output q_L^* at D. Such a contract will be rejected by a firm with a c_H realisation because D is on a lower iso-profit locus than that through π^*. The c_H firm at A breaks even, while the c_L firm at D earns positive profits because its iso-profit locus is flat enough to intercept the vertical axis above π^*.

Thus we can pull our general results together as follows. If the firm has a high-cost parameter realisation it truthfully announces this by selecting a contract with a high price (corresponding marginal cost plus incentive correction) and a low transfer payment, producing low output below the corresponding first best for this realisation and just breaking even. If the firm has a low-cost parameter realisation it truthfully announces this by selecting a contract with a low price equal to the corresponding marginal cost and a high transfer payment and producing the first-best output that corresponds to low marginal cost. It makes abnormal profits above the breakeven level by doing this and hence would not opt for a high-price contract because such an option entails an output too low to make abnormal profits. If the firm had a high cost realisation it would never opt for the low-price contract because the price and transfer payment combination it would receive would put it on an iso-profit contour below π^*.

The policy instruments work by the regulator sharing the high-cost firm's costs but in doing so setting a price so high that output is too small to be attractive to the firm with a low-cost realisation. The low-cost firm is capped at marginal cost and produces first-best output, but is subsidised by T large enough to ensure $\pi > \pi^*$ to cover its informational rents, i.e. it continues to make some abnormal profit which reflects its monopoly of information. In a manner of speaking the optimal regulatory mechanism trades off market power against informational monopoly by offering a menu of contracts that associates low output with breakeven performance and high output with abnormal profits. The degree of incentive correction is entirely dependent on the regulator's social welfare weightings and her prior beliefs about the probability distribution of c_i, and it is these factors which differentiate this outcome from the LM mechanism.

9.7   INCENTIVES IN PRINCIPAL–AGENT RELATIONSHIPS

Adverse selection is only one of these issues in regulation under asymmetric information, and we now consider a more general treatment. This is a description of the fundamental principal–agent model, with a particular emphasis on moral hazard problems, and is based on Sappington (1991). Again this is a Bayesian approach to regulatory mechanism design incorporating the regulator's probabilistic beliefs about the firm's environment.

Using Sappington's notation, let P be the principal (regulator) and A be the agent (utility). Both P and A are assumed to be risk-neutral, and both share the same prior beliefs about a random productivity variable, r. High realisations of r raise output, Z. A's expected output performance also depends on A's effort, e, which remains unknown to P. Thus, in expected value notation, (where $E(x)$ is the expected value of a random variable x):

$$E(Z) = f(r, e); \partial f/\partial r > 0; \partial f/\partial e > 0$$

while P's valuation of output is:

$$V = V(Z), V' > 0; V'' \leq 0$$

The structure of the game is then

(i) P designs a contract to pay A for performance: $p = p(Z)$; and this contract is offered to A.
(ii) A accepts or rejects, (if A rejects, the game ends).
For A to accept, he must expect a utility of payment, U, at least as large as his reservation utility, U^*. Hence, A will accept only if $E(U(p(Z))) \geq U^*$.
(iii) If A accepts, A starts work, and observes the realisation of r.
(iv) A decides on the level of e.
(v) The realisation of Z is observed, and payment is made, according to $p = p(Z)$.

For any Z to be produced, the opportunity cost of U^* must be incurred. The first-best, full information equilibrium for P is where

(i) A chooses the value of e which, given the value of r, maximises P's expected surplus: $E(V(Z))$ – cost of effort including U^*. This is $e^*(r)$.
(ii) P collects all the surplus leaving A with U^*.

In Figure 9.6 A has a utility function $U(e, p)$ and therefore indifference curves between effort ('bad') and payment ('good'): e.g. U' and U^* where U' represents a higher level of utility than the

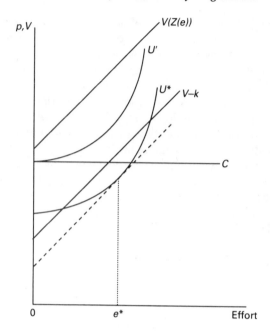

FIGURE 9.6   Incentives and principal–agent contracts

reservation level U^*. P's valuation of output rises as output rises, which in turn rises as effort increases, for a given value of r. This is represented by the $V(Z(e))$ line with positive slope. In the first-best, full information equilibrium which assumes that P can directly observe A's effort, effort is at e^* where P's surplus, $[V(Z) - U^*]$, is maximised, and A just participates at utility level U^*. This first-best outcome is located where the broken line parallel to $V(Z(e))$ is tangent to U^* thus maximising the vertical distance between V and U^*. Now hold the random productivity variable constant to examine the moral hazard issue. The first-best outcome is no longer attainable since we will now assume more realistically that effort cannot be observed. With unobservable effort (hidden action) A will have an incentive to be x-inefficient. Suppose P pays A a fixed sum, C, to produce output. C is represented in Figure 9.6 by a horizontal line. A seeks to reach his highest indifference curve subject to the constraint represented by the flat fee, C, and does so at a corner solution gaining utility U' with zero effort.

How can P induce an effort level of e^*? Instead of a flat fee, A is made to be the franchisee to the output production, and is given the residual claim to the surplus above a fixed franchise fee, k, payable to the principal. Thus A becomes the residual claimant to $V - U^* - k$. The vertical distance between $V - k$ and U^* is maximised by A by choosing effort level e^*. But P, even without observing effort, can choose k to be any level which leaves A as residual claimant to U^* or more. Therefore P is able to claim all the surplus herself, leaving A to deliver e^* in order to reach U^*. Note that P has no incentive to devote resources to gathering additional information.

In the UK regulatory system, the most celebrated residual claimant contract is the *RPI-X* price cap. Section 9.8 below explains how this works and why it can be interpreted as a residual claimant contract. The flat fee contract by contrast is equivalent to a profits-confiscation contract, such as the instruction to price at marginal cost.

Sappington shows the foregoing solution to depend on four critical assumptions:

(1) *Symmetry of pre-contractual beliefs about r*. However, the agent may know more about the likely value of r than the principal, and then A can lie about whether he has high or low productivity. This introduces an adverse selection problem. Rather than giving A all of the surplus to reveal his type, P may then use a sharing contract, in which the agent gets less than 100 per cent of improved performance, but bears less than 100 per cent of the costs of low productivity.

(2) *Risk-neutrality of the agent*. If the agent is risk-averse, while the principal is risk-neutral, an efficient sharing of risk improves on the solution which gives A all the risk. In fact A will want more than U^* to participate in the game if he is risk-averse. Instead of giving A a larger guaranteed U, P may prefer to bear some of the risk herself.

(3) *Complete commitment ability i.e. neither P nor A can renege on the contract if realised r turns out to be low*. Again a sharing contract may persuade A to perform even when r is low and the possibility of reneging exists. Sharing contracts have a parameter,

α, which represents the fraction of cost overruns or suplus gains taken by P. If $\alpha = 1$ there is a cost plus contract, while if $\alpha = 0$ there is a fixed price (residual claimant) contract. In adverse selection problems there may be a menu of sharing contracts, from high U^* and low α, to high α and low U^*. This is a form of separating equilibrium in which different types of agents self-select different contracts.

(4) *A's output performance (including quality aspects) is observable*. Without complete observability P has to gather additional information. The signals may be imperfect and impose additional risks on A, which require sharing. One useful form of residual claimant contract is to relate the franchise fee to the 'yardstick' performance of other agents. This may lead to duplicate sourcing, or permitting the entry of more than the socially-optimal number of agents to the industry, e.g. several firms in a natural monopoly network utility like telecommunications. With risk-aversion sharing is still needed. Two difficult issues which however then arise are collusion and comparability problems for the principal when applying yardsticks amongst the multiple supplying agents.

Finally, where the game is repeated, it may be very difficult to persuade the agent to divulge any information by a sharing contract because of a ratchet effect. This would occur if every time an agent revealed information about his characteristics or chose a maximal effort level, the principal could be expected to use this information to establish higher standards of attainment in the next round of the game. The agent will have an added incentive to perform badly in early stages of the game to reduce the stringency of performance standards sought by the regulator later in the game. Only large guaranteed surpluses to the agent may produce any participation at all – a characteristic of centrally planned economies. We will see an example of this outcome in a repeated game in the next section of the chapter.

9.8 PRICE-CAP MECHANISMS AND *RPI-X*

We have already seen that marginal cost pricing and cost of service regulation are seen as cost plus mechanisms. Price caps may be fixed price mechanisms, and they may also be regarded as residual claimant contracts under a moral hazard situation. They may further be seen as simple *non-Bayesian* incentive mechanisms when the regulator lacks all but the most elementary published historical accounting data. It all depends on the nature of the regulatory review. Critical points to note in what follows are that in general we assume the utilities are multiproduct natural monopolies, and the regulator is interested less in the structure of prices than in their level.

The basic theoretical model is the Vogelsang–Finsinger (1979) (hereafter V–F) mechanism (see also Vogelsang, 1990). They asked: how could a regulator push a utility towards Ramsey prices, if the regulator's only information consists of last year's profit and loss accounts? She does not even know the shape or position of the demand curve, nor is she going to attempt any difficult Bayesian contract design.

First, V–F assume that the regulator's objective is the maximisation of unweighted social surplus:

$$W(p) = S(p) + \pi(p)$$

In Figure 9.7, we have iso-profit and iso-welfare contours drawn in price space together with the corresponding demand schedules, (recall that we are dealing with multiproduct utilities). The demand schedules are unknown to the regulator but she can observe the quantities sold at last year's prices. In the prices quadrant, higher profit lies to the northeast, while higher consumer surplus lies to the southwest. The iso-welfare contour corresponding to $\pi(p) = 0$ is just the contour representing $S(p)$ alone. The slope of the $S(p)$ contour is $-[q_1/q_2]$. The tangency between the $S(p)$ contour and the $\pi(p) = 0$ contour at E gives the Ramsey prices. To emphasise this refer back to the discussion of equation (9.13), and Figure 9.2. The slope along any of the iso-profit contours is: $-[(\partial\pi/\partial p_1)/(\partial\pi/\partial p_2)] = -[(MR_1 - MC_1)/(MR_2 - MC_2)]$ and if we evaluate marginal revenue and cost with respect to price changes, this can be written:

$$-[q_1 + (p_1 - MC_1)(dq_1/dp_1)]/[q_2 + (p_2 - MC_2)(dq_2/dp_2)]$$

However at the Ramsey prices the conditions of equation (9.13)

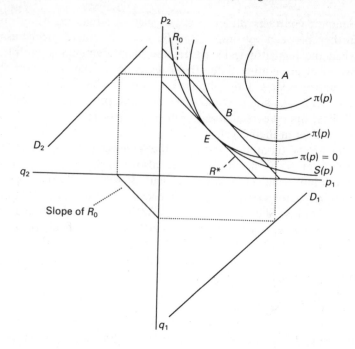

FIGURE 9.7   Vogelsang–Finsinger mechanism

hold so that the $\pi(p) = 0$ iso-profit contour's slope at the Ramsey point E is:

$$-[q_1 - (\lambda/1 + \lambda)q_1]/[q_2 - (\lambda/1 + \lambda)q_2] = -q_1/q_2$$

and is therefore equal to the slope of the $S(p)$ iso-welfare contour at that point.

In Figure 9.7, the unregulated profit-maximising utility is initially observed at the point A. The ratio of the quantities sold at these prices gives the tangent slope of an $S(p)$ contour through A. The regulator says that the utility in the next period must put consumers on a $S(p)$ contour nearer the origin. She does this by stipulating that it can choose any prices in the region, R_0, whose boundary has the same slope as the $S(p)$ contour through A. In Figure 9.7 this region is shown as the set of price pairs between the origin and the linear boundary through B. Thus the regulator leaves the structure of prices entirely to the utility–price structure is deregulated–but the level of prices is reduced by being constrained to be an element of the set R_0. Next period the utility chooses price structure B by locating the tangency between the boundary of the price constraint set R_0 and the highest attainable $\pi(p)$ iso-profit contour. The regulator now chooses the slope of the next period's price boundary to be equal to the ratio of the current quantities: $-q_1/q_2$, but locates the boundary even closer to the origin. The process is repeated as the utility chooses in each period a new price structure to reach the highest attainable iso-profit contour. Each period the regulator transfers last period's profits to this period's consumers by pushing the boundary inwards but always keeping its slope tangential to the previous iso-welfare contour. In this way the boundary of each period's price set, R, represents a linear approximation to last period's welfare contour but displaced closer to the origin.

Eventually the regulator will push the boundary so close to the origin, (e.g. at R^*), that the highest attainable iso-profit contour for the utility is $\pi(p) = 0$. The utility will choose to locate at a point where the $\pi(p) = 0$ contour is tangent to the limiting price boundary, but since the slope of the boundary is $-[q_1/q_2]$, the chosen point must be at E corresponding to the tangency between the $\pi(p) = 0$ contour and an $S(p)$ iso-welfare contour. As we already know this is exactly the point which corresponds to the Ramsey prices. We conclude therefore that by each period's self-selection of the profit-maximising prices subject only to locating on a boundary with slope $-[q_1/q_2]$ the regulated utility converges in the limit on the Ramsey prices.

Formally, the region R is defined as: $R = \{p_t: \Sigma q_{it-1} p_{it} - C(q_{it-1}) \leq 0\}$. This says that R is a region in price space such that total revenue from last period's quantities evaluated at this period's regulated prices cannot exceed last period's reported costs. Note that since last period's costs can be treated as a datum, C_{t-1}, the slope of a boundary in the two-product case defined by the equation: $p_1 q_{1t-1} + p_2 q_{2t-1} - C_{t-1} = 0$ is simply $dp_2/dp_1 = -[q_{1t-1}/q_{2t-1}]$, and this reflects the mechanism sketched in Figure 9.7 without requiring the regulator to know more than last period's accounting data.

Suppose all prices are measured in real terms: $[p_1, \ldots p_n]$. The regime leaves $[p_1, \ldots p_n]$ unregulated, but caps an index of the real prices: M, where the weights are last year's quantities, q_{it-1}. That is,

$$M = \Sigma q_{it-1} p_{it}; \quad M_t = M_{t-1}[1 - X] \qquad (9.21)$$

The X factor is then last year's profit as a percentage of turnover: $[\pi_{t-1}/\Sigma q_{it-1} p_{it-1}]$. The explanation goes as follows. The definition of last year's profit $[\Sigma q_{it-1} p_{it-1} - C(q_{it-1})] = \pi_{t-1}$ can be used in conjunction with the definition of R to write:

$$\Sigma q_{it-1} p_{it} - C(q_{it-1}) \leq 0 \equiv \Sigma q_{it-1} p_{it-1} - C(q_{it-1}) - \pi_{t-1}$$

and now cancelling the costs and dividing through both sides of the identity by last year's turnover, we obtain:

$$[\Sigma q_{it-1} p_{it}]/[\Sigma q_{it-1} p_{it-1}] \leq 1 - [\pi_{t-1}]/[\Sigma q_{it-1} p_{it-1}] \qquad (9.22)$$

The expression on the left is a Laspeyres, base-weighted chain index of the utility's prices and the expression on the right shows that this is falling at the lagged rate of profits as a percentage of turnover. The V–F mechanism then corresponds to 100 per cent confiscation, (V–F use 'sharing') of last year's profits.

Figure 9.8 illustrates the single-product case, though this loses the main point of the analysis which is to leave the structure of prices unregulated, while capping the level of prices.

Applying the V–F algebra: the regulator observes p_0, q_0, c_0 in year 0. She sets $p_1 = c_0$, so that:

$$p_1/p_0 = c_0/p_0,$$

so that in turn, $[p_1 - p_0]/p_0 = [c_0 q_0 - p_0 q_0]/p_0 q_0 = -\pi_0/p_0 q_0$

Figure 9.9 presents Sappington's (1980) critique of the V–F mechanism. The firm may be surprised by the first application of the V–F mechanism, but in the second period, now anticipating the regulation, it has an incentive to waste resources in order to be given a higher price cap. Note that this is a two-edged sword, because wasted resources are sacrificed profits although they may be used to enhance the utility of the firm's managers (yet another

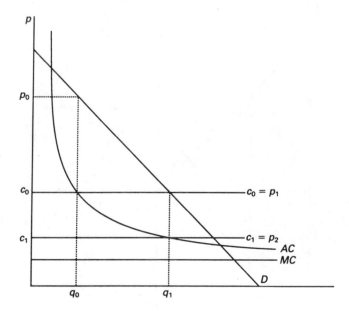

FIGURE 9.8 **Single-product *V-F* mechanism**

version of a principal–agent problem) and all that the firm can do is delay the approach to the Ramsey optimum. In Figure 9.9, the firm begins with an unregulated price p_1, and announces costs of c.

The regulator imposes a second-period price of $p_2 = c$, with output $q(c)$. The firm can raise the second period's price cap by indulging in the waste level, w, achieving output level q_2. It is then trading off two present-value profit streams (with discount rate ρ):

$$PV(1) = [p_1 - c]q_1 + [0/(1 + \rho)];$$
$$PV(2) = [p_1 - c - w]q_1 + wq_2/(1 + \rho) \tag{9.23}$$

and waste will be incurred ($PV(1) < PV(2)$ with $w > 0$) if $[(q_2/q_1) - 1] > \rho$.

The essence of the Sappington critique is that the V–F mechanism assumes that the utility is myopic, whereas it is likely to behave strategically, maximising the present value of its future income stream. It is encapsulated in the familiar complaint that if a utility

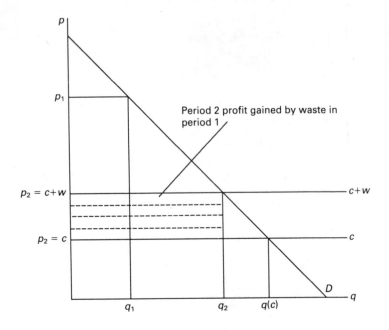

FIGURE 9.9   Sappington's critique of the *V–F* mechanism

declares large profits it should be made to lower its prices. If the utility had been subject to a residual claimant contract and then came to believe this profits-confiscation contract would be imposed on it, it would simply never declare large profits again, and the x-efficiency gains of the residual claimant contract would be lost.

Finsinger and Vogelsang (1982) present an extension to the dynamic case to cope with this Sappington critique. The essence is still confiscation of last year's profits but with an offsetting subsidy which is larger the closer the utility gets to allocative efficiency. In each year the utility's regulated income, I_t, consists of its current profits minus last year's profits plus a subsidy which is positive only if it reduces prices this year compared with last year:

$$I_t = \pi_t - \pi_{t-1} + q_{t-1}(p_{t-1} - p_t) \tag{9.24}$$

In the static case, the utility can completely recover its confiscated profits by reducing this year's price to last year's unit cost. In the dynamic case the convergence to allocative efficiency takes longer. Assume the utility seeks to maximise the present value of its income stream by choosing a profile of output levels:

$$\max \sum_{t=0}^{t=\infty} [\pi_t - \pi_{t-1} + q_{t-1} (p_{t-1} - p_t)](1 + \rho)^{-t} \qquad (9.25)$$

The first-order conditions then include pairs of consecutive terms such as:

$$[\partial \pi_t / \partial q_t - q_{t-1}(dp_t/dq_t)](1 + \rho)^{-t} - [\partial \pi_t / \partial q_t - p_t - q_t$$
$$(dp_t/dq_t) + p_{t+1}](1 + \rho)^{-(t+1)} = 0 \qquad (9.26)$$

Recognising that $\partial \pi_t / \partial q_t = p_t - MC_t + q_t(dp_t/dq_t)$, this yields with some rearranging:

$$(\rho/(1 + \rho))[q_t(dp_t/dq_t) + p_t - MC_t] - q_{t-1}(dp_t/dq_t) +$$
$$(1/(1 + \rho))[p_t - p_{t+1} + q_t(dp_t/dq_t)] = 0$$

If a steady state solution in which $q_t = q_{t+1} = q_{t+2} = \cdots$. exists for these difference equations, then it must include: $p_t = MC_t$ as t approaches ∞. In other words this is a regulatory mechanism which could converge to marginal cost pricing in the limit. Baron (1989) has neatly categorised such mechanisms as the dynamic equivalent of LM, with the dynamic subsidy repayment replacing the auction mechanism of the static case.

The issue of profits confiscation versus x-efficiency remains in all these non-Bayesian mechanisms, in which the price cap diminishes in a way that confiscates previous profits. The alternative x-efficient mechanism is simply to fix X exogenously when the utility is changed from public ownership to investor owned utility status. This is a residual claimant contract which may allow the utility to make large profits while still reducing costs and prices. It is represented by the Littlechild (1983) *RPI-X* mechanism (see also Beesley and Littlechild, 1989), and takes the form, (where M is now an index of the utility's *nominal* prices):

$$M = \Sigma q_i p_i, \text{ and: } M_t = M_{t-1} [1 + RPI - X] \qquad (9.27)$$

Note the tariff basket issue here: V–F and some UK utilities' *RPI-X* contracts have *last year's* quantities as weights, which are therefore out of the utility's current control (but which, nevertheless, could be subject to forward-looking strategic manipulation). Other UK utilities have *this year's* quantities as weights, which are therefore endogenous to the utility. It can be shown that this latter 'average revenue' cap means no convergence to Ramsey prices (Bradley and Price, 1989).

The policy dilemma in price-cap regulation (i.e. should X be equal to the previous profit rate as in V–F or set exogenously as in Littlechild) re-emerges when the utility is due for regulatory review of its X factor. How is the X factor to be set for a natural monopoly utility? The polar cases appear to be as follows: a cost plus cap, or a fixed price cap. The first is price-efficient, but x-inefficient and it could be based on (i) the rate of profit over previous years as in the V–F mechanism, or (ii) the achieved rate of return on capital. The second is x-efficient, but the firm retains a share of its profits which may appear to ordinary consumers to be excessively large. The cap could be based on (i) an exogenous target for efficiency, or (ii) yardstick comparisons.

Yardstick comparisons with other comparable utilities are an attractive possibility for an incentive-based price cap that will not grossly distort allocative efficiency. One form of such a fixed price contract is that suggested by Shleifer (1985), in which each of a group of comparable regional monopolists has a price cap determined by the mean unit cost of the others in the group. This delivers a first-best outcome which satisfies the participation and incentive compatibility constraints on the regulated firms. When the firms differ in certain characteristics, the regulator can still obtain the first-best result by handicapping the firms according to the impact of these characteristics on the firm's unit costs.

Figure 9.10 illustrates the case of two monopolists with different unit cost curves, c_i, each of which depends on the amount of effort expended by the firm [$c_i = c_i(e_i)$]. This effort brings disutility to the firm's managers. Under yardstick regulation the firms' initial prices, p_i^*, may be capped at the mean observed unit cost, m. Alternatively, if the regulator believes the firms differ because of the impact of some exogenous characteristic of the operating environment, z, the price cap is [$m + bz_i$] where b is the slope coefficient in a regression of c_i against z_i. In Figure 9.10, firm 1

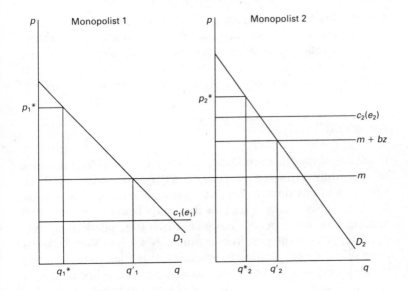

FIGURE 9.10 Yardstick competition

keeps the residual profit from having its unit cost below the price cap, although it clearly must produce a higher output, an effect which is welfare-improving. Firm 2 is in a more equivocal position. To beat the price cap even after allowance for the differential factor, z, it must increase effort to reduce costs, as well as expanding output. Otherwise it will make a loss, which violates the participation constraint in the regulator's optimisation programme. Increasing effort is costly for managers, so the firm has an incentive to adopt strategic behaviour to alter the impact of z in its favour if it can. This may involve attempting to ensure that z is a variable over which it has some control. Alternatively, in the UK case, it may seek judicial review of the regulator's cost comparisons. As Besanko and Sappington (1987, p. 64), argue 'When firms differ according to immutable observable characteristics, the [yardstick] incentive scheme . . . can be readily modified to effect the handicapping necessary to ensure the social optimum. When firms differ in ways that are not readily observable by the regulator, however, it will generally not be possible to implement the social optimum'. Wherever any leeway exists in the regulator's ability to impose an exogenous handicapping system, then the firm has a dimension of strategic behaviour which it may prefer to the option of reducing costs through additional effort. Hence the incentive compatibility constraint in the regulator's problem is violated, and the first-best efficient outcome does not emerge.

9.9 CONCLUSIONS

It will be obvious that regulatory economics is a large and complex subject, only a limited part of the surface of which has been scratched in this review. Positive regulation models of how regulators do behave rather than how they could behave have not been addressed, and the public choice approach to regulation has only been hinted at in the governance structures section. Very little has been said about regulation in practice rather than in theory, and no empirical studies have been examined. These are all highly relevant issues which the reader will need to explore for himself or herself. Undoubtedly however the lion's share of the recent literature has been devoted to incentive issues and the principal–agent model of regulator–utility interactions under asymmetric information. This has revolutionised the way economists think about regulatory problems, and it is an approach which is still rapidly evolving.

10 Linear and Non-linear Models of Economic Time Series: An Introduction with Applications To Industrial Economics

J. D. BYERS AND D. A. PEEL

10.1 INTRODUCTION

Cubbin and Geroski (1987) propose a mechanism by which the profits of firms in an industry converge to a long-run equilibrium. Their model focuses on the interaction between profits and entry or exit of firms. To illustrate, consider the following simplified version,

$$E_t = \alpha \rho_{t-1} + u_t \tag{10.1}$$

$$\rho_t = \beta E_t + \beta_1 \rho_{t-1} + \varepsilon_t \tag{10.2}$$

where E_t is some measure of entry or exit of firms into an industry, ρ_t is the deviation of observed profit rates from long-run or normal profit rates, α, β and β_1 are constants and u_t and ε_t are random disturbance terms. Substitution of equation (10.1) into (10.2) yields:

$$\rho_t = (\alpha\beta + \beta_1)\rho_{t-1} + \beta u_t + \varepsilon_t \tag{10.3}$$

Equation (10.3), which is the time-series process for profit rates, is called an autoregressive process of order one. As with equations (10.1) and (10.2), many structural models describing, for instance, industries, firms or other agents, will generate reduced-form time-series processes. In principle, such time-series processes can be estimated.

Estimates of the parameters of the time-series processes can be informative about the nature of the underlying structural model. If, for example, we found that profits were significantly related to profits not only in the previous period but also to those two periods before, then we could infer that the specification of the structural model (10.1) and (10.2) is inadequate. Similarly, if we found empirical evidence that lagged profits squared were significant determinants of current profits, we could reject a linear specification of the underlying structural model.

The empirical application and development of methods in time-series analysis have made a major impact on empirical research, particularly in macroeconomics and finance, over the last few years. More recently, such methods have begun to appear with increasing frequency in the industrial economics literature and, with the accumulation of data sets which permit time-series analysis, we would expect this trend to continue. The purpose of this chapter is to introduce and briefly review some of the salient literature.

In the next section we consider first stationary and non-stationary stochastic processes. The analysis is extended to a discussion of multivariate processes and the theory of cointegration. A further section introduces non-linear models and chaotic processes.

10.2   STOCHASTIC PROCESSES[1]

Stationary stochastic processes

A time series is a set of measurements on some variable taken at different, usually consecutive, points of time. We regard a T-element time series of observations on a variable, X, as a random drawing from the joint probability distribution of a collection of random variables indexed by time and denoted $X_t, t = 1, 2 \ldots, T$.

The problem is to estimate or test (a subset of) the parameters of this distribution. However, since there is usually no possibility of drawing more than one observation from the relevant joint distribution, i.e. of acquiring more than one observation on X for any time period, statistical inference requires that the observations through time provide information on the distribution of X_t at each point in time and can be used to estimate the parameters of the distribution. This is called the *ergodic property*. The assumption of *covariance stationarity* is sufficient for estimating the linear properties of the process generating the X_t, i.e. its means, variances and covariances.

Covariance stationarity requires (a) that the mean of X is constant, (b) that the variance, $V(X_t)$, is a finite constant and (c) that the covariance between X_t and X_{t+s}, for any s, $\text{cov}(X_t, X_{t+s})$, depends only upon s. We can write these as:

$$E(X_t) = \mu \text{ all } t \tag{10.4a}$$

$$V(X_t) = E(X_t - \mu)^2 = \sigma_x^2 \text{ all } t \tag{10.4b}$$

$$\text{cov}(X_t, X_{t+s}) = E(X_t - \mu)(X_{t+s} - \mu) = \gamma(s) \text{ all } s, t \tag{10.4c}$$

where E is the expectations operator. Stationarity implies $\gamma(s) = \gamma(-s)$ so that the function $\gamma(s)$, known as the *autocovariance function* (ACVF), is symmetrical about the origin. Using $\gamma(0) = \sigma_x^2$ we define the *autocorrelation function* (ACF) as:

$$\rho(s) = \frac{\text{cov}(X_t, X_{t+s})}{V(X_t)^{1/2} V(X_{t+s})^{1/2}}$$

$$= \frac{\text{cov}(X_t, X_{t+s})}{V(X_t)} \qquad \text{(using (10.4b))}$$

$$= \gamma(s)/\gamma(0) \tag{10.5}$$

As will be discussed below, the ACF can be used to decide which of a set of possible models is appropriate for modelling a particular time series.

Although most empirical time series exhibit serial dependence, a basic building block for modelling time series processes is the stationary, serially-uncorrelated, process known as *white noise*, which we will denote ε_t. White noise satisfies the conditions,

$$E(\varepsilon_t) = 0 \quad \text{all } t \tag{10.6a}$$

$$V(\varepsilon_t) = \sigma^2 \quad \text{all } t \tag{10.6b}$$

$$\text{cov}(\varepsilon_t, \varepsilon_{t+s}) = 0 \quad \text{all } t \tag{10.6c}$$

A stronger assumption is that ε_t is independently distributed. If, in addition, ε_t is normally distributed we refer to it as Gaussian white noise.

A *linear stochastic process* is a linear combination of its own past values and of the current and past values of other processes. *Autoregressive processes* are linear combinations of their own past values plus ε_t and *moving average processes* are linear combinations of current and past values of ε_t. The autoregressive process of order p, denoted AR(p), is written:

$$X_t = \phi_1 X_{t-1} + \phi_2 X_{t-2} + \phi_3 X_{t-3} + \ldots$$
$$+ \phi_p X_{t-p} + \varepsilon_t \tag{10.7}$$

or $\phi(L)X_t = \varepsilon_t$
where the lag polynomial $\phi(L) = 1 - \phi_1 L - \phi_2 L^2 \ldots - \phi_p L^p$ and L is the lag operator. The moving average process of order q, denoted MA(q), is written,

$$X_t = \varepsilon_t - \theta_1 \varepsilon_{t-1} - \theta_2 \varepsilon_{t-2} - \theta_3 \varepsilon_{t-3} - \ldots - \theta_q \varepsilon_{t-q} \tag{10.8}$$

or $X_t = \theta(L)\varepsilon_t$
with lag polynomial $\theta(L) = 1 - \theta_1 L - \theta_2 L^2 - \ldots - \theta_q L^q$
Both (10.7) and (10.8) can be written in the form,

$$X_t = \sum_{i=0}^{\infty} \beta_i \varepsilon_{t-i} = \beta(L)\varepsilon_t \tag{10.9}$$

which is referred to as the *general linear process*.

The MA(q) process is always stationary since, from the properties of ε_t, it follows that $E(X_t) = 0$ and

$$V(X_t) = (1 + \theta_1^2 + \theta_2^2 + \theta_3^2 + \ldots \theta_q^2)\sigma^2 \qquad (10.10)$$

It is easy to show that $\text{cov}(X_t, X_{t+s})$ depends only on s (see e.g. Harvey, 1981b, ch. 2). Things are more tricky when q is infinite. The mean of X_t will still be zero but its variance is

$$V(X_t) = \sigma^2 \sum_{i=0}^{\infty} \beta_i^2 \qquad (10.11)$$

which will be finite only if the infinite sum of the β_i^2 converges. The AR(p) process is stationary if the roots of the autoregressive lag polynomial are greater than unity in absolute value if real and have modulus exceeding unity if complex, i.e. if they lie outside the unit circle. If this condition is fulfilled an AR(p) process can be written as an infinite moving average. Similarly, an MA(q) process can be written as an infinite autoregressive process if the roots of the moving average polynomial lie outside the unit circle. These are known as the *invertibility conditions*.

So far the processes considered have had a constant mean of zero, something which is obviously not of wide applicability. This defect can be remedied by including a *deterministic component* such as a constant, a polynomial time trend or seasonal dummies in the process. The Wold Decomposition Theorem (see e.g. Priestley, 1981, pp. 755–60) establishes that any stationary process can be written as the sum of two mutually uncorrelated processes one of which is a linear deterministic function of time and one of which is purely indeterministic or stochastic and takes the form of an infinite MA as in (10.9). The latter can often be written as, or approximated by, the ratio of two finite order polynomials. Thus if the deterministic component is $f(t)$ and $\beta(L) = \theta(L)/\phi(L)$ we can write

$$X_t = f(t) + \beta(L)\varepsilon_t = f(t) + [\theta(L)/\phi(L)]\varepsilon_t \qquad (10.12)$$

or

$$\phi(L)[X_t - f(t)] = \theta(L)\varepsilon_t$$

This is an *autoregressive moving average model of order* (p, q) or ARMA (p, q).

Consider the stationary AR(1) process with a deterministic component, μ',

$$X_t - \mu' = \phi(X_{t-1} - \mu') + \varepsilon_\tau \tag{10.13}$$

where $|\phi| < 1$ is required for stationarity. If $\varepsilon_t = 0$ for all t then (10.13) can be treated as a first-order deterministic difference equation in a variable, $X_t - \mu'$, which measures the deviation of X_t from μ'. Since $|\phi| < 1$, $X_t - \mu'$ approaches zero as t approaches infinity and we can therefore think of μ' as the equilibrium value of X_t. All stationary processes share the characteristic that the effect of past shocks, ε_{t-k}, declines as k increases – implying that the autocorrelation function declines to zero – and can be thought of as being in stochastic equilibrium, with the current deviation from equilibrium being the outcome of the past history of shocks, and with forces tending to eliminate the gap between the current value and the equilibrium value.

The autocorrelation function for a stationary stochastic process declines in a manner characteristic to each specific process. It is this which enables the time series analyst to select or *identify* a statistical model to fit an observed time series. The MA(q) process, for example, is uncorrelated with all ε_{t-k} for $k > q$, implying that the ACF is non-zero only for k no greater than q. Subject to sampling variability, then, the autocorrelation function calculated from the data should have the first q values non-zero and zero sample autocorrelations thereafter. The ACF of an AR(p) process follows a p th-order homogeneous difference equation,

$$\rho(k) = \phi_1\rho(k-1) + \phi_2\rho(k-2) + \ldots \phi_k\rho(k-p) \tag{10.14}$$

for $k > p$. This difference equation is stable (i.e. $\rho(k)$ goes to zero) if the stationarity conditions are satisfied. The AR(1) process, for instance, has an ACF given by $\rho(k) = \phi^k$ with $\rho(0) = 1.0$. The ACF of a second-order process follows a second-order difference equation and its behaviour will depend upon the roots of this equation. One possibility is that the roots are complex conjugates. In this case the ACF behaves as a damped cycle. In general the ACF of a stationary p th -order autoregressive process consists of a mixture of damped exponentials and cycles so that, while a first-order process is pretty easy to spot, it is not so easy to differentiate between, say, a fifth-order process and a seventh-order process. In these cases the *partial autocorrelation function* (*PACF*) provides useful information. The PACF at lag k measures the additional information on X_t provided by X_{t-k} after the influence of the intervening lags is accounted for. It turns out that the AR(p) process has a PACF which 'cuts off' at lag p while the PACF of a moving average process of order q follows a qth-order difference equation.

Non-stationary processes

Many techniques for identifying, estimating and testing time-series models can be applied only to stationary stochastic processes.[2] Unfortunately economic time series frequently exhibit non-stationary behaviour, having a mean level which varies through time perhaps trending steadily upwards or varying from season to season. Non-stationarity is easily handled if it arises in the deterministic component of a time-series process, since one can use standard regression methods to estimate the parameters of the deterministic component, then remove if from the data and continue the analysis using the adjusted series. Processes which are stationary after a deterministic trend has been removed are called *trend stationary processes*.

A second type of non-stationarity arises if the roots of the autoregressive polynomial do not satisfy the stationarity condition outlined above. Consider the AR(1) process (10.13). If we write $\mu = (1 - \phi)\mu'$ this becomes

$$X_t = \mu + \phi X_{t-1} + \varepsilon_t \tag{10.15}$$

Suppose that $\phi = 1$. Equation (10.15) then defines a process known as a '*random walk with drift*'. Repetitive substitution for past values of X_t yields

$$X_t = \mu t + \varepsilon_t + \varepsilon_{t-1} + \varepsilon_{t-2} + \ldots + \varepsilon_1 + X_0 \tag{10.16}$$

where X_0 is the initial value of X_t. Consequently, the mean of X changes through time and its variance, which is $t\sigma^2$, also grows as t increases. Clearly the random walk with drift is non-stationary in both mean and variance. Even if $\mu = 0$, the ACF of such a process will not exhibit a tendency to die away since the influence of the past does not decline. However we can obtain a stationary process by the simple expedient of taking the first difference of X_t, since

$$\Delta X_t = X_t - X_{t-1} = \varepsilon_t \tag{10.17}$$

from which we see that the first difference of a random walk process is white noise. Comparison of equations (10.16) and (10.17) shows that differencing and summation are inverse operations. As a consequence processes of this form are frequently referred to as *integrated processes* or as *difference stationary processes*.

The random walk model is a special case but its implications carry over into more general models. Suppose that the characteristic polynomial, $\phi(z)$, of an AR(p) process had d roots of unity and $p - d$ roots lying outside the unit circle. We could then write the process as:

$$\phi^*(L)(1 - L)^d X_t = \varepsilon_t \tag{10.18}$$

where $\phi^*(L)$ contains all of the stationary roots. This means that d^{th} difference of X_t is a stationary autoregressive process of order $p - d$. We say that X_t is *integrated of order d*, denoted $I(d)$.

If we know that an AR(p) process has exactly d roots of unity in the autoregressive polynomial then we can estimate the remaining $p - d$ stationary roots by regressing the dth difference on its lagged values. Typically, of course, we need to test for the number of roots of unity. A widely-used approach to testing for unit root non-stationarity is that of Dickey and Fuller (1979, 1981) (hereafter, DF) (Dickey, Bell and Miller, 1986, review the tests). In the simplest case the problem is to test the null hypothesis that ϕ in the purely stochastic AR(1) process

$$X_t = \phi X_{t-1} + \varepsilon_t \tag{10.19}$$

equals unity against the stationary alternative that $\phi < 1.0$. The test can be carried out by regressing X_t on X_{t-1} and calculating either the t-statistic for the null hypothesis that $\phi = 1.0$ or the 'normalised coefficient statistic' $T(\hat{\phi} - 1)$ where $\hat{\phi}$ is the OLS estimate of ϕ. If X_t is stationary the calculated values of either statistic will be 'large' and negative and the question is how large the value must be to reject the null. The calculated values of the test statistics cannot be compared with standard tables of critical values but Fuller (1976, pp. 371, 373) provides asymptotic critical values and critical values for a number of sample sizes.[3] Subtracting X_{t-1} from both sides of (10.19) we get,

$$X_t - X_{t-1} = (\phi - 1)X_{t-1} + \varepsilon_t \qquad (10.20)$$

so that under the null hypothesis the coefficient on X_{t-1} equals zero. Since standard econometric packages typically print out the t-statistic for the null of zero the DF test is usually carried out by regressing the first difference of X_t on the first lag of X_t. The test can be extended to higher order autoregressive processes, in which case it is referred to as the *Augmented Dickey–Fuller* or ADF test. The critical values are the same as those for the DF test. For an autoregressive process of known order, p, one simply regresses the first difference of X_t on its lagged level and $p - 1$ lagged differences plus, if necessary, a deterministic component. When p is not known one includes enough lagged first differences to render the regression residual empirical white noise.[4] The test can also be applied to moving average and more general processes by using an autoregressive approximation subject to the proviso that the number of lagged differences increases with the sample size.[5] Dickey and Fuller (1981) extend the approach to tests on parameters other than that on X_{t-1}[6] and to joint tests of regression parameters.[7]

The *Guardian*'s market share

To illustrate some techniques of univariate time series modelling we analyse the market share of the *Guardian* newspaper over the period January 1963–November 1989.[8] The series is plotted in Figure 10.1. Since we assume a data generating mechanism which enables the observed variable to take any real value and since a market share is constrained to lie between zero and unity, we use the logit transformation, i.e. we analyse

$$x_t = \log\left(\frac{X_t}{1 - X_t}\right) \qquad (10.21)$$

where X_t is the *Guardian*'s market share. Clearly x_t approaches

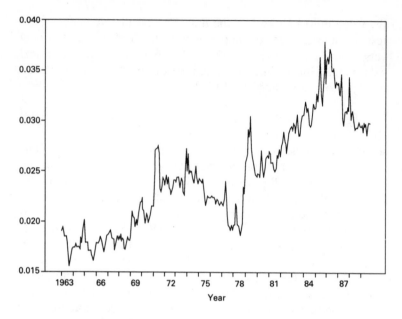

FIGURE 10.1 *Guardian* **market share**

plus infinity as X_t approaches unity and minus infinity while X_t tends to zero, and so can take any real value.

Several features can be noted from Figure 10.1. Firstly the series appears to be non-stationary, experiencing successive periods of rising and falling trends although the behaviour around trend in each segment seems similar. Secondly, there is evidence of seasonality. Thirdly, there appears to be an anomalous period from January 1971 to June 1971 when market share rose from around 2 per cent to 2.7 per cent. We handle the latter via a dummy variable which is unity for the period in question and zero otherwise. Preliminary analysis suggests that the seasonality is adequately handled by including a set of seasonal dummies rather than by the inclusion of seasonal autoregressive or moving average terms. The DF τ_τ test takes the value -2.78 when a linear trend and one lagged difference are included in the test regression. Since the relevant 95 per cent critical value is -3.43 we cannot reject the hypothesis that x_t is difference stationary. On the basis of these results we analyse the first difference of the logit of the *Guardian*'s market share as the sum of a deterministic component which includes seasonal dummies and a stationary stochastic process.

We isolate the latter by regressing Δx_t on a constant, a set of seasonal dummies and the dummy for the anomalous months of 1971. The sample autocorrelations and partial autocorrelations of the residuals from this regression, denoted S_t, are given in Table 10.1. As a rough guide, any value in excess of $2/\sqrt{T}$ can be regarded as significant.

The results are consistent with either an AR(1) process or an MA(1) process. In fact, the former gives a slightly better fit, yielding:

$$S_t = -0.206 \, S_{t-1} \qquad R^2 = 0.047 \qquad (10.22)$$
$$(0.055)$$

If the model is adequate the residuals from (10.22) should be indistinguishable from white noise so the residual autocorrelations should be individually and collectively zero. These are reported in the last row of Table 10.1. None of the residual autocorrelations are significant at 5 per cent. To test whether the autocorrelations are jointly zero we note that in large samples the autocorrelations are independently and normally distributed with a mean of zero and variance $1/T$ so that:

$$Q_K = T \sum_{K=1}^{K} r_K^2 \sim \chi_K^2$$

This is the Box–Pierce Portmanteau test statistic for departures from white noise (Box and Pierce, 1970). A variant of this, the Ljung–Box Q-statistic (hereafter LBQ) (Ljung and Box, 1978) has been found to perform better in small samples. The LBQ is distributed as a χ^2 variate, with $K - p - q$ degrees of freedom, where p is the number of AR parameters estimated and q is the number of MA parameters estimated. Using 12 lagged residuals the LBQ for the estimated model has the value 9.898 compared to a value of 19.677 obtained from χ^2 tables for $K - 1 = 11$ degrees of freedom and a significance level of 5 per cent. Hence the residuals seems to be empirical white noise. In a more detailed analysis we would investigate other properties of the residuals, testing e.g. for normality and heteroscedasticity.[9]

238

TABLE 10.1 Sample and partial autocorrelations

Row	Lag											
	1	2	3	4	5	6	7	8	9	10	11	12
(a)	−0.217	0.022	0.083	−0.074	0.004	−0.029	−0.060	0.048	−0.011	0.105	0.004	0.004
(b)	−0.217	−0.026	0.087	−0.038	−0.022	−0.041	−0.069	0.022	0.010	−0.107	−0.017	0.015
(c)	−0.004	−0.002	0.079	−0.060	−0.017	−0.043	−0.060	0.038	−0.021	−0.104	0.015	−0.018

Note: Rows (a) and (b) give the sample autocorrelations and partial autocorrelations respectively from the regression of the logit of the *Guardian's* market share on a constant, seasonal dummies and a dummy for January–June 1991. Row (c) gives the autocorrelations for model (10.22).

Multivariate analysis

Granger and Newbold (1974) used a simulation approach to show that it was possible to regress one random walk on another and to uncover a high degree of correlation, as measured by the R^2, despite the random walks being independent. Granger and Newbold referred to this as the 'spurious regression' problem and pointed out that a low Durbin–Watson (hereafter DW) statistic provides a warning signal.[10] Since the high apparent correlation disappears when regressions are run in first differences it is tempting to conclude that one should estimate equations in first differences. However, this induces a further problem in that there is nothing to pin down the levels of the variables. To be somewhat more concrete, suppose that theory suggest that Y_t is related to X_t but that both are difference stationary variables. An investigator who regresses Y_t on X_t may discover a high R^2 but a low DW and, suspecting a spurious regression problem, respond by regressing ΔY_t on ΔX_t or, more generally, by regressing ΔY_t on a number of current and lagged values of ΔX_t, and lagged values of ΔY_t, sufficient to ensure that the regression residuals cannot be empirically distinguished from white noise. The latter equation indicates how changes in Y_t are related to changes in X_t and enables one to calculate the eventual rate of change of Y_t if X_t settles down to grow at a constant rate, but does not tell us what value Y_t settles at if X_t is constant for a sufficiently long period of time. Considerations such as these led to the development of *Error Correction Models* (ECMs) which contain terms involving both levels and first differences of variables.[11]

As an illustration consider the *autoregressive distributed lag* (ADL) specification,

$$Y_t = \alpha_1 Y_{t-1} + \alpha_2 Y_{t-2} + \beta_1 X_{t-1} + \beta_2 X_{t-2} + \varepsilon_t \qquad (10.23)$$

where the variables are in logs and $\alpha_1 + \alpha_2 < 1$ if the stochastic difference equation is stable. Subtracting Y_{t-1} from both sides and rearranging the right-hand side we obtain,

$$\Delta Y_t = \alpha(Y_{t-1} - \beta X_{t-1}) + \phi \Delta Y_{t-1} + \theta \Delta X_{t-1} + \varepsilon_t \qquad (10.24)$$

where $\alpha = \alpha_2 - \alpha_1 - 1$, $\beta = (\beta_1 + \beta_2)/(\alpha_2 - \alpha_1 - 1)$, $\phi = -\alpha_2$ and θ

$= -\beta_2$. Stability implies that $\alpha < 0$. The term in parentheses on the right-hand side is the error correction term. Its role is to bring Y_t back on to track by eliminating the discrepancy between Y_t and X_t. Since α is negative Y_t will tend to be below Y_{t-1} if Y_{t-1} exceeds βX_{t-1} and vice-versa.

The error correction framework received formal support with the development of the concept of *cointegration*.[12] Two stochastic processes X_t and Y_t are said to be cointegrated if there exists a linear combination which is integrated of a lower order than the two processes. In the case usual in economic applications, Y_t and X_t are integrated of order 1, or $I(1)$, and there is a linear combination which is integrated of order zero, i.e. is stationary. The definition extends in an obvious way to the case of more than two variables. The attraction of the concept of cointegration lies in its similarity to commonly-held views about the presence of equilibrating forces in economic systems. If two $I(1)$ variables are cointegrated then even though each can wander arbitrarily far from its mean, they cannot wander arbitrarily far from each other. The existence of a stationary linear combination imposes a constraint on the long-run behaviour of the system. The connection with the error correction mechanism analysed above should be apparent. Stationarity of $Y_t - \beta X_t$ implies that the equilibrium value of Y_t is βX_t. We can think of βX_t as the target value of Y at time t. As X moves through time, Y adjusts to follow the target. We refer to the vector $(1, -\beta)$ as the 'cointegrating vector'.

Suppose we have two series, Y_t and X_t, and wish to test if they are cointegrated. The simplest case occurs when theoretical considerations suggest the appropriate cointegrating vector since we could then form the putative stationary linear combination and apply a unit root test. If the null is rejected the two series are cointegrated. Typically we do not have such information and must investigate a number of candidate vectors. One way to do this is via an OLS regression of Y_t on X_t. Essentially, this procedure discovers the cointegrating parameter because it minimises the error variance over all possible values of the regression slope, and only by choosing the cointegrating parameter as the slope estimator can the error variance remain finite. All other linear combinations are non-stationary, implying increasing variance as the sample size increases. Since the regression residuals estimate the candidate stationary linear combination, the test for cointegration is simply the test for the regression residuals to have a unit root. The most commonly used test for cointegration is the ADF test, though because the cointegrating parameter is estimated rather than known the critical values differ from those in the standard test, being somewhat larger. Critical values are found in Engle and Granger (1987) and McKinnon (1991). The test can also be used in cases where there are more than two variables. However, in a multivariate situation there may be several cointegrating vectors and there is a problem in finding all of them. Alternative approaches have been suggested by Johansen (1988, 1991) and Bossaerts (1988).

Many results relating to cointegrating systems of variables are summarised in the Granger Representation theorem. Amongst the most important is that cointegrated variables are related by an error correction mechanism or ECM. In the two-variable case, cointegration of X_t and Y_t implies that we can write an ECM for Y_t of the form

$$\Delta Y_t = \gamma(Y_{t-1} - \lambda X_{t-1}) + \sum_{i=1}^{m} \phi_i \Delta Y_{t-i} + \sum_{j=1}^{n} \theta_j \Delta X_{t-j} + u_t \qquad (10.25)$$

where u_t is a stationary ARMA error, γ is less than one in absolute value and λ is the cointegrating coefficient. Given that Y_t and X_t are cointegrated all of the terms in (10.25) are stationary and so standard techniques of inference can be applied. However (10.25) is non-linear in variables. It can be estimated by non-linear least squares or by a two-step procedure which uses OLS.[13] Step 1 is to regress Y_t on X_t and test for cointegration. If cointegration is not rejected the OLS estimate of the cointegration parameter is used instead of the true parameter in (10.25), implying that the term in parentheses on the right-handside (10.25) is replaced by the lagged cointegrating regression residual (CRR). Step 2 is to regress the first difference of Y_t on the lagged CRR and a number of lags of ΔY_t and ΔX_t. In practice, one uses a sufficient number of lags to render the residual in (10.25) empirical white noise.

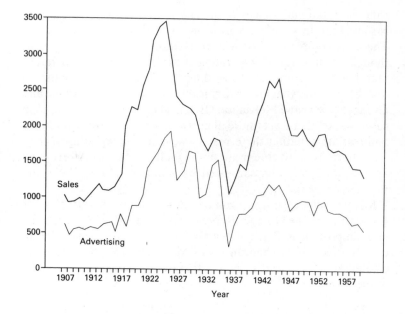

FIGURE 10.2 **Lydia Pinkham sales and advertising**

The advertising–sales relationship

In this section we use the foregoing concepts to analyse a well-known proposition relating a monopolist's advertising and sales – the Dorfman–Steiner condition (Dorfman and Steiner, 1954). We investigate this proposition using the Lydia Pinkham data set. The data series and how it became available are described in Palda (1964) and has been analysed in a cointegration framework by Baghestani (1991) who briefly surveys previous work. The data set, which is plotted in Figure 10.2, consists of sales and advertising expenditure for the Lydia Pinkham Company over the period 1907–60, which is rather short for time series analysis. In addition, it is not obvious that the firm's advertising policies can be regarded as constant over the period. Indeed, the data became available as a result of a disagreement over advertising spending. However, the data set has become something of a test bed for empirical techniques and it does refer to a product which did not change much over time and over which the producer exerted a degree of monopoly power.

The Dorfman–Steiner condition is:

$$\frac{A}{S} = a\frac{(P - C_Q)}{P} = \frac{a}{E} \tag{10.26}$$

where a is the elasticity of sales revenue, S, with respect to advertising, A, E is the price elasticity of demand and P is the price level. C_Q is the derivative of costs, C, with respect to output, Q. In a static environment (10.26) specifies that for given a and E the firm chooses a constant ratio of advertising expenditure to sales. We interpret (10.26) as a long-run equilibrium condition. In the short run other, unspecified, factors shift the firm from this optimal value and the firm responds by adjusting advertising sales to achieve the desired ratio. Let R be the ratio of advertising to sales, then the above argument implies that R is a stationary variable with a mean value of a/E. Alternatively, it implies that A and S are cointegrated, but notice that there are two ways in which the cointegration relation can be tested. Either we can regress A on S (or S on A), in which case the cointegration parameter is a/E and there is no constant in the regression, or we can regress the logarithm of A on the logarithm of S, in which case the cointegration parameter is specified as unity and there is a constant equal to $\log(a/E)$.

In Table 10.2 we report autocorrelations for the untransformed series, A_t and S_t, and their log transforms, LA_t and LS_t. These decline rather more rapidly than is consistent with non-stationarity although the pattern of decline suggests no obvious model. However, the advertising–sales ratio does seem to be stationary. Table 10.3 reports the ADF τ_μ tests, based on five lagged differences and the Phillips and Perron test which is denoted $Z(\tau_\mu)$ and uses a lag truncation parameter of five. Baghestani reports the former but excludes intercepts from the test regressions, thereby treating the series as zero-mean processes. This has the effect of reducing the (absolute) values of the test statistics as may be seen by comparing the first column of Table 10.3, in which an intercept is excluded from the test regressions, with the second where an intercept is included. The 5 per cent critical value for these tests, based upon McKinnon (1990), is -2.917 so the null hypothesis of

TABLE 10.2   Autocorrelations

Lag	A_t	LA_t	S_t	LS_t	R_t	LR_t
1	0.809	0.796	0.910	0.909	0.555	0.509
2	0.599	0.590	0.706	0.768	0.257	0.261
3	0.529	0.496	0.598	0.625	0.209	0.167
4	0.497	0.447	0.432	0.478	0.313	0.227
5	0.317	0.307	0.251	0.302	0.234	0.203
6	0.123	0.122	0.069	0.132	−0.007	−0.029
7	0.049	0.032	−0.084	−0.013	−0.088	−0.114
8	0.010	−0.013	−0.218	−0.148	−0.109	−0.169
9	−0.087	−0.096	−0.334	−0.274	−0.211	−0.169
10	−0.225	−0.223	−0.424	−0.376	−0.330	−0.346
11	−0.272	−0.262	−0.493	−0.449	−0.308	−0.321
12	−0.341	−0.334	−0.523	−0.480	−0.289	−0.300

TABLE 10.3   Unit root tests

Variable	τ	τ_μ	$Z(\tau_\mu)$
A	−0.655	−2.239	−2.298
S	−0.643	−2.874	−2.057
LA	−0.124	−2.405	−2.314
LS	−0.131	−2.921	−2.027
R	–	−3.801	−3.938
LR	–	−4.060	−4.209

a unit root is not rejected except, marginally, in the case of the ADF test on the logged sales series. We proceed on the basis that all four series are non-stationary in levels.

Table 10.4 contains the results of OLS testing for cointegration between advertising and sales based upon running regressions in each direction for both pairs of variables. The cointegration test is the Phillips–Perron-adjusted DF test, $Z(\tau)$, on the regression residuals. The 5 per cent critical value for the null hypothesis of no cointegration (McKinnon, 1990, is − 3.491. The upper part Table 10.4 gives the results of OLS estimation and the lower part gives the results of using OLS with semiparametric corrections for serial correlation and endogeneity using the procedure suggested by Phillips and Hansen (1990). The uncorrected OLS procedure

TABLE 10.4 **Cointegration tests**

Variable	Regressor	β	R^2	$Z(\tau)$
		OLS estimation		
A	S	0.496	0.711	−3.711
S	A	1.435	0.711	−3.158
LA	LS	0.979	0.762	−4.203
LS	LA	0.778	0.762	−3.569
		Modified OLS estimation		
A	S	0.511	0.710	−3.720
		(0.057)		
S	A	1.487	0.710	−3.283
		(0.185)		
LA	LS	0.974	0.761	−4.212
		(0.094)		
LS	LA	0.831	0.758	−3.877
		(0.089)		

leads, in general, to biased estimators and *t*-ratios (Phillips and Loretan, 1991), but the corrected OLS is asymptotically efficient and provides asymptotic standard errors which allow conventional *t*-tests to be conducted. Results in Hansen and Phillips (1990) and Phillips and Hansen (1990) indicate that these tests perform adequately in samples as small as that used here given a small number of variables in the cointegrating regression. Thus, in the lower part Table 10.4 we also report asymptotic standard errors. The results from the two procedures are similar and, for the former, very close to those reported by Baghestani. Several things stand out. Firstly, the values of R^2 are rather low for cointegrated variables – though this could be due to the small number of observations. Secondly, the divergence between the estimated cointegration parameter, β, for the different directions of regression, which is particularly marked for the regressions involving untransformed variables. Thirdly, the test statistic for sales on advertising is not significant. These lend support to the proposition that one should seek cointegration between the log levels rather than the levels of advertising and sales.

Table 10.5 gives preferred specifications for the single-equation ECMs estimated by instrumental variables using lags one to three of the differenced variables plus any other predetermined variables in the equation. In these equations ZX represents the 'equilibrium error' as measured by the Phillips–Hansen residuals – these are close to the OLS residuals – $\Delta 2X$ stands for the second difference of variable X and $\Delta X2$ stands for the squared first difference. Second differences are included because lags of the relevant variables had opposite but roughly equal coefficients and the null of opposite but equal coefficients could not be rejected. Squared first differences were included to allow for non-linearity. Dummies for certain years are included to account for large residuals which would otherwise lead one to adopt a more complicated dynamic structure. The various tests of model adequacy reported in Table 10.5 again support the logarithmic specification.

10.3 NON-LINEAR DYNAMICS

Non-linear time series

In the previous sections we have assumed that the data generating process can be described by a linear stochastic model though there is often no theoretical reason why the underlying data generating process should be linear. In recent years there has been a growing interest in the study of non-linear dynamics. The reasons for this are perhaps threefold: (i) the discovery (see, e.g. May, 1976) that relatively simple non-linear deterministic difference equations can generate highly complex behaviour including that referred to as *chaos*, (ii) a number of economic models have been developed which suggest that economic relationships can be described by non-linear and, possibly, chaotic processes, and (iii) new empirical tests have been developed for detecting non-linear (possibly chaotic) data generating processes in observed data series (see, e.g. Brock, *et al.*, 1991). Our purpose here is to review briefly some non-linear stochastic time-series models. In addition, we provide an introduction to the subject area of chaos and give examples which illustrate its potential relevance in industrial economics.

To date, there has been limited estimation of non-linear time-series models in industrial economics, principally because of the inadequate length of time series available to the researcher. However, a number

TABLE 10.5   Single-equation ECMs

	ΔA		ΔS
$ZA\ (-1)$	−0.613	$ZS\ (-1)$	−0.116
	(6.032)		(1.189)
$\Delta 2A\ (-1)$	0.209	$\Delta S\ (-1)$	0.291
	(2.500)		(3.262)
$\Delta 2S\ (-1)$	0.237	$\Delta S\ (-3)$	0.221
	(2.623)		(1.988)
$\Delta A2\ (-1)$	0.765E−3	ΔA	0.529
	(3.310)		(3.056)
$CONST$	−28.512	$CONST$	3.856
	(1.234)		(0.200)
$D36$	−595.12	$D18$	641.32
	(3.303)		(4.642)
		$D26$	−683.53
			(4.823)
R^2	0.622		0.732
$SC(1)$	0.981		2.786
$RESET$	12.423*		0.303
$NORM$	0.459		11.209*
HET	1.202		0.918

	ΔLS		ΔLS
$ZLA\ (-1)$	−0.371	$ZLS\ (-1)$	−0.199
	(2.575)		(1.904)
ΔLS	0.719	$\Delta LS\ (-1)$	0.185
	(1.873)		(2.443)
$\Delta LA\ (-2)$	0.502	$\Delta LS\ (-3)$	0.289
	(2.035)		(3.221)
$CONST$	−0.004		0.401
	(0.167)		(3.589)
$D18$	−0.528	$D18$	0.427
	(2.432)		(6.577)
$D36$	−1.007	$D26$	−0.227
	(2.613)		(3.596)
R^2	0.722		0.799
$SC(1)$	1.648		0.002
$RESET$	0.208		0.093
$NORM$	0.718		0.115
HET	1.613		2.289

Notes: D18 and D36 are dummy variables which take the value 1.0 in 1918 and 1936 respectively and zero otherwise. $SC(1)$ is the LM test for first-order serial correlation, distributed as X_1. *RESET* is Ramsey's test for functional form, distributed as X_1. *NORM* is the Jarque–Bera normality test, distributed as X_2, and *HET* tests for heteroscedasticity due to squares of the fitted values.
* denotes significance at 5 per cent.

of theories have been developed which suggest that linear stochastic models may not always adequately capture the underlying data generating mechanism. For example, there are models which suggest non-linear response of price changes to demand changes (see, e.g. Stigler and Kindahl, 1970). Gould (1970) sets out a model in which advertising expenditures add to the stock of goodwill in a non-linear manner. There are also models where a firm's response to price or quantity changes by other firms is asymmetric, and dependent on price or quantity changes crossing some endogenously determined critical threshold (see, e.g. Porter, 1983; Green and Porter, 1984). Finally non-linear reduced-form behaviour is not precluded on theoretical grounds. For example the Cubbin and Geroski (1987) model discussed in the Introduction assumes that entry responds linearly to profits, but if we replace equation (10.1) by

$$E_t = \alpha \rho_{t-1} + \alpha_1 \rho_{t-1}^2 + u_t \tag{10.27}$$

the reduced form for ρ_t is

$$\rho_t = (\alpha \beta + \beta_1) \rho_{t-1} + (\beta \alpha_1) \rho_{t-1}^2 + \beta u_t + \varepsilon_t \tag{10.28}$$

which is a non-linear stochastic equation. More generally this example shows that there are, in principle, an infinite number of non-linear models that can be specified, since the entry function $E = f(\rho)$ can take an infinite number of forms. In practice, unless the theory is informative as to the precise functional form, then we must employ non-linear models which approximate the 'correct' underlying non-linear time-series representation. A number of non-linear stochastic models have been suggested in the literature (see, e.g. Priestley, 1988; Ullah, 1988). We focus on two models.

The first is the bilinear model. This is discussed in, for example, Granger and Andersen (1978) and Subba Rao and Gaber (1984), and has had some limited application in economics (see, e.g. Maravall, 1983; Weiss 1986). It can be demonstrated that a bilinear process is a reasonably general non-linear model in that it is an arbitrarily close second order approximation to any underlying non-linear process. The general bilinear process is given by:

$$y_t + \sum_{i=1}^{P} a_i y_{t-i} + \sum_{j=1}^{N} \beta_j \varepsilon_{t-j} = \alpha + \sum_{i=1}^{M} \sum_{j=1}^{Q} b_{ij} y_{t-i} \varepsilon_{t-j} + \varepsilon_t \tag{10.29}$$

where ε_t is a sequence of i.i.d. random variables (10.29) is a generalisation of the univariate ARMA model to include cross-product terms of lagged variable and errors. In the special case, where the b_{ij} are all zero, we obtain the standard ARMA model. To illustrate the potential complexity of the processes captured by (10.29) consider the simple bilinear model:

$$y_t = \alpha + by_{t-1}\varepsilon_{t-1} + \varepsilon_t \tag{10.30}$$

Since $\varepsilon_{t-1} = y_{t-1} - \alpha - by_{t-2}\varepsilon_{t-2}$, we can substitute for ε_{t-1} and then similarly for ε_{t-2} to obtain:

$$\begin{aligned} y_t &= \alpha + by_{t-1}^2 - \alpha by_{t-1} - b^2 y_{t-1} y_{t-2}^2 + \alpha b^2 y_{t-1} y_{t-2} \\ &\quad + b^3 y_{t-1} y_{t-2} y_{t-3} \varepsilon_{t-3} + \varepsilon_t \end{aligned} \tag{10.31}$$

We could continue this process substituting for ε_{t-3} and so on, but it is already clear from inspection of (10.31) that (10.28) implies that y_t is a complicated non-linear function of lagged values of y.

To illustrate the potential applicability of the bilinear model we have estimated the most parsimonious bilinear model of changes in the percentage market share of the *Daily Express* newspaper, employing monthly data over the period 74:04–89:11.

$$y_t = -0.07 - 0.51y_{t-1} - 0.142\varepsilon_{t-1}y_{t-1} + \varepsilon_t \tag{10.32}$$

where y_t denotes the per-period change in the market share. The variance of the residuals from (10.32) was 0.329. The most parsimonious linear model was estimated as

$$y_t = -0.11 - 0.49y_{t-1} + \varepsilon_t \tag{10.33}$$

with a residual variance of 0.367 and residuals which were not statistically different from white noise. Thus the bilinear model has a residual variance lower by some 11 per cent relative to the linear model. Given that the bilinear model has only one additional estimated parameter this turns out to be a highly significant reduction in variance. It would appear that the hypothesis that the market share of the *Daily Express* has a non-linear time series structure has some validity and merits further investigation.

The second model we consider is the threshold autoregressive model introduced by Tong (1990). A threshold model may be regarded as a piecewise linear approximation to the general non-linear kth-order autoregresive model:

$$y_t = f(y_{t-1}, y_{t-2} \ldots y_{t-k}) + \varepsilon_t \qquad (10.34)$$

The threshold autoregressive model takes the form:

$$y_t = a_0^{(j)} + \sum_{i=1}^{k_j} a_i^{(j)} X_{t-i} + e_j^{(j)} \qquad X_{t-d} \, \varepsilon \, R^{(j)} \, j = 1, \ldots L \quad (10.35)$$

where $k_1, k_2, \ldots, k_L$ denote the orders of the autoregressions in the L threshold regions and the $e_j^{(j)}$ are each i.i.d. random variables. The following process is a simple example of a threshold model:

$$y_t = \alpha + \beta y_{t-1} + \gamma y_{t-2} + \varepsilon_t \qquad y_{t-1} < r \qquad (10.36a)$$

$$y_t = \theta + u_t \qquad\qquad\qquad y_{t-1} \geq r \qquad (10.36b)$$

where $\alpha, \beta, \gamma, \theta$ and k are constants and ε_t and u_t are i.i.d. disturbances. In this model, y_t follows an autoregression of order 2 when y_{t-1} is less or equal to the constant r. When y_{t-1} is greater or equal to r, y_t is a constant, θ, plus white noise.[14]

The threshold model is the only 'general' non-linear model which is able to model parsimoniously data which embodies asymmetric limit cycles. It is therefore a particularly appropriate model if the data generating process exhibits cyclical behaviour. In addition it will be useful in economic modelling if the thresholds could be related to some underlying economic decisions such as transaction bands in asset market analysis or 'target' levels as described in the market share models of Porter *et al.* referred to above. To illustrate, we estimated a threshold model for changes in the market share of the *Daily Express*, obtaining

$$y_t = -0.0445 - 0.24y_{t-1} + \varepsilon_t^1 \qquad y_{t-1} < -0.1287 \qquad (10.37a)$$

$$y_t = 0.0124 - 0.9161y_{t-1} + \varepsilon_t^2 \qquad y_{t-1} \geq -0.1287 \qquad (10.37b)$$

The residual variance for the threshold model is 0.322. The final choice between the bilinear and threshold models will be based on in-sample reduction of residual variance, theoretical priors and accuracy of out-of-sample forecasts.

Estimation of linear or non-linear stochastic models naturally carries the implication that the data generating process can be adequately captured by such processes. We next consider non-linear processes for which, under certain circumstances, the data generating process cannot be adequately captured by any stochastic process.

Chaotic models

The equation

$$X_t = AX_{t-1}(1 - X_{t-1}) \tag{10.38}$$

where A is a constant has been termed the simplest non-linear difference equation. It is useful to note that the more general equation:

$$Z_t = a + b Z_{t-1} + c Z_{t-1}^2 \tag{10.39}$$

where a, b and c are constants, can be written in the form (10.38) by employing the transformation[15]

$$Z_t = \lambda X_t + \gamma \tag{10.40}$$

where λ and γ are constants and

$$c\gamma^2 + (b - 1)\gamma + a = 0$$
$$\lambda = -A/c$$
$$A = 2c\gamma + b$$

and

$$A^2 - 2A + 2b - b^2 + 4ac = 0.$$

In order to analyse the dynamic behaviour of equation (10.38), we note that it has two fixed points $(\bar{X})$ where $X_{t+1} = X_t = \bar{X}$. By

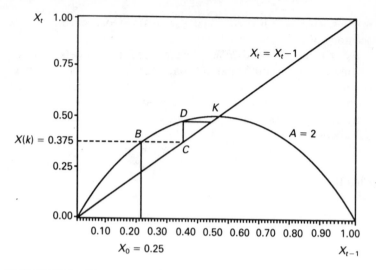

FIGURE 10.3 Phase curve relating X_t+ and X_t

substitution in (10.38) we find that these are $\bar{X} = 0$ and $\bar{X} = (A - 1)/A$. Since the slope of the function is

$$\frac{dX_t}{dX_{t-1}} = A - 2A\,X_{t-1} \tag{10.41}$$

there is a maximum at $X_{t-1} = 1/2$.

The reader will readily find from plotting a few points that the relationship between X_{t+1} and X_t – called the phase curve – for a given value of A is hill-shaped. By changing the parameter A, we can adjust the height and steepness of the hill. It turns out that the 'tuning parameter' A is crucial for the dynamics of the system. The value of A also is sometimes called the 'knob setting'. In order to examine the dynamics of the system, we draw on the phase curve a 45°-ray to give the points where $X_{t+1} = X_t$. This is shown in Figure 10.3, for $A = 2$.

To illustrate the dynamic behaviour of this equation we start the system at the initial value $X_0 = 0.25$. This value generates a value of $X(1) = 0.375$ in the next period (point B). We now wish to repeat the process, this time commencing from $X(1)$. To do this we move horizontally to point C on the 45°-line. The point vertically below C is $X(1)$ on the horizontal axis, because the two coordinates of any point of the 45°-line must be equal. From $X(1)$, we move directly to point D on the phase curve. Continuing in this fashion we will trace out the path of X_t. In this case the path converges to the equilibrium point K where $X = 0.5$

In order that we converge on an equilibrium point it is necessary that the slope of the phase curve at the equilibrium point has modulus less than unity. (Note also that for any starting values of X_{t-1}, which do not begin in the unit interval (i.e. between 0 and 1) the system tends to negative infinity. Try $X_0 = -1$ in (10.38) and substitute a couple of periods.)

The slope of the phase curve at the two equilibrium points is

$$\frac{dX_{t+1}}{dX_t} = A \qquad (\bar{X} = 0) \tag{10.42}$$

and

$$\frac{dX_{t+1}}{dX_t} = 2 - A \quad \left(\bar{X} = 1 - \frac{1}{A}\right) \tag{10.43}$$

It follows that for $0 < A < 1$, the equilibrium point of the system is zero.

For the case $1 < A < 3$, we find that the equilibrium point, $(A - 1)/A$, is stable or 'attracting', whilst that for $\bar{X} = 0$ is 'repelling'. In other words, any deviation from zero causes the system to move further away, whilst any paths in the neighbourhood of $(A - 1)/A$ converge on the equilibrium point. We note further that for $2 < A < 3$ $\frac{dX_{t+1}}{dX_t}$ will be negative, implying stable oscillations in the trajectory of X_t from any initial condition apart from equilibrium.

When A is greater than or equal to 3, the slope at the equilibrium point becomes unstable. In the case of a linear equation if the slope is greater than one in absolute value the oscillations will be explosive (i.e., X_t will tend to infinity). However, with the hill-shaped phase curve, this cannot occur because, as the oscillations increase, the path will eventually 'expand into' the positively-sloping side of the hill and produce a value of X_{t+j} closer to the

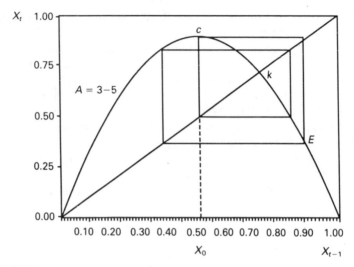

FIGURE 10.4   Unstable equilibrium with $A > 3$

equilibrium point than some earlier point X_{t+j-k}. From this point the cyclical path will begin converging towards the equilibrium point. However, since the equilibrium point is unstable, convergence cannot occur so that the path will once again at some point begin to diverge. This is illustrated in Figure 10.4, where we note that starting from initial condition X_0, point C is closer to the equilibrium point ($K = 0.714$) than is point E.

The plethora of different dynamic paths of the system as A is gradually increased between 3 and 4 was not understood until recent developments in the theory of chaos.

For A equal to or just greater than 3 the path converges on a stable two-period cycle. As A is gradually increased, the two-period limit cycle becomes unstable and exactly at this point a stable four-period cycle emerges (also illustrated in Figure 10.2). As we continue to increase A the four-period cycle itself becomes unstable and at this point is replaced by a stable eight-period cycle. As A is further increased the process continues until ultimately the path of X evolves into an infinite number of cycle lengths. Feigenbaum (1980) demonstrated that the interval of A over which a cycle is stable shrinks at a geometric rate. In particular, each interval is approximately 4.669 times smaller than the previous interval. He also showed that this property is universal for all functions that have 'hill-shaped' maps (for example, a sine wave). The period doublings as A increases are known as 'period doubling bifurcations'. At points of bifurcation the system under consideration changes discontinuously. This is one possible path to chaos. Although the cycles initially only have even periods it turns out that cycles with odd number of periods eventually begin to appear. Initially these will have very long periods, but in due course they are joined by cycles of shorter and shorter duration which encompass every positive odd integer.

As we continue to increase A we find that there are essentially an infinite number of initial values of A for which the time path of A never repeats itself. When a system starting from an initial value never repeats itself it is said to exhibit *aperiodic motion*. Aperiodic motion does not imply that the observed patterns appear to have no structure. It is possible, for example, to distinguish patterns which look like cycles but which disappear after a number of periods. Systems exhibiting aperiodic motion can be thought of as chaotic.[16]

The different types of dynamic behaviour which we observe as we vary A illustrates the notion of an attractor. An attractor in a linear system is a point, more generally a subspace, to which the system converges. The fixed-point equilibrium is defined as an attractor of period one. Limit cycles of whatever period are also types of equilibrium of a system, and are known as *periodic attractors*. When the system is in the chaotic region we have another type of attractor known as a *strange attractor*. The strange attractor is an attractor for all paths in its neighbourhood. Unlike limit cycles, trajectories within the strange attractor are not periodic, and no point is ever visited twice.

In Figure 10.5 we plot a segment of the path for a value $A = 3.9$, which is within the chaotic region. We notice that X appears quite volatile but always remains within the 0–1 range. We also see that periods of relatively large cyclical oscillations can be followed by periods of relative stability (e.g. observations around 2340). Such abrupt qualitative changes in the path of X are characteristic of chaotic systems (and non-linear stochastic equations).

Chaotic systems possess a number of other interesting properties. One is that the time path of X is highly sensitive to initial conditions (X_0 in our systems). Table 10.6 illustrates this property. In row 1 we set out, for a value of A of 3.95 (within the chaotic region), the values

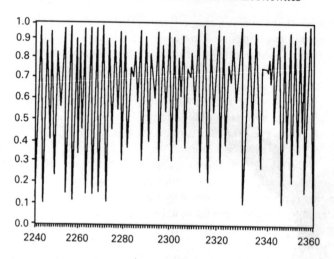

FIGURE 10.5 **Segment of the time path of X_t for $A = 3.9$**

that X takes after 10, 23 and 72 from a starting value of 0.3. In row 2 we set the starting value of A at 0.30001. We observe that after ten periods to five decimal places the paths are close together, but after 23 periods the values are becoming different.

In fact, after 500 iterations the correlation coefficient between the two series (R^2) is -0.02 and quickly approaches zero. In rows 3 and 4 we carry out a similar experiment with $A = 3.10$ (outside the chaotic region). Now the values of X remain close together and the R^2 after 500 iterations is approximately 1.0. The sensitive dependence of the path of X on the initial conditions in a chaotic region of a model was termed the 'butterfly effect' by Lorenz (1963) in reference to the possibility that if the weather system is chaotic, a butterfly flapping its wings may set off a sequence of meteorological events that result in tornadoes, the sensitivity of the system being such that minute changes in initial conditions give rise to outcomes which are dramatically different. We also note that since equation (10.38) is deterministic, the path of X is totally predictable if we know the exact initial condition. However, the sensitivity to initial conditions informs us that in all practical situations, where there will almost inevitably be errors in measurement and rounding errors in computation, it will almost certainly not be possible to make long-term forecasts.[17]

TABLE 10.6 Time path of X_t

Row	Value A	x_0	x_{10}	x_{23}	x_{72}
1	3.95	0.3	0.41538	0.45516	0.06589
2	3.95	0.3001	0.38369	0.69396	0.09839
3	3.1	0.3	0.62339	0.75924	0.58104
4	3.1	0.3001	0.62362	0.75918	0.58104
5	3.95001	0.30	0.41471	0.24035	0.41117

A second interesting feature of chaotic systems is that the time path exhibits sensitivity to small changes in parameter values. This is also illustrated in Table 10.6 where in row 5 we set out values of X at various points on the path for a value of A of 3.95001, and starting value of 0.3. The value can be contrasted with those in row 1 where A has the value 3.95. The values soon become quite different.

A third feature of chaotic processes (shared by some other non-chaotic deterministic processes) is that the observed time paths appear to be random, or, as a linear/non-linear system subject from time to time to 'very large' random shocks. Frank and Stengos (1988) illustrate the first possibility by considering the autocorrelation function of the logistic equation for the first 1000 iterations with $X_0 = 0.3$ and $A = 4$. On the basis of usual statistics, we would accept that the series is random.

Although the dynamic paths that can occur in mathematical models typified by chaos are of great interest, the question naturally arises as to their potential applicability in economics (or elsewhere). A number of statistical methods now exist which, given a sufficiently large number of observations, can determine whether an observed time series is chaotic (see, e.g. Grassberger and Procaccia, 1983). However, there is, to date, no convincing empirical evidence of chaotic behaviour in economic series (mostly asset prices or macroeconomic series) though many appear non-linear. In the industrial economics area, formal statistical tests for chaos have not been feasible for want of long series of data. However, a number of theoretical models generating chaos have been developed.

To illustrate, we consider two models. The first was developed for expositional purposes by Baumol and Quandt (1985), and is a model of advertising expenditures. Baumol and Quandt hypothesise that with no expenditure on advertising the firm's sales are zero. As advertising expenditure is increased, net profits first increase, then gradually level off and then decline, yielding a hill-shaped profit curve. For simplicity, the relationship between net profit π_t and advertising (G_t) is given by:

$$\pi_t = aG_t(1 - G_t) \tag{10.44}$$

It is further assumed that the firm devotes a fixed proportion, λ, of its current (real profit) to advertising in the following period, so that:

$$G_t = \lambda\pi_{t-1} \tag{10.45}$$

It is clear from substitution of (10.45) into (10.44) that we have equation (10.38) with $A = a\lambda$. Consequently, advertising can exhibit chaotic behaviour in the Baumol and Quandt model.

The second model, developed by ourselves, also assumes that the firm follows a 'rule of thumb'. Suppose the firm sets price (p_t) on the basis of a markup, μ, of average cost (AC_t) in the previous period,

$$p_t = \mu AC_{t-1} \tag{10.46}$$

For simplicity let demand ($=$ output supplied q_t) be given by the linear schedule:

$$p_t = a - bq_t \tag{10.47}$$

where a, b are constants and that average cost is given by the 'U'-shaped function,

$$AC_t = \gamma_0 - \gamma_1 q_t + \gamma_2 q_t^2 \tag{10.48}$$

where γ_0, γ_1 and γ_2 are positive constants. Substituting (10.46), (10.47) and (10.48) we obtain

$$q_t = \frac{a - \mu\gamma_0}{b} + \frac{\mu\gamma_1}{b}q_{t-1} - \frac{\mu\gamma_2}{b}q_{t-1}^2 \tag{10.49}$$

Equation (10.49) can be transformed into the logistic equation using (10.40). Chaotic behaviour is feasible (try, e.g. $a = 20$, $b = 2$, $\mu = 3/2$, $\gamma_1 = 12$, $\gamma_2 = 1$, $\gamma_0 = (93 - (A^2 - 2A))4/9$, (where A is the parameter desired in the logistic map.

Although the two illustrative examples are simplistic, they do illustrate how complicated non-linear behaviour can be readily generated in simple models of the firm. Furthermore, other models exist in the domain of industrial economics which embody deeper theoretical underpinnings which also can generate chaotic dynamics. For instance, Dana and Montrucchio (1986) demonstrate that with small rates of discount, chaotic dynamic paths can readily arise in a dynamic oligopoly model. Also Benhabib and Day (1981) demonstrate that when consumer preferences are determined endogenously and are allowed to evolve as a result of past consumption patterns, consumer choices can fluctuate dramatically without relying on explanations which involve 'random influences on tastes'.

10.4 CONCLUSIONS

The purpose in this chapter has been to introduce and review some of the methods now available for the analysis of linear and non-linear economic time series.[18] These methods have already had an impact in areas of economics such as macroeconomics and finance. We confidently anticipate a similar development in industrial economics as data sets which can exploit such methods become available.

End-Notes

CHAPTER 2

* The author would like to thank John Cable for his comments on an earlier draft.
1. A special issue of the *Journal of Law and Economics* (34, 2, part 2, 1991) on 'Contracts and the Activities of Firms' includes investigations of contracts in the US gas and railroad industries.
2. A less technical discussion, which also uses this example, is provided by Moore (1991). A related paper is Grossman and Hart (1986).
3. The quadratic form has the unfortunate general property that utility eventually declines with $(s-d)$, but it is increasing over the relevant range in this example.
4. This desirability to provide the most insurance consistent with an incentive to supply effort means that even the suggested salary contract is not in fact the optimal one because the incentive compatibility constraint is not binding. That is, there is still some scope to provide more insurance for M – by reducing the differential between S_L and S_H – whilst still providing an incentive to work hard. The need for insurance similarly rules out the option of the manager taking on the role of residual claimant. To see this, suppose the status of residual claimant is transferred to M for a fee of 12.8 (so that A is indifferent between this arrangement and the contract above). M now gets $u(5 - 2 - 12.8)$ with probability 0.1 and $u(20 - 2 - 12.8)$ with probability 0.9. This gives an expected utility of 6.76, compared with 26.2 from the salary contract.
5. Another possibility is monitoring of the managers' actions by owners. This involves costs and therefore is likely to be more effective when there are shareholders with a significant proportion of the total stock (and thus an entitlement to a significant share of the benefits from monitoring. An additional external constraint may be the managerial labour market. Fama (1980) argues that managers may be dissuaded from deviating from owners' interests because to do so would lower the value on the labour market and hence reduce their expected lifetime income. For a general discussion of the constraints on managers see Helm (1989).
6. For further discussion of these and other defensive tactics see Jarrell, Brickley and Netter (1988).

7. For further discussion see Chapter 9 by Weyman-Jones in this volume, and also Tirole (1988, pp. 41–2).
8. For an explanation of iso-profit curves, see Chapter 4 by Fraser in this volume.
9. For further discussion of two-stage games, including applications, see Shapiro (1989).

CHAPTER 3

* The author gratefully acknowledges useful comments from Peter Abell, William Bartlett, John Cable and Paul Geroski. Any remaining errors are his own.
1. In practice, organisations may combine some elements of several categories. For example, the successful group of cooperatives in Mondragon, Spain are partly collectively and partly individual equity owned (see Bradley and Gelb, 1983).
2. If profits are zero, labour-managed and capitalist firms produce exactly the same output, and pay the same wages. Since zero profits are bought about by competition, it comes as no surprise that the general equilibria of the two systems are equivalent (see Vanek, 1970; Dreze, 1976).
3. For an alternative formulation, see Ireland and Law, 1982.
4. That is to say, returns to scale do not vary with factor proportions.
5. In practice the adjustment of output and factor proportions when technology is non-homothetic is simultaneous rather than step-wise as suggested by this illustration. Thus the move to the new output X_1^* would imply a further change in the choice of technique, and so on.
6. It has been argued that the reduction of employment in response to price increases can be justified only if such behaviour is consistent with democratic procedures. Estrin (1991) discusses how it could be consistent with the method of majority voting provided layoffs are based on seniority rules. If layoffs are random, the collective will not reduce employment when earnings exceed outside wages, provided individuals are risk-averse.
7. There have been a number of other approaches to relaxing the assumptions. For example, Ireland and Law (1981) analyse short-run adjustment when the supply of effort is variable, and deduce a positive effort response to price increases but a continued decline in labour demand. In the case of price uncertainty, labour demand is still inversely related to the (expected) price if the labour-managed firm is assumed to maximise expected average earnings (see Bonin, 1984).
8. It should be noted that the contract curve *BCD* is not necessarily upward-sloping; it can be vertical if workers are risk-neutral, or backward-sloping if workers are risk-takers (see Svejnar, 1982; Ben-Ner and Estrin, 1991).

CHAPTER 4

1. See e.g. Cowling and Waterson (1976) for details of the derivation.
2. See Bulow, Geneakopolos and Klemperer (1985). Firm i's output is a strategic substitute for firm j's when an increase in q_i decreases the marginal profit j obtains from an increase in q_j. For the case of constant marginal costs, this is equivalent to j's marginal revenue decreasing as q_i increases. Strategic complementarity is defined analogously.
3. The reaction functions are drawn linearly for convenience. However, they will be linear if the demand function is linear and the cost function is either linear or quadratic.
4. In a Nash equilibrium each decision-maker is maximising its objective function, given what its counterparts are doing. In the Cournot–Nash case the decision variables are output levels; in the Bertrand–Nash case they are price levels.
5. This point is well made in many places. See e.g. Shapiro (1989) and Tirole (1989).
6. Note that the first firm might then be imputing *optimality* to the rivals' responses, for given beliefs by the rivals w.r.t. its own behaviour, but not *rationality* – as these beliefs need not be very reasonable ones to have in the first place.
7. Note that the reaction functions for the rivals should, for consistency, subsume optimal responses to all their rivals responses to their response to i. Waterson (1984) speaks of 'reduced-form' reaction functions in this context.
8. Cf. Jacquemin and Slade (1988).
9. Cubbin thus identifies the perfectly collusive outcome as prices moving in tandem although, with differentiated products, such behaviour need not preserve market shares nor, necessarily, relative profits.
10. In many respects, this need to specify out-of-equilibrium behaviour resembles a similar requirement in sequential or perfect equilibria. See Kreps and Wilson (1982).
11. Much of Ulph's paper is actually concerned with consistent duopoly behaviour involving boundary equilibria, i.e., with one output equal to zero.
12. Under the efficient rationing rule, it is assumed that consumers placing the highest valuation on the relevant commodity purchase from the lowest-priced firm. Thus, if the capacity of the lowest-price firm is denoted $\bar{q}$, the higher-priced firm, charging price p_2, would face demand equal to $D(p_2) - \bar{q}$.
13. Further experiments under 'incomplete information' were also run, without materially affecting this main conclusion or the average price. Incomplete information led mainly to less dispersion of the prices across experiments.
14. See Jacquemin and Slade (1988). Also see Cubbin (1983) for

alternative expressions for λ_i, based on his measures of apparent collusion in differentiated goods contexts.

15. Breshnahan (1989, p. 1051) tabulates the Lerner indices obtained from empirical work on a number of industries.

16. Of course, the deadweight loss associated with oligopoly is but one aspect of more general distributional issues arising from various forms of market structure. Cowling (1981) provides a discussion of some of these issues in relation to the CV model.

17. I am indebted to Morten Hviid for this reference.

CHAPTER 5

1. The exceptions were Kamerschen (1966) and Cowling and Mueller (1978).

2. For details see Chapter 4 above, and Ulph (1983).

3. Fringe firms assume $dp_j/dx_i = 0$ *with* $p_j = p_i$, where j is the dominant firm and $i = 1, 2, \ldots, n$ is a member of an n-firm fringe.

4. Figure 5.1 is not drawn for this case where, as was seen, B, RCE, D_1 and D_2 would converge on SO.

5. Since $H = \dfrac{1}{n} + \sigma_n^2$ where n is the number of firms in the industry, the minimum H value in our case is 0.5, obtained whenever $x_1 = x_2$.

6. Parameter values underlying Figure 5.2 are $\alpha_1 = 20$; $\alpha_2 = 22$; b_1, $b_2 = 1$; $c_1 = 6.0$, $c_2 = 6.6$.

7. Dominant-firm equilibrium is not reported in Table 5.2 for the reasons given.

8. The structural criteria under the 1984 regulations can be severe. For example, mergers among non-dominant competitors are likely to be challenged where the post-merger industry Herfindahl exceeds 1000 and the increase due to the merger is more than 100 (monopoly = 10 000).

9. For a review of new ideas about strategic competition among the few, in which structure is endogenous, and results are not necessarily socially desirable, see e.g. Vickers (1985).

CHAPTER 6

* This chapter is based upon my (1989) survey paper 'Models of Product Differentiation' which appeared in the *Bulletin of Economic Research*, 41, pp. 1–27. The original paper was written whilst I was spending a year at the University of Sydney. I am grateful to Roger Sherman, Noel Gaston, and other participants at the University of Sydney day workshop in March 1988, and an anonymous referee for the *Bulletin*, for helpful comments on an earlier draft.

1. Though as long ago as 1919, Marshall noted a developing trend towards what he called 'multiform' standardisation.
2. However, on this issue see Mussa and Rosen (1978).
3. He also extends the analogy to choice between political parties, and this has itself generated a considerable literature; see e.g. Mueller (1976).
4. There is also the issue of 'general-purpose' products which can be thought of either in a multidimensional context, or as having lower transport costs than special purpose products; see von Ungern-Sternberg (1988).
5. Assuming these are the same for all firms.
6. In this case, but not necessarily with other distance metrics. For existence, we require a quasi-concave profit function.
7. Though the comparison is slightly misleading, because the equilibria cannot coexist. The nature of results (6.10) and (6.11) leads to unusual comparative static behaviour at the 'kink' between the two.
8. Moreover, it can be extremely inconvenient, since equilibrium would appear never to exist in a *closed* entry model with simultaneous determination of prices and location (see Jaskold Gabszewicz and Thisse, 1986).
9. Thing are rather more complex where an outside good has to be taken into consideration, as in Figure 6.2. If the *szpe* is a monopoly one, it remains so when we impose deterrence. On the other hand, if the *szpe* is competitive, $2A_c > A_m$, which would imply a monopoly deterrence equilibrium (at least at given prices).
10. Notice that the element in round brackets is the shaded area in Figure 6.3. It is x, not p, which matters.
11. Though see also Bonanno (1987) on this issue.
12. Schmalensee (1978) solves this artificially by assuming that the established manufacturers were caught out by a change in tastes.
13. As before, we neglect the integer problem regarding firm numbers here.
14. Notice that equation (6.13) is C.E.S. in form.
15. For example, given that uncertainty is absent, it is questionable whether we may consider (6.19) as a continuous function, since the higher-quality product might capture all sales at equal prices. This issue is resolved in very different ways in the two special cases, as we see below.
16. If the optimal quality imbedded in each unit is a constant, which it will be if $p_{uq} = 0$, then these problems do not exist, but this is a very special case.
17. The demand-side assumption may be generalised slightly – see Spence (1975, p. 422, n. 8), and also see Waterson (1984, p. 109) regarding cost conditions. Swan (1970) develops a dynamic model.
18. We shall shortly find that some care has to be exercised regarding the lowest-quality good marketed, there being more than one solution equation.
19. The equation of the inverse demand curve is found by straightforward methods using (6.3) to be $p_1 = (1/D_1)(b - q_1/s)$ for $q_1 < s(b - a)$.

20. This may or may not be plausible formulation, but it would be a candidate from the stability viewpoint.
21. Indeed, what is surprising is that there seem to be practical cases (e.g. TV programming) for which Hotelling's original model nevertheless seems relevant. It may be interesting for the reader to speculate why this is so.
22. To take two examples, considerable volumes to intra-industry trade can only really arise in the presence of product differentiation (see e.g. Greenaway, 1987); and the practice whereby manufacturers impose vertical restraints on retailers is amenable to analysis using the types of tools developed here, see e.g. Waterson (1986) for an exposition.

CHAPTER 7

* This chapter draws on Geroski (1991), where the interested reader can find a more extensive discussion and a much fuller set of references. I am obliged to Filippo Dell'Osso, Scott Barrett, Stefan Szymanski and John Cable for helpful comments on an earlier draft, but the usual disclaimer applies.

CHAPTER 8

1. This is not the same thing as saying that the loser is forced out of the market. A loser may still be able to make non-negative profits in the resulting market equilibrium.
2. Auctions can come in many forms. An English auction is one in which the bidding for an object starts at a low price and rises until there is only one bidder left active. It is to be distinguished from a Dutch auction where the auctioneer starts at a high price and reduces it until someone bids for the object at that price. That first bidder is successful. Another form of auction is the sealed-bid auction. Potential bidders put there bids in a sealed envelope. When the envelopes are opened, the object goes to the person who bid the most.
3. That is, quantity rather than price is a firm's decision variable. When price is the decision variable, product market competition is Bertrand.
4. An analysis of the effect of the size of the initial cost asymmetry between firms and of the size of the innovation is contained in Beath, Katsoulacos and Ulph (1993).
5. This statement is not true for the case of increasing marginal costs. However, the result that industry profits are increasing in the size of the cost gap continues to hold.
6. A product is said to be *vertically differentiated* if, when its various varieties are offered for sale at the same price, all consumers choose

to purchase the same one: that of the highest quality.

7. This is assumed to be zero, so we can equally refer to such goods as having a zero price.

8. We note in passing that $1/\Sigma x_j$ is the expected date of success.

9. It is worth pointing out that the large-numbers contractual-cost case is explored in Beath *et al.* (1989b). The discussion there and that in the present section are thus highly complementary.

10. Notice that in this case the competitive threat *exceeds* the profit incentive and the R&D reaction functions are *positively-sloped*.

11. This inequality is a 'stability' condition. Note that $\phi_h = \partial x^e/\partial h$. Thus the condition says that if all other firms, in aggregate, increase their R&D effort by one unit, the firm in question should increase its effort by less than that.

12. R&D activity will not be concentrated on a single project for two reasons: rising marginal costs and the uncorrelated nature of potential research strategies.

13. The key parameters are r and g and the table of results focuses on these.

CHAPTER 10

1. Pindyck and Rubinfeld (1991) contains an introduction to time-series models for economists. The classic reference is Box and Jenkins (1976). Harvey (1981a, 1981b) deals with many issues from an econometric point of view. Sargent (1979) illustrates the use of time-series methods in theoretical economics. For more detailed treatments see Priestley (1981) and Granger and Newbold (1986). Many of the procedures discussed here are implemented, or easy to implement, on standard econometric packages such as RATS, TSP, PC-GIVE, and MICROFIT.

2. See Granger and Newbold (1986, Ch. 3). Some recent results on implications for estimation are discussed in Stock and Watson (1988).

3. Guilkey and Schmidt (1989) supply more detailed tables.

4. The DF tests assume only one unit root in the process. One often sees the test incorrectly applied by authors who first test the levels series for a unit root and then the differenced series. The correct procedure is to test downwards from the largest possible number of unit roots. See Dickey and Pantula (1987).

5. See Said and Dickey (1984), Solo (1984) and Hall (1989).

6. A frequent application is to test trend versus difference stationarity. Perron (1989, 1990) discusses the case where the trend and intercept change. For an alternative approach to carrying out unit root tests see Phillips (1987), Perron and Phillips (1987), Phillips and Perron (1988) and Perron (1988).

7. See Cochrane (1988, 1991), Schwert (1987) and Christiano and

Eisenbaum (1990) for critical views on unit root testing. Dejong and Whiteman (1991) argue that the tests use a prior which attaches a very low probability to trend stationary alternatives, and so tends to favour finding unit roots.

8. We are grateful to John Cable for providing the data which, in its original form, had no observations for October and November 1979. To obtain a continuous series we replaced the missing values using a simple linear interpolation.

9. For more detailed discussions of tests of specification and misspecification and general issues of dynamic modelling see Harvey (1981a, 1981b). See also papers by Hendry and Richard (1982), Hendry (1983) and Hendry *et al.* (1984).

10. Phillips and Durlauf (1986) provide theoretical support for these results.

11. The intellectual lineage can be traced back to Phillips (1954) and Sargan (1964). The recent literature stems from Davidson *et al.* (1978). See also Hendry and Richard (1982), Hendry (1983), Hendry, Pagan and Sargan (1984).

12. Engle and Granger (1987) ignited an explosion of research into the implications of common trends in economic time series. See articles by Granger and Hendry in *Oxford Bulletin of Economics and Statistics* 48, Pt 3 (1986). See also Phillips and Durlauf (1986), Engle and Yoo (1987). The journals are full of empirical applications. For an example see Campbell and Schiller (1987). A useful survey of cointegration and related issues is Psaradakis (1989).

13. See Engle and Granger (1987); Stock (1987), Phillips and Loretan (1991).

14. It is interesting to note that the threshold model is similar to the asymmetric moving average model developed by Wecker (1981), which was motivated by the analysis of Stigler and Kindahl (1970).

15. For example, $Z_t = 4 + 6Z_{t-1} + Z_{t-1}^2 - 1$ can be transposed to $X_t = 4X_{t-1}(1 - X_{t-1})$ by employing the transformation $Z_t = -4X_{t-1} - 1$ other illustrative examples are: $Z_t = -1.95 Z_{t-1} + Z_{t-1}^2$, $Z_t = 3.95X_t + 2.95$ $A = 3.95$

16. See Baumol and Benhabib (1989) for a fuller exposition. Some understanding is obtained by consideration of the different equilibria. For instance, consider the equilibrium for the two-period limit cycle. This occurs when $X_t = X_{t+2}$, $X_{t+1} = X_{t+3}$. By substitution

$$X_{t+2} = A\{AX_t(1 - X_t)(1 - AX_t(1 - X_t))\}$$
$$= X_{t+2} = f^2(y_t)$$

After some manipulation this can be written at the equilibrium point $(\overline{X})$ as:

$$\overline{X}(A\overline{X} - A + 1)(A^2\overline{X}^2 - (A^2 + A)\overline{X} + A + 1) = 0$$

The first two roots of this correspond to the original one-period equilibrium. The last parenthesis contains a quadratic equation. The roots of this equation are given by:

$$\overline{X} = \frac{A^2 + A \pm A \sqrt{A^3 - 3 - 2A}}{2A^2}$$

For $A < 3$ the roots of this equation are complex and consequently play no role in the dynamics. However, for $A > 3$ we obtain real values which provide the two new stationary points (every other period). The four-period cycles ($X_{t+4} = X_t$, $X_{t+1} = X_{t+5}$, etc.) are obtained in a similar way. We solve the equation $X_{t+4} = f^4(y_t)$. Initially the roots will be complex, but as A increases will become real, giving the points of the new four-period cycle.

It is also of interest to note that if white noise is added to a non-linear system then the possibility of observing aperiodic motion is increased even for ranges of behaviour in which the deterministic component of the model would generate stable cycles in the absence of additions of the random noise (see, e.g. Lines, 1989).

17. We should, however, note that new methods are being developed which show promise in forecasting chaotic systems in the short run (see e.g. Farmer and Sidorowich, 1988).

18. A major area which has been omitted is that of Autoregressive Conditional Heteroscedasticity (ARCH) and the many consequent developments. For a summary see Bollerslev *et al.* (1992).

References

Alchian, A. A. and Demsetz, H. (1972) 'Production, Information Costs, and Economic Organization', *American Economic Review*, 62, pp. 777–95.

Amit, R., Domowitz, I. and Fershtman, C. (1988) 'Thinking One Step Ahead: The Use of Conjectures in Competitor Analysis', *Strategic Management Journal*, 9, pp. 431–42.

Appelbaum, E. (1979) 'Testing Price-Taking Behaviour', *Journal of Econometrics*, 9, pp. 283–94.

———— (1982) 'The Estimation of the Degree of Oligopoly Power', *Journal of Econometrics*, 19, pp. 287–99.

Archibald, G. C., Eaton, B. C. and Lipsey, R. G. (1986) 'Address Models of Value Theory', in J. E. Stiglitz and G. F. Mathewson (eds), *New Developments in the Analysis of Market Structure*, London: Macmillan.

Archibald, G. C. and Rosenbluth, G. (1975) 'The "New" Theory of Consumer Demand and Monopolistic Competition', *Quarterly Journal of Economics*, 89, pp. 569–90.

Arrow, K. (1962) 'Economic Welfare and the Allocation of Resources for Inventions', in R. Nelson (ed.), *The Rate and Direction of Inventive Activity*, Princeton: Princeton University Press, pp. 609–24.

d'Aspremont, C., Jaskold Gabszewicz, J. and Thisse, J. F. (1979) 'On Hotelling's Stability in Competition', *Econometrica*, 47, pp. 1045–50.

Averch, H., and Johnson, L. L., (1962) 'Behaviour of the Firm under Regulatory Constraint', *American Economic Review*, 52, pp. 1052–69.

Axelrod, R. (1981) 'The Emergence of Cooperation among Egoists', *American Political Science Review*, 15, pp. 306–18.

Baghestani, H. (1991) 'Cointegration Analysis of the Advertising–Sales Relationship', *Journal of Industrial Economics*, 39, pp. 671–81.

Bailey, E. (1976) 'Price and Productivity Changes Following Deregulation: The US Experience', *Economic Journal*, 96, pp. 1–17.

Bain, J. S. (1956) *Barriers to New Competition*, Cambridge, MA: Harvard University Press.

———— (1959) *Industrial Organization*, New York: Harvard University Press.

Baron, David (1989) 'Design of Regulatory Mechanisms and Institutions', in R. Schmalensee and R. D. Willig (eds), *Handbook of Industrial Organization*, vol. II, Amsterdam: North-Holland.

Bartlett, W., Cable, J. Estrin, S., Jones, D. C. and Smith, S. C. (1992) 'Labor-Managed Cooperatives and Private Firms in North-Central Italy: An Empirical Comparison', *Industrial and Labor Relations Review*, 46, pp. 103–19.

Barzel, Y. (1968) 'Optimal Timing of Innovations', *Review of Economics and Statistics*, 50, pp. 348–55.

Baumol, W. J. (1959) *Business Behavior, Value and Growth*, New York: Macmillan.

————, and Benhabib, J. (1989) 'Chaos: Significance, Mechanism, and Economic Applications', *Journal of Economic Perspectives*, 3, pp. 77–105.

————, Panzar, J. and Willig, R. (1982) *Contestable Markets and the Theory of Market Structure*, New York: Harcourt, Brace & Jovanovic.

————, and Quandt, R. E. (1985) 'Chaos Models and their Implications for Forecasting', *Eastern Economic Journal*, 11, pp. 3–15.

Beath, J., Katsoulacos, Y. and Ulph, D. (1987) 'Sequential Product Innovation and Industry Evolution', *Economic Journal (Supplement)*, 97, pp. 32–43.

———— (1989a) 'Strategic R&D Policy', *Economic Journal* (Supplement), 99, pp. 74–83.

———— (1989b) 'The Game-Theoretic Analysis of Innovation: A Survey', *Bulletin of Economic Research*, 42, pp. 163–84.

———— (1991) 'The Efficiency of Market Equilibrium in a Tournament Model of Technological Competition', University of Bristol (mimeo).

———— (1992) 'Sequential Product Innovation with Endogenous Market Structure', in A. Gee and G. Norman., (eds), *Market Structure and Market Strategy*. London: Wheatsheaf, pp. 329–350.

———— (1993) 'Strategic Innovation', in M. Bacharach, M. Dempster and J. Enos (eds), *Mathematical Models in Economics* Oxford: Oxford University Press.

Beath, J. and Ulph, D. (1990) 'The Trade-Off Between Static and Dynamic Efficiency in a Non-Tournament Model of Innovation', University of Bristol, *Discussion Paper*, 90/286.

Beesley, M. and Littlechild, S. (1989) 'The Regulation of Privatized Monopolies in the United Kingdom', *Rand Journal of Economics*, 20(3), pp. 454–72.

Benhabib, J. and Day, R. H. (1981) 'Rational Choice and Erratic Behaviour', *Review of Economic Studies*, 48, pp. 459–72.

Ben-Ner, A. (1984) 'On the Stability of the Cooperative Type of Organisation', *Journal of Comparative Economics*, 8, pp. 247–60.

———— (1988) 'Comparative Empirical Observations on Worker-Owned and Capitalist Firms', *International Journal of Industrial Organisation*, 6, pp. 7–31.

Ben-Ner, A. and Estrin, S. (1991) 'What Happens When Unions Run Firms?', *Journal of Comparative Economics*, 15, pp. 65–88.

Berman, K. V. and Berman, M. D. (1989) 'An Empirical Test of the

Theory of the Labor-Managed Firm', *Journal of Comparative Economics*, 13, pp. 281–300.

Bernheim, D. (1984) 'Strategic Deterrence of Sequential Entry into an Industry', *Rand Journal of Economics*, 15, pp. 1–11.

Bertrand, J. (1883) 'Review of "Theorie Mathématique de la Richesse Social" and "Recherches sur les Principes Mathematiques de la Théorie des Richesses"', *Journal des Savants*, pp. 499–508.

Besanko, D. and Sappington, D. (1987) *Designing Regulatory Policy with Limited Information*, London: Harwood Academic Publishers.

Bevan, A. (1974) 'The UK Potato Crisp Industry, 1960–72: A Study of New Entry Competition', *Journal of Industrial Economics*, 22, pp. 281–97.

Biggadike, E. (1976) *Entry, Strategy and Performance*, Harvard University, Division of Research, Harvard Graduate School of Business.

Blinder, A. S. (ed.) (1990) *'Paying for Productivity: A Look at the Evidence*, Washington, DC: Brookings Institution.

Bollerslev, T., Chou, R. Y. and Kroner, K. F. (1992) 'ARCH Modelling in Finance: A Review of Theory and Empirical Evidence', *Journal of Econometrics*, 52, pp. 5–59.

Bonanno, G. (1987) 'Location Choice, Product Proliferation and Entry Deterrence', *Review of Economic Studies*, 54, pp. 37–45.

Bonin, J. P. (1984) 'Membership and Employment in an Egalitarian Cooperative', *Economica*, 51, pp. 295–305.

————, and Fukuda, W. (1986) 'The Multifactor Illyrian Firm Revisited', *Journal of Comparative Economics*, 10, pp. 171–80.

————, and Putterman, L. (1987) *Economics of Cooperation and the Labor-Managed Economy (Fundamentals of Pure and Applied Economics*, 14) London: Harewood Academic Publishers.

Bossaerts, P. (1988) 'Common Nonstationary Components of Asset Prices', *Journal of Economic Dynamics and Control*, 12, pp. 347–64.

Box, G. E. P. and Jenkins, G. M. (1976) 'Time Series Analysis: Forecasting and Control', San Francisco: Holden-Day, 2nd edn.

Box, G. E. P. and Pierce, D. A. (1970) 'Distribution of Residual Autocorrelations in Autoregressions: Integrated Moving Average Time Series Models,' *Journal of the American Statistical Association*, 65, pp. 1509–26.

Boyer, M. and Moreaux, M. (1983) 'Conjectures, Rationality and Oligopoly Theory', *International Journal of Industrial Organisation*, 1, pp. 23–43.

Bradley, I. and Price, C. (1989) 'The Economic Regulation of Private Industries by Price Constraints', *Journal of Industrial Economics*, 37, pp. 9–106.

Bradley, K., Estrin, S. and Taylor, S. (1990) 'Employee Ownership and Company Performance in the John Lewis Partnership', *Industrial Relations*, 29, pp. 385–403.

Bradley, K. and Gelb A. (1983) *Cooperation At Work*, London: Heinemann.

Bramness, G. (1979) 'The General Conjectural Model of Oligopoly:

Some Classical Points Revisited', *Warwick Economic Research Paper*, 142.

Brander, J. A. and Eaton, J. (1984) 'Product Line Rivalry', *American Economic Review*, 74, pp. 323–34.

Brander, J. and Spencer, B. (1983) 'Strategic Commitment with R&D: The Symmetric Case', *Bell Journal of Economics*, 14, pp. 225–35.

Bresnahan, T. F. (1981) 'Duopoly Models with Consistent Conjectures', *American Economic Review*, 71, pp. 934–45.

———— (1989) 'Empirical Studies of Industries with Market Power', in R. Schmalensee and R. D. Willig (eds), *Handbook of Industrial Organisation*, vol. II, Amsterdam: North-Holland.

————, and Reiss, P. (1988) 'Do Entry Conditions Vary Across Markets?', *Brookings Papers on Economic Activity*, 3, pp. 833–81.

————, and Schmalensee, R. (1987) 'The Empirical Renaissance in Industrial Economics: An Overview', *Journal of Industrial Economics*, 35, pp. 371–8.

Brock, G. (1975) *The US Computer Industry: A Study of Market Power*, Cambridge, MA: Ballinger.

Brock, W. A., Hsieh, D. A. and LeBaron, B. (1991) *Nonlinear Dynamics, Chaos and Instability*, Cambridge, MA: MIT Press.

Brown, R. (1978) 'Estimating Advantages to Large Scale Advertising', *Review of Economics and Statistics*, 60, pp. 428–37.

Bulow, J., Geanakopolos, J. and Klemperer, P. (1985) 'Multimarket Oligopoly: Strategic Substitutes and Complements', *Journal of Political Economy*, 93, pp. 488–511.

Burton, M. (1991) 'Some Implications of Chaos for Models in Agricultural Economics', University of Manchester (mimeo).

Cable, J. (1984) 'Employee Participation and Firm Performance: A Prisoners' Dilemma Framework', *European University Institute Working Paper*, 84/126, Florence.

Cable, J. and Fitzroy, F. (1980) 'Cooperation and Productivity – Some Evidence from West German Experience', *Kyklos*, 33, pp. 100–21.

Campbell, J. Y. and Schiller, R. J. (1987) 'Cointegration and Tests of Present Value Models', *Journal of Political Economy*, 95, pp. 1062–87.

Carlsson, B. (1989) 'Flexibility and the Theory of the Firm', *International Journal of Industrial Organisation*, 7, pp. 179–204.

Caves, R. E. and Porter, M. (1977) 'From Entry Barriers to Mobility Barriers: Conjectural Decisions and the Contrived Deterrence to New Competition', *Quarterly Journal of Economics*, 97, pp. 247–61.

Caves, R. E. and Williamson, P. J. (1985) 'What is Product Differentiation, Really?', *Journal of Industrial Economics*, 34, pp. 113–32.

Chamberlin, E. H. (1933) *The Theory of Monopolistic Competition*, Cambridge, MA: Harvard University Press.

Christiano, L. J. and Eichenbaum, M. (1990) 'Unit Roots in Real GNP: Do We Know and Do We Care?', *Carnegie Rochester Series in Public Policy*, 32, pp. 7–62.

Clarke, R. and Davies, S. W. (1982) 'Market Structure and Price-Cost Margins', *Economica*, 49, pp. 277–87.

Cochrane, J. H. (1988) 'How Big is the Random Walk in G.N.P.?', *Journal of Political Economy*, 96, pp. 893–920.

———— (1991) 'A Critique of the Application of Unit Root Tests', *Journal of Economic Dynamics and Control*, 15, pp. 275–84.

Cohen, W. and Levinthal, D. (1989) 'Innovation and Learning: The Two Faces of R&D', *Economic Journal*, 99, pp. 569–96.

Comanor, W. S. and Wilson, T. A. (1967) 'Advertising, Market Structure and Performance', *Review of Economics and Statistics*, 49, pp. 423–40.

————, (1974) *Advertising and Market Power*, Cambridge, MA: Harvard University Press.

———— (1979) 'The Effect of Advertising on Competition: A Survey', *Journal of Economic Literature*, 17, pp. 453–76.

Cournot, A. (1863) *Recherches sur les Principes Mathématiques de la Théorie des Richesses*, Paris: Hachette.

Cowing, Thomas G. (1978) 'The Effectiveness of Rate of Return Regulation: an empirical test using profit functions', in Daniel McFadden (ed.), *Production Economics: A Dual Approach To Theory And Applications*, vol 2, Amsterdam: North-Holland.

Cowling, K. G. (1981) 'Oligopoly, Distribution and the Rate of Profit', *European Economic Review*, 15, pp. 195–224.

————, Cable, J., Kelly, M. and McGuinness, T. (1975) *Advertising and Economic Behaviour*, London: Macmillan.

————, and Mueller D. C. (1978) 'The Social Costs of Monopoly Power', *Economic Journal*, 88, pp. 727–48.

————, and Waterson, M. J. (1976) 'Price-cost Margins and Market Structure', *Economica*, 43, pp. 267–74.

Crew, M. and Kleindorfer, P. (1986) *The Economics of Public Utility Regulation*, London: Macmillan.

Cubbin, J. (1983) 'Apparent Collusion and Conjectural Variations in Differentiated Oligopoly', *International Journal of Industrial Organisation*, 1, pp. 155–63.

————, (1988) *Market Structure and Performance: The Empirical Research*, London and Chur: Harwood Academic Publishers.

————, and Geroski, P. (1987) 'The Convergence of Profits in the Long Run: Inter-firm and Inter-Industry Comparisons', *Journal of Industrial Economics*, pp. 427–36.

Dana, R. A. and Montrucchio, L. (1986) 'Dynamic Complexity in Duopoly Games', *Journal of Economic Theory*, 40, pp. 40–56.

Dasgupta, P. and Stiglitz, J. (1980) 'Industrial Structure and the Nature of Innovative Activity', *Economic Journal*, 90, pp. 266–293.

Daskin, A. J. (1991) 'Deadweight Loss in Oligopoly: A New Approach', *Southern Economic Journal*, 58, pp. 171–85.

Daughety, A. (1985) 'Reconsidering Cournot: The Cournot Equilibrium is Consistent', *Rand Journal*, 16, pp. 368–80.

Davidson, C. and Deneckere, R. (1986) 'Long-run Competition in Capacity, Short-Run Competition in Price and the Cournot Model', *Rand Journal of Economics*, 17, pp. 405–15.

Davidson, J. E. H., Hendry, D. F., Srba, F. and Yeo, S. (1978) 'Econometric Modelling of the Aggregate Time Series Relationship between Consumers' Expenditure and Income in the United Kingdom', *Economic Journal*, 88, pp. 661–92.

Davies, S., Geroski, P., and Vlassopoulos, A. (1991) 'The Dynamics of Market Leadership in UK Manufacturing Industry', Report for the Centre of Business Strategy, London Business School.

Davis, E. (1984) 'Express Coaching since 1980: Liberalization in Practice', *Fiscal Studies*, 5, pp. 76–86.

Dejong, D. N. and Whiteman, C. H. (1991) 'Reconsidering Trends and Random Walks in Macroeconomic Time Series', *Journal of Monetary Economics*, 28, pp. 221–54.

Demsetz, Harold (1968) 'Why Regulate Utilities?', *Journal of Law and Economics*, 11, pp. 55–65.

Dickey, D. A., Bell, W. A. and Miller, R. B. (1986) 'Unit Roots in Time Series Models: Tests and Implications', *American Statistician*, 40, pp. 12–26.

Dickey, D. A. and Fuller, W. A. (1979) 'Distribution of the Estimators for Autoregressive Time Series with a Unit Root', *Journal of the American Statistical Association*, 74, pp. 427–31.

——— (1981) 'Likelihood Ratio Statistics for Autoregressive Time Series with a Unit Root', *Econometrica*, 49, pp. 1057–72.

Dickey, D. A. and Pantula, S. G. (1987) 'Determining the Order of Differencing in Autoregressive Processes', *Journal of Business and Economic Statistics*, 5, pp. 455–61.

Dixit, A. K. (1979) 'A Model of Duopoly Suggesting a Theory of Entry Barriers', *Bell Journal of Economics*, 10, pp. 20–32.

——— (1980) 'The Role of Investment in Entry Deterrence', *Economic Journal*, 90, pp. 95–106.

——— (1982) 'Recent Developments in Oligopoly Theory', *American Economic Review Papers and Proceedings*, 72, pp. 12–17.

———, and Stern, N. (1982) 'Oligopoly and Welfare: A Unified Presentation with Applications to Trade and Development', *European Economic Review*, 19, pp. 123–43.

———, and Stiglitz, J. E. (1977) 'Monopolistic Competition and Optimum Product Diversity', *American Economic Review*, 67, pp. 297–308.

Dolbear, F. T., Lave, L. B., Bowman, G., Lieberman, A., Prescott, E. C., Rueter, F. and Sherman, R. (1968) 'Collusion and Oligopoly: An Experiment on the Effects of Numbers and Information', *Quarterly Journal of Economics*, 82, pp. 240–59.

Domar, E. D. (1966) 'The Soviet Collective Farm as a Producers' Cooperative', *American Economic Review*, 56, pp. 734–57.

Dorfman, R. and Steiner, P. O. (1954) 'Optimal Advertising and Optimal Quality', *American Economic Review*, 44, pp. 826–36.

Drèze, J. (1976) 'Some Theory of Labor Management and Participation', *Econometrica*, 44, pp. 1125–39.

Dunne, T., Roberts, M. and Samuelson, L. (1988) 'Patterns of Firm Entry and Exit in US Manufacturing Industries', *Rand Journal of Economics*, 19, pp. 495–515.

Durlauf, S. N. and Phillips, P. C. B. (1988) 'Trends versus Random Walks in Time Series Analysis', *Econometrica*, 56, pp. 1333–54.

Eaton, B. C. (1972) 'Spatial Competition revisited', *Canadian Journal of Economics*, 5, pp. 268–78.

————, and Lipsey, R. G. (1978) 'Freedom of Entry and the Existence of Pure Profits', *Economic Journal*, 88, pp. 455–69.

———— (1979) 'The Theory of Market Pre-emption: the Persistence of Excess Capacity and Monopoly in Growing Spatial Markets', *Economica*, 46, pp. 149–58.

EEC (1988) 'The Economics of 1992', *European Economy*, 35, pp. 1–222.

Engle, R. F. and Granger, C. W. J. (1987) 'Cointegration and Error Correction: Representation, Estimation and Testing', *Econometrica*, 55, pp. 251–76.

Engle, R. F. and Yoo, B. S. (1987) 'Forecasting and Testing in Cointegrated Systems', *Journal of Econometrics*, 35, pp. 143–59.

Erickson, W. (1976) 'Price Fixing Conspiracies: Their Long Term Impact', *Journal of Industrial Economics*, 26, pp. 189–202.

Estrin, S. (1982) 'Long Run Supply Responses under Labor-Management', *Journal of Comparative Economics*, 6, pp. 363–78.

———— (1983) *Self-management: Economic Theory and Yugoslav Practice*, Cambridge: Cambridge University Press.

———— (1986) 'The Role of Producer Cooperatives in Employment Creation', *Economic Analysis and Workers' Management*, 19, pp. 345–84.

———— (1991) 'Some Reflections on Self-Management, Social Choice and Reform in Eastern Europe', *Journal of Comparative Economics*, 15, pp. 349–66.

————, Grout, P. and Wadhwani, S. B. (1987) 'The Share Economy: A Critical Evaluation', *Economic Policy*, April, pp. 14–62.

————, and Jones, D. C. (1988) 'Do Employee-owned Firms Invest Less?', London School of Economics, Centre for Labour Economics, Working Paper 956.

————, (1991) 'The Viability of Employee-Owned Firms: Evidence from France', *Industrial and Labor Relations Review*.

————, and Svejnar J. (1987) 'The Productivity Effects of Worker Participation: Producer Cooperatives in Western Economies', *Journal of Comparative Economics*, II, pp. 40–61.

Fagerberg, J. (1988) 'International Competitiveness', *Economic Journal*, 98, pp. 355–74.

Fama, E. (1980) 'Agency Problems and the Theory of the Firm', *Journal of Political Economy*, 88, pp. 288–307.

Farmer, J. D. and Sidorowich, J. (1988) 'Can New Approaches to Non-linear Modelling Improve Economic Forecasts?', in P. W. Anderson, K. J. Arrow and D. Pines (eds), *The Economy as an Evolving Complex System*, New York: Addison-Wesley.

Farrell, M. G. (1957) 'The Measurement of Productive Efficiency', *Journal of the Royal Statistical Society*, series A, 120, pp. 253–81.

Feigenbaum, M. J. (1980) 'Universal Behaviour in Non-linear Systems', *Los Alamos Science*, 1, pp. 4–27.

Finsinger, J. and Vogelsang, I. (1982) 'Performance Indices for Public

Enterprises', in L. P. Jones (ed.), *Public Enterprise in Less Developed Countries*, Cambridge: Cambridge University Press.

Fisher, F. (1987) 'Pan-American to United: the Pacific Division Transfer Case', *Rand Journal of Economics*, 18, pp. 492–508.

Flaherty, M. (1980) 'Industry Structure and Cost-Reducing Investment', *Econometrica*, 48, pp. 1187–1209.

Frank, M. and Stengos, T. (1988) 'Chaotic Dynamics in Economic Time-Series', *Journal of Economic Surveys*, 2, pp. 103–33.

Friedman, J. W. (1971) 'A Non-cooperative Equilibrium for Super-games', *Review of Economic Studies*, 38, pp. 1–12.

Friedman, M. (1953) 'The Methodology of Positive Economics', in M. Friedman, *Essays in Positive Economics*, Chicago: Chicago University Press.

Fudenberg, D., Gilbert, R., Stiglitz, J. and Tirole, J. (1983) 'Preemption, Leapfrogging and Competition in Patent Races', *European Economic Review*, 22, pp. 3–31.

Fudenberg, D. and Tirole, J. (1986) *Dynamic Models of Oligopoly*, Chur: Harwood Academic Publishers.

Fuller, W. A. (1976) *Introduction to Statistical Time Series*, New York: John Wiley.

Furubotn, E. and Pejovich, S. (1970) 'Property Rights and the Behaviour of the Firm in a Socialist State: The Example of Yugoslavia', *Zeitschrift für Nationalökonomie*, 30, pp. 431–54.

Futia, C. (1980) 'Schumpeterian Competition', *Quarterly Journal of Economics*, 93, pp. 675–95.

Geroski, P. (1989a) 'The Effect of Entry on Profit Margins in the Short and Long Run', *Annales d'Economie et de Statistique*, 15–16, pp. 333–53.

———— (1989b) 'Entry, Innovation and Productivity Growth', *Review of Economics and Statistics*, 71, pp. 572–8.

———— (1990) 'Entry, Exit and Structural Adjustment in European Industry', in K. Cool, D. Neven and I. Walter (eds), *European Industrial Restructuring in the 1990s*, London: Macmillan.

———— (1991) *Market Dynamics and Entry*, Oxford: Basil Blackwell.

————, and Murfin, A. (1990) 'Advertising and the Dynamics of Market Structure: the UK Car Industry 1958–1983', *British Journal of Management*, 1, pp. 77–90.

————, Gilbert, R. and Jacquemin, A. (1990) *Barriers to Entry and Strategic Competition*, London: Harwood Academic Publishers.

Gilbert, R. (1989) 'Pre-emptive Competition', in R. Schmalensee and R. Willig (eds), *Handbook of Industrial Organization*, Amsterdam: North-Holland.

————, and Newbery, D. (1982) 'Preemptive Patenting and the Persistence of Monopoly', *American Economic Review*, 72, pp. 514–26.

Gollop, F. and Roberts, M. J. (1979) 'Firm Interdependence in Oligopolistic Markets', *Journal of Econometrics*, 10, pp. 323–31.

Gorecki, P. (1986) 'The Importance of Being First: the Case of Prescription Drugs in Canada', *International Journal of Industrial Organization*, 4, pp. 371–96.

Gort, M. and Klepper, S. (1982) 'Time Paths in the Diffusion of Product Innovations', *Economic Journal*, 92, pp. 630–53.

Gould, J. P. (1970) 'Diffusion Processes and Optimal Advertising Policy', in E. Phelps (ed.), *Microeconomic Foundations of Employment and Inflation Theory*, New York: W. W. Norton, pp. 338–68.

Grabowski, H. and Vernon, J. (1982) 'The Pharmaceutical Industry', in R. Nelson (ed.), *Government and Technical Progress*, Oxford: Pergamon Press.

Granger, C. W. J. and Andersen, A. P. (1978) *An Introduction to Bilinear Time Series Models*, Göttingen: Vanderhoeck and Ruprecht.

Granger, C. W. J. and Newbold, P. (1974) 'Spurious Regressions in Econometrics', *Journal of Econometrics*, 2, pp. 189–203.

———— (1986) *Forecasting Economic Time Series*, London: Academic Press, 2nd edn.

Grassberger, P. and Procaccia, I. (1983) 'Measuring the Strangeness of Strange Attractors', *Physica*, 9D, pp. 189–208.

Gravelle, H. and Rees R. (1981) *Microeconomics*, Harlow: Longman.

Green, E. J. and Porter, R. H. (1984) 'Noncooperative Collusion under Imperfect Price Infomation', *Econometrica*, 52, pp. 87–100.

Greenaway, D. (1987) 'The New Theories of Intra-Industry Trade', *Bulletin of Economic Research*, 39, pp. 95–120.

Grindley, P. and McBryde, R. (1989) 'The Use of Product Standards in Business Strategy: Video Cassette Recorders', London Business School (mimeo).

Grossman, S. and Hart O. (1980) 'Takeover Bids, the Free Rider Problem and the Theory of the Corporation', *Bell Journal of Economics*, 11, pp. 42–64.

———— (1986) 'The Costs and Benefits of Ownership: A Theory of Vertical and Lateral Integration', *Journal of Political Economy*, 94, pp. 691–719.

Grossman, G. and Shapiro, C. (1987) 'Dynamic R&D Competition', *Economic Journal*, 97, pp. 327–87.

Guilkey, D. K. and Schmidt, P. (1989) 'Extended Tabulations for Dickey–Fuller Tests', *Economics Letters*, 31, pp. 355–57.

Hall, A. (1989) 'Testing for a Unit Root in the Presence of Moving Average Errors', *Biometrika*, 76, pp. 49–56.

Hansen, B. E. and Phillips, P. C. B. (1990) 'Estimation and Inference in Models of Cointegration: A Simulation Study', *Advances in Econometrics*,

Harberger, A. (1954) 'Monopoly and Resource Allocation', *American Economic Review Papers and Proceedings*, 44, pp. 73–87.

Harris, C. and Vickers, J. (1987) 'Racing with Uncertainty', *Review of Economic Studies*, 54, pp. 1–21.

Hart, O. and Holmstrom B. (1987) 'The Theory of Contracts', in T. Bewley (ed.), *Advances in Economic Theory, Fifth World Congress*, Cambridge: Cambridge University Press.

Hart, O. and Moore J. (1990) 'Property Rights and the Nature of the Firm', *Journal of Political Economy*, 98, pp. 1119–58.

Harvey, A. C. (1981a) *The Econometric Analysis of Time Series*, Oxford: Phillip Allan.

———— (1981b) *Time Series Models*, Oxford: Phillip Allan.

Hay, D. A. (1976) 'Sequential Entry and Entry-deterring Strategies in Spatial Competition', *Oxford Economic Papers*, 28, pp. 240–57.

————, and Morris, D. J. (1991) *Industrial Economics and Organisation: Theory and Evidence*, Oxford: Oxford University Press.

Helm, D. (1989) 'Mergers, Takeovers, and the Enforcement of Profit Maximization', in J. Fairburn and J. Kay (eds), *Mergers and Merger Policy*, Oxford: Oxford University Press.

Henderson, J. M. and Quandt, R. E. (1980) *Microeconomic Theory*, New York: McGraw-Hill, 3rd edn.

Hendry, D. F. (1983) 'The Econometric Analysis of Economic Time Series', *International Statistical Review*, 51, pp. 111–163.

————, Pagan, A. R. and Sargan, J. D. (1984) 'Dynamic Specification', in Z. Griliches and M. Intriligator (eds), *Handbook of Econometrics*, Amsterdam: North-Holland.

Hendry, D. F. and Richard, J. F. (1982) 'On the Formulation of Empirical Models in Dynamic Econometrics', *Journal of Econometrics*, 20, pp. 3–33.

Holt, C. A. (1985) 'An Experimental Test of the Consistent Conjectures Hypothesis', *American Economic Review*, 75, pp. 314–25.

Horvat, B. (1982) *The Political Economy of Socialism*, Armonk, NY: M. E. Sharpe.

Hotelling, H. (1929) 'Stability in Competition', *Economic Journal*, 39, pp. 41–7.

Ireland, N. J. (1987) *Product Differentiation and Non-price Competition*, Oxford: Basil Blackwell.

————, and Law, P. J. (1981) 'Efficiency, Incentives, and Individual Labor Supply in the Labor-Managed Firm', *Journal of Comparative Economics*, 5, pp. 1–23.

———— (1982) *The Economic Analysis of Labour Managed Enterprise*, London: Croom Helm.

Iwata, G. (1974) 'Measurement of Conjectural Variations in Oligopoly', *Econometrica*, 42, pp. 947–66.

Jacquemin, A. and Slade, M. E. (1988) 'Cartels, Collusion and Horizontal Mergers', in *Handbook of Industrial Organisation*, vol. I, R. Schmalensee and R. D. Willig (eds), Amsterdam: North-Holland.

Jarrell, G. A., Brickley, J. A. and Netter, J. M. (1988) 'The Market for Corporate Control: The Empirical Evidence Since 1980', *Journal of Economic Perspectives*, 2, pp. 49–68.

Jaskold Gabszewicz, J. and Thisse J. F. (1979) 'Price Competition, Quality and Income Disparities', *Journal of Economic Theory*, 20, pp. 340–59.

———— (1980) 'Entry (and Exit) in a Differentiated Industry', *Journal of Economic Theory*, 22, pp. 327–38.

———— (1986a) 'Spatial Competition and the Location of Firms', in J. Jaskold Gabszewicz, J. F. Thisse, M. Fujita and U. Schweizer, *Loca-*

tion Theory, Chur: Harwood Academic Publishers.

———— (1986b) 'Spatial Competition and the Market: the Monopolist's Optimal Product Mix', *Journal of Economic Theory*, 39, pp. 273–89.

Johansen, S. (1988) 'Statistical Analysis of Cointegration Vectors', *Journal of Economic Dynamics and Control*, 12, pp. 231–54.

———— (1991) 'Estimation and Testing of Cointegration Vectors in Gaussian Vector Autoregressive Models', *Econometrica*, 59, pp. 1551–80.

Jong, H. W. de (1986) 'European Industrial Organization: Entrepreneurial Economics in an Organizational Setting', in H. W. de Jong and W. G. Shepherd (eds), *Mainstreams in Industrial Organization, Book I*, Boston: Kluwer.

Joskow, P. (1987) 'Contract Duration and Relationship-Specific Investments: The Case of Coal', *American Economic Review*, 77, pp. 168–85.

————, and Schmalensee, R. (1986) 'Incentive Regulation for Electric Utilities', *Yale Journal on Regulation*, 4(1), pp. 1–49.

Judd, K. L. (1985a) 'Credible Spatial Preemption', *Rand Journal of Economics*, 16, pp. 153–66.

———— (1985b) 'On the Performance of Patents', *Econometrica*, 53, pp. 567–85.

Kamerschen, D. R. (1966) 'An Estimation of the "Welfare Losses" from Monopoly in the American Economy', *Western Economic Journal* (Summer) pp. 221–36.

Kamien, M. and Schwartz, N. (1971) 'Timing of Innovations under Rivalry', *Econometrica*, 40, pp. 43–60.

————, (1983) 'Conjectural Variations', *Canadian Journal of Economics*, 16, pp. 191–211.

Kaplinsky, R. (1983) 'Firm Size and Technical Change in a Dynamic Context', *Journal of Industrial Economics*, 32, pp. 39–60.

Katsoulacos, Y. and Ulph, D. (1990a) 'R&D Rivalry under Product Differentiation: Market Equilibria and Social Optimum', University of Liverpool, *Discussion Paper*.

———— (1990b) 'Social Welfare Losses under Product Differentiation and R&D Rivalry', University of Bristol, *Discussion Paper*, 90/285.

Katz, M. L. and Shapiro, C. (1987) 'R&D Rivalry with Licensing or Imitation', *American Economic Review*, 77, pp. 402–420.

Kessides, I. (1986) 'Advertising, Sunk Costs and Barriers to Entry', *Review of Economics and Statistics*, 68, pp. 84–95.

Kihlstrom, R. E. and Levhari, D. (1977) 'Quality, Regulation and Efficiency', *Kyklos*, 30, pp. 214–34.

Koutsoyiannis, A. (1979), *Modern Microeconomics*, London: Macmillan.

Kreps, D. and Scheinkman, J. (1983) 'Quantity Pre-commitment and Bertrand Competition Yield Cournot Outcomes', *Bell Journal of Economics*, 14, pp. 326–37.

————, and Wilson, R. (1982) 'Sequential Equilibrium', *Econometrica*, 50, pp. 863–94.

Laitner, J. (1980) 'Rational Duopoly Equilibrium', *Quarterly Journal of Economics*, 95, pp. 641–62.

Lancaster, K. (1966) 'A New Approach to Consumer Theory', *Journal of Political Economy*, 74, pp. 132–57.

————— (1971) *Consumer Demand: a New Approach*, New York: Columbia University Press.

————— (1974) 'Socially Optimal Product Differentiation', *American Economic Review*, 65, pp. 567–85.

————— (1979) *Variety, Equity and Efficiency*, New York: Columbia University Press.

Lee, B. (1988) *Productivity and Employee Ownership: The Case of Sweden*, Stockholm: Trade Union Institute for Economic Research.

Lee, T. and Wilde, L. (1980) 'Market Structure and Innovation: A Reformulation', *Quarterly Journal of Economics*, 94, pp. 429–36.

Leffler, K. B. and Rucker, R. R. (1991) 'Transactions Costs and the Efficient Organization of Production: A Study of Timber Harvesting Contracts', *Journal of Political Economy*, 99, pp. 1060–87.

Leibeinstein, H. (1966) 'Allocative Efficiency vs. X-Efficiency', *American Economic Review*, 56, pp. 392–415.

Lerner, A. (1934) 'The Concept of Monopoly and the Measurement of Monopoly Power', *Review of Economic Studies*, 1, pp. 157–75.

Levhari, D. and Peles, Y. (1973) 'Marker Structure and Durability', *Bell Journal of Economics*, 4, pp. 244–8.

Lieberman, M. (1984) 'The Learning Curve and Pricing in the Chemical Processing Industries', *Rand Journal of Economics*, 15, pp. 213–28.

Lines, M. (1989) 'Environmental Noise and Non-linear Models', *Economic Notes*, 3, pp. 376–94.

Lipsey, R. G. and Rosenbluth, G. (1971) 'A Contribution to the New Theories of Demand: A Rehabilitation of the Giffen Good', *Canadian Journal of Economics*, 4, pp. 121–63.

Littlechild, Stephen (1983) *Regulation of British Telecommunications Profitability*, London: HMSO.

Ljung, G. M. and Box, G. E. P. (1978)'On a Measure of Lack of Fit in Time Series Models', *Biometrika*, 65, pp. 297–303.

Loeb, M. and Magat, W. (1979) 'A Decentralized Method for Utility Regulation', *Journal of Law and Economics*, 22, pp. 399–404.

Lorenz, E. N. (1963) 'Deterministic Non-Periodic Flow', *Journal of Atmospheric Science*, 20, pp. 130–48.

Loury, G. (1979) 'Market Structure and Innovation', *Quarterly Journal of Economics*, 93, pp. 395–410.

Lucas Jr, R. (1971) 'Optimal Management of a Research and Development Project', *Management Science*, 17, pp. 679–97.

Makowski, L. (1987) 'Are "Rational Conjectures" Rational?', *Journal of Industrial Economics*, 36, pp. 35–48.

Mankiw, G. B. and Whinston, M. D. (1986) 'Free Entry and Social Efficiency', *Rand Journal of Economics*, 17, pp. 48–58.

Mansfield, E., Schwartz, M. and Wagner, S. (1981) 'Imitation Costs and Patents: An Empirical Study', *Economic Journal*, 91, pp. 903–18.

Maravall, A. (1983) 'An Application of Non-linear Time Series Forecasting', *Journal of Business and Economic Statistics*.

Marshall, A. (1919) *Industry and Trade*, London: Macmillan.

Marris, R. (1964) *The Economic Theory of 'Managerial' Capitalism*, London: Macmillan.

———— (1982) 'Stochastic Dynamic Limit Pricing: An Empirical Test', *Review of Economics and Statistics*, 64, pp. 413–23.

Mason, E. S. (1957) *Economic Concentration and the Monopoly Problem*, Cambridge Mass: Harvard University Press.

Masson, R. and Shaanan, J. (1984) 'Social Costs of Oligopoly and the Value of Competition', *Economic Journal*, 94, pp. 520–35.

May, R. M. (1976) 'Simple Mathematical Models with Very Complicated Dynamics', *Nature*, 261, pp. 59–467.

McDonald, I. M. and Solow, R. M. (1981) 'Wage Bargaining and Employment', *American Economic Review*, 71, pp. 896–908.

McKinnon, J. G. (1991) 'Critical Values for Cointegration Tests', University of California, in Engle, R. F. and Granger, C. W. J. *Long Run Economic Relationships: Readings in Cointegration*, Oxford: Oxford University Press.

Meade, J. E. (1972) 'The Theory of Labour-Managed Firms and of Profit Sharing', *Economic Journal*, 32, pp. 402–28.

Milgrom, P. and Roberts, J. (1982) 'Limit Pricing and Entry Under Incomplete Information: An Equilibrium Analysis', *Econometrica*, 50, pp. 443–59.

———— (1992) *Economics, Organization and Management*, Englewood Cliffs, NJ: Prentice-Hall.

Modigliani, F. (1958) 'New Developments on the Oligopoly Front', *Journal of Political Economy*, 66, pp. 215–32.

Moore, J. (1991) 'The Firm as a Collection of Assets', Discussion Paper, TE/91/234, Suntory-Toyota Centre for Economics and Related Disciplines, London School of Economics.

Mueller, D. C. (1976) 'Public Choice: a Survey', *Journal of Economic Literature*, 14, pp. 395–433.

————, (1986) *Profits in the Long Run*, Cambridge: Cambridge University Press.

————, (ed.) (1990) *The Dynamics of Company Profits*, Cambridge: Cambridge University Press.

Mussa, M. and Rosen, S. (1978) 'Monopoly and Product Quality', *Journal of Economic Theory*, 18, pp. 301–17.

Neven, D. (1985) 'Two Stage (Perfect) Equilibrium in Hotelling's Model', *Journal of Industrial Economics*, 33, pp. 317–25.

Norman, G. and La Manna, M. (1992) 'Introduction', in G. Norman and M. La Manna (eds), *The New Industrial Economics*, Aldershot: Edward Elgar.

OECD (1985) *Costs and Benefits of Protection*, Paris: OECD.

Orr, D. (1974) 'The Determinants of Entry: A Study of the Canadian Manufacturing Industry', *Review of Economics and Statistics*, 61, pp. 58–66.

Osborne, D. K. (1976) 'Cartel Problems', *American Economic Review*, 66, pp. 835–44.

Palda, K. S. (1964) *The Measurement of Cumulative Advertising Effects*, Englewood Cliffs, NJ: Prentice-Hall.

de Palma, A., Ginsburgh, V., Papageorgiou, Y. Y. and Thisse, J. F. (1985) 'The Principle of Minimum Differentiation Holds Under Sufficient Heterogeneity', *Econometrica*, 53, pp. 767–81.

Park, J. (1987) 'Dynamic Patent Races with Risky Choices', *Management Science*, 33, pp. 1563–72.

Perron, P. (1988) 'Trends and Random Walks in Macroeconomic Time Series: Further Evidence from a New Approach', *Journal of Economic Dynamics and Control*, 12, pp. 297–332.

———— (1989) 'The Great Crash, the Oil Price Shock and the Unit Root Hypothesis', *Econometrica*, 57, pp. 1361–1401.

———— (1990) 'Testing for a Unit Root in a Time Series with a Changing Mean', *Journal of Business and Economic Statistics*, 8, pp. 153–62.

————, and Phillips, P. C. B. (1987) 'Does GNP have a Unit Root?', *Economics Letters*, 23, pp. 139–45.

Perry, M. K. (1982) 'Oligopoly and Consistent Conjectural Variations', *Bell Journal of Economics*, 13, pp. 197–205.

Pfouts, R. and Rosefelde, S. (1986) 'The Firm in Illyria: Market Syndicalism Revisited', *Journal of Comparative Economics*, 10, pp. 160–70.

Phillips, A. (1976) 'A Critique of Empirical Studies of the Relationship between Market Structure and Profitability', *Journal of Industrial Economics*, 24, pp. 214–19.

Phillips, A. W. (1954) 'Stabilisation Policy in the Closed Economy', *Economic Journal*, 64, pp. 290–323.

Phillips, P. C. B. (1987) 'Time Series Regressions with a Unit Root', *Econometrica*, 55, pp. 473–95.

————, and Durlauf, S. N. (1986) 'Multiple Time Series with Integrated Processes', *Review of Economic Studies*, 53, pp. 473–95.

————, and Hansen, B. E. (1990) 'Statistical Inference in Instrumental Variable Regression with I(1) Processes', *Review of Economic Studies*, 57, pp. 9–125.

————, and Loretan, M. (1991) 'Estimating Long Run Economic Equilibria', *Review of Economic Studies*, 58, pp. 407–36.

————, and Perron, P. (1988) 'Testing for a Unit Root in Time Series Regressions', *Biometrika*, 75(2), pp. 335–46.

Pindyck, R. S. and Rubinfeld, D. S. (1991) *Econometric Models and Economic Forecasts*, New York: McGraw-Hill, 3rd edn.

Plott, C. R. (1989) 'An Updated Review of Industrial Organization: Applications of Experimental Methods', in R. Schmalensee and R. D. Willig (eds), *Handbook of Industrial Organization*, vols 1 and 2, Amsterdam: North-Holland.

Porter, R. H. (1983) 'Optimal Cartel Trigger Price Strategies', *Journal of Economic Theory*, 29, pp. 313–38.

Priestley, M. B. (1981) *Spectral Analysis and Time Series*, London: Academic Press.

———— (1988) *Non-linear and Non-Stationary Time Series Analysis*, London: Academic Press.

Prescott, E. C. and Visscher, M. (1977) 'Sequential Location Among Firms with Foresight', *Bell Journal of Economics*, 8, pp. 378–93.

Psaradakis, Z. G. (1989) 'The Econometrics of Cointegrated Time Series: A Survey', University of Southampton, Department of Economics, *Discussion Paper*.

Rand, D. (1978) 'Exotic Phenomena in Games and Duopoly Models', *Journal of Mathematical Economics*, 5, pp. 173–84.

Reinganum, J. (1981) 'Dynamic Games of Innovation', *Journal of Economic Theory*, 25, pp. 21–41 (also (1985) 'Corrigendum', *Journal of Economic Theory*, 35, pp. 196–7).

———— (1982) 'A Dynamic Game of R&D: Patent Protection and Competitive Behaviour', *Econometrica*, 50, pp. 671–88.

———— (1983) 'Uncertain Innovation and the Persistence of Monopoly', *American Economic Review*, 73, pp. 741–8.

———— (1985) 'Innovation and Industry Evolution', *Quarterly Journal of Economics*, 100, pp. 81–99.

Rizzo, J. and Zeckhauser, R. (1990) 'Advertising and Entry: The Case of Physicians' Services', *Journal of Political Economy*, 98, pp. 476–500.

Roberts, D. J. (1987) 'Battles for Market Share: Incomplete Information Aggressive Pricing and Competitive Dynamics', in T. Bewley (ed.), *Advances in Economic Theory, Fifth World Congress*, Cambridge: Cambridge University Press.

Robinson, J. (1967) 'The Soviet Collective Farm as a Producer Cooperative: Comment', *American Economic Review*, 57, pp. 222–3.

Rogerson, W. (1982) 'The Social Costs of Monopoly and Regulation: A Game-Theoretic Analysis', *Bell Journal of Economics*, 13, pp. 391–401.

Rothschild, R. (1976) 'A Note on the Effect of Sequential Entry on Choice of Location', *Journal of Industrial Economics*, 24, pp. 313–20.

Russell, R. (1985) *Sharing Ownership in the Workplace*. Albany: State University of New York Press.

Said, S. E. and Dickey, D. A. (1984) 'Testing for Unit Roots in Autoregressive-Moving Average Time Series of Unknown Order', *Biometrika*, 71, pp. 599–607.

Salop, S. C. (1979a) 'Monopolistic Competition with Outside Goods', *Bell Journal of Economics*, 10, pp. 141–56.

———— (1979b) 'Strategic Entry Deterrence', *American Economic Review Papers and Proceedings*, 69, pp. 335–8.

————, and Scheffman, D. (1983) 'Raising Rival's Costs', *American Economic Review*, 73, pp. 267–71.

Samuelson, P. A. (1967) 'The Monopolistic Competition Revolution', in R. Kuenne (ed.), *Monopolistic Competition Theory*, New York, Wiley.

Sappington, D. (1980) 'Strategic Firm Behaviour under a Dynamic Regulatory Adjustment Process', *Bell Journal of Economics*, 11, pp. 360–72.

———— (1991) 'Incentives in Principal Agent Relationships', *Journal of Economic Perspectives* (Spring) pp. 1–30.

Sargan, D. J. D. (1964) 'Wages and Prices in the United Kingdom: A Study in Econometric Methodology', reprinted in D. F. Hendry and K.

F. Wallis (eds), *Econometrics and Quantitative Economics*, Oxford: Basil Blackwell.

Sargent, T. J. (1979) *Macroeconomic Theory*, London: Academic Press.

Scherer, F. M. (1967) 'Research and Development Resource Allocation under Rivalry', *Quarterly Journal of Economics*, 81, pp. 359–94.

———— (1980) *Industrial Market Structure and Economic Performance*, New York, Rand-McNally, 2nd edn.

———— (1988) Review of Hay, D. and Vickers, J. *The Economics of Market Dominance*, Basil Blackwell: Oxford, 1987 in *International Journal of Industrial Organisation*, 6, pp. 517–18.

————, and Ross, T. (1990) *Industrial Market Structure and Economic Performance*, Boston: Houghton Mifflin.

Schmalensee, R. (1972) *The Economics of Advertising*, Amsterdam: North-Holland.

————, (1978) 'Entry Deterrence in the Ready-to-eat Breakfast Cereal Industry', *Bell Journal of Economics*, 9, pp. 305–27.

————, (1982a) 'The New Industrial Organization and the Economic Analysis of Modern Markets', in W. Hildenbrand (ed.), *Advances in Economic Theory*, Cambridge: Cambridge University Press.

———— (1982b) 'Product Differentiation Advantages of Pioneering Brands', *American Economic Review*, 72, pp. 349–65.

———— (1988) 'Industrial Economics: An Overview', *Economic Journal*, 98, pp. 643–81.

———— (1989) 'Inter-Industry Studies of Structure and Performance', in R. Schmalensee and R. D. Willig (eds), *Handbook of Industrial Organization*, vols 1 and 2, Amsterdam: North-Holland.

Schwartz, M. and Thompson E. A. (1986) 'Divisionalization and Entry Deterrence', *Quarterly Journal of Economics*, 101, pp. 307–21.

Schwert, G. W. (1987) 'Effects of Model Specification on Tests for Unit Roots in Macroeconomic Data', *Journal of Monetary Economics*, 20, pp. 3–103.

Scitovsky, T. (1943) 'A note on Profit-Maximization and its Implications', *Review of Economic Studies*, 11, pp. 57–60.

Selten, R. (1975) 'Reexamination of the Perfectness Concept for Equilibrium Points in Extensive Games', *International Journal of Game Theory* 4, pp. 25–55.

Sertel, M. R. (1982) *Workers and Incentives*, Amsterdam: North-Holland.

Shaffer, S. (1991) 'Consistent Conjectures in a Value-Maximising Duopoly', *Southern Economic Journal*, 57, pp. 993–1009.

———— (1983). 'Natural Oligopolies', *Econometrica*, 51, pp. 1469–84.

———— (1984). 'Natural Oligopolies and International Trade', in H. Kierzkowski (ed.) *Monopolistic Competition and International Trade*, Oxford: Oxford University Press.

Shaked, A. and Sutton, J. (1986) 'Relaxing Price Competition through Product Differentiation', *Review of Economic Studies*, 49, pp. 3–13.

———— (1987). 'Product Differentiation and Industrial Structure', *Journal of Industrial Economics*, 36, pp. 131–46.

Shapiro, C. (1989) 'Theories of Oligopoly Behaviour', in R. Schmalensee and R. D. Willig (eds) *Handbook of Industrial Organisation*, vol. I, Amsterdam: North-Holland.

Shaw, R. (1973) 'Investment and Competition from Boom to Recession: A Case Study in the Process of Competition – The Dry Cleaning Industry', *Journal of Industrial Economics*, 21, pp. 308–24.

Shleifer, A. (1985) 'A Theory of Yardstick Competition', *Rand Journal of Economics*, 16, pp. 319–27.

Slade, M. E. (1987) 'Interfirm Rivalry in a Repeated Game: An Empirical Test of Tacit Collusion', *Journal of Industrial Economics*, 35, pp. 499–516.

Smithies, A. (1940) 'Optimum Location in Spatial Competition', *Journal of Political Economy*, 49, pp. 423–9.

Solo, V. (1984) 'The Order of Differencing in ARIMA Models', *Journal of the American Statistical Association*, 79, pp. 916–21.

Spence, A. M. (1975) 'Monopoly, Quality and Regulation', *Bell Journal of Economics*, 6, pp. 417–29.

———— (1977) 'Entry, Capacity, Investment and Oligopolistic Pricing', *Bell Journal of Economics*, 8, pp. 534–44.

———— (1978) 'Efficient Collusion and Reaction Functions', *Canadian Journal of Economics*, 11, pp. 527–33.

———— (1980) 'Notes on Advertising, Economies of Scale, and Entry Barriers', *Quarterly Journal of Economics*, 95, pp. 493–504.

———— (1984) 'Cost Reduction, Competition and Industrial Performance', *Econometrica*, 52, pp. 101–22.

Stackelberg, H. von (1952) *The Theory of the Market Economy*, Oxford: Oxford University Press, a translation of the German original (1934).

Stern, N. H. (1972) 'The Optimum Size of Market Areas', *Journal of Economic Theory*, 4, pp. 154–73.

Stewart, G. (1989) 'Profit-Sharing in Cournot Oligopoly', *Economics Letters*, 31, pp. 221–4.

Stigler, G. J. (1964) 'A Theory of Oligopoly', *Journal of Political Economy*, 72, pp. 44–61.

———— (1968a) *The Organization of Industry*, Homewood: Irwin.

———— (1968b) 'Barriers of Entry, Economies of Scale and Firm Size', in G. Stigler, *The Organisation of Industry*, Homewood: Irwin.

———— and Kindahl, J. K. (1970) *The Behaviour of Industrial Prices* New York: National Bureau of Economic Research.

Stiglitz, J. E. (1986) 'Towards a More General Theory of Monopolistic Competition', in M. H. Peston and R. E. Quandt (eds), *Prices, Competition and Equilibrium*, Oxford: Philip Allen.

Stock, J. H. (1987) 'Asymptotic Properties of Least Squares Estimators of Cointegrating Vectors', *Econometrica*, 55, pp. 1035–56.

———— and M. W. Watson, (1988) 'Variable Trends in Economic Time Series', *Journal of Economic Perspectives*, 2, pp. 147–74.

Subba Rao, T. and Gaber, M. M. (1984) 'An Introduction to Bispectral Analysis and Bilinear Time Series Models', *Lecture Notes on Statistics*, 24, New York: Springer.

Sutton, J. (1986) 'Vertical Product Differentiation: Some Basic Themes', *American Economic Review Papers and Proceedings*, 76, pp. 393–8.

————— (1991) *Sunk Costs and Market Structure*, Cambridge, MA: MIT Press.

Svejnar, J. (1982) 'On the Theory of a Participatory Firm', *Journal of Economic Theory*, 27, pp. 313–30.

Swan, P. L. (1970) 'Durability of Consumption Goods', *American Economic Review*, 60, pp. 884–94.

Tilton, J. (1971) *International Diffusion of Technology: The Case of Semi-Conductors*, Washington, DC: Brookings Institution.

Tirole, J. (1988) *The Theory of Industrial Organization*, Cambridge, MA: MIT Press.

Tong, H. (1990) *Non-linear Time Series. A Dynamical System Approach*, Oxford Science Publications, Oxford: Clarendon Press.

Ullah, A. (1988) 'Non-Parametric Estimation of Econometric Functionals', *Canadian Journal of Economics*, pp. 625–58.

Ulph, D. (1983) 'Rational Conjectures in the Theory of Oligopoly', *International Journal of Industrial Organisation*, 1, pp. 131–54.

Ulph, A. and Ulph, D. (1988) 'Bargaining Structures and the Delay in Innovation', *Scandinavian Journal of Economics*, 90, pp. 475–91.

————— (1989) 'Labor Markets and Innovation', *Journal of Japanese and International Economics*, 3, pp. 403–23.

————— (1990) 'Labour Markets and Innovation: Ex-Post Bargaining', University of Southampton, *Discussion Paper, 9010*.

von Ungern-Sternberg, T. (1988) 'Monopolistic Competition and General Purpose Goods', *Review of Economic Studies*, 55, pp. 231–46.

Urban, G., Carter, T., Gaskin, S. and Mucha, Z. (1984) 'Market Share Rewards to Pioneering Brands', *Management Science*, 32, pp. 645–59.

US Department of Justice (1984) *Merger Guidelines*, 49 Fed. Reg. 26, 823, reprinted in E. T. Sullivan and H. Ovenkamp, *Antitrust Law: Policy and Proceedings*, Charlottesville, VA, Michie Co. (1985).

Vanek, J. (1970) *The General Theory of Labor-Managed Market Economies*, Ithaca, NY: Cornell University Press.

Vickers, J. (1985a) 'Delegation and the Theory of the Firm', *Economic Journal*, 95, Supplement, pp. 138–47.

————— (1985b) 'Strategic Competition Among the Few: Some Recent Developments in the Economics of Industry', *Oxford Review of Economic Policy*, 1, pp. 39–62.

————— (1986) 'The Evolution of Industry Structure when there is a Sequence of Innovations', *Journal of Industrial Economics*, 35, pp. 1–12.

Vogelsang, I. (1990) *Public Enterprise in Monopolistic and Oligopolistic Industries*, London: Harwood Academic Publishers.

Vogelsang, I. and Finsinger, J. (1979) 'A Regulatory Adjustment Process for Optimal Pricing by Multiproduct Firms', *Bell Journal of Economics*, 10, pp. 157–71.

Ward, Benjamin (1958) 'The Firm in Illyria: Market Syndicalism', *American Economic Review*, 68, pp. 566–89.

Ware, R. (1985) 'Inventory Holdings as a Strategic Weapon to Deter Entry', *Economica*, 52, pp. 93–102.

Waterson, M. (1984) *Economic Theory of the Industry*, Cambridge: Cambridge University Press.

———— (1985) 'Locational Mobility and Welfare', *Economic Journal*, 95, pp. 774–7.

———— (1986) 'The Economics of Vertical Restraints on Retailers', in G. Norman (ed.), *Spatial Competition and Differentiated Markets*, London: Pion Press.

Webb, S. and Webb, B. (1920) *A Constitution for the Socialist Commonwealth of Great Britain*, London: Longmans: Green.

Wecker, W. E. (1981) 'Asymmetric Time Series', *Journal of the American Statistical Association*, 76, pp. 16–21.

Weiss, A. A. (1986) 'ARCH and Bilinear Time Series Models: Comparison and Combination', *Journal of Business and Economic Statistics*, 4, pp. 59–70.

von Weisäcker, C. (1980) 'A Welfare Analysis of Barriers to Entry', *Bell Journal of Economics*, 11, pp. 399–420.

Williamson, O. E. (1964) *The Economics of Discretionary Behavior: Managerial Objectives in a Theory of the Firm*, Englewood Cliffs, NJ: Prentice-Hall.

———— (1976) 'Franchise Bidding for Natural Monopolies – in general and with respect to CATV', *Bell Journal of Economics*, 7, pp. 73–104.

———— (1985) *The Economic Institutions of Capitalism*, New York: Free Press.

———— (1989) 'Transaction Cost Economics', in R. Schmalensee and R. D. Willig, (eds) *Handbook of Industrial Organization*, Amsterdam: North-Holland.

Yarrow, G. K. (1985) 'Welfare Losses in Oligopoly and Monopolistic Competition', *Journal of Industrial Economics*, 33, pp. 515–29.

Author Index

Subject Index

Current issues in industrial
economics